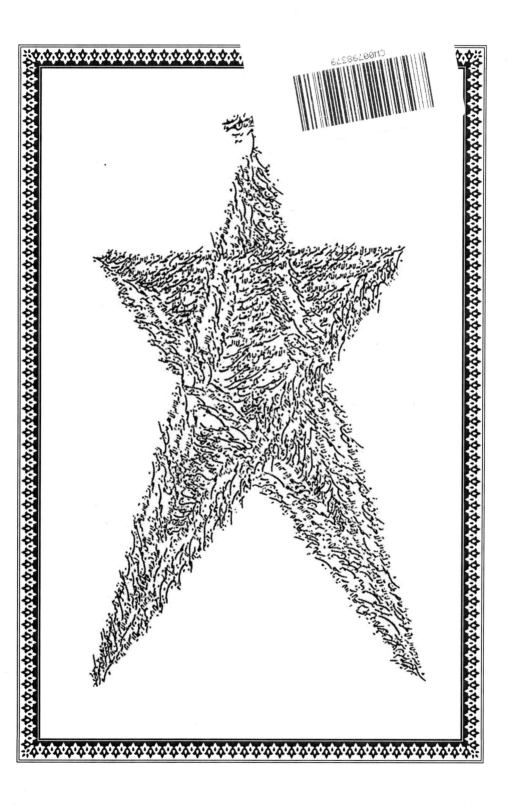

ABOUT THE AUTHORS

Nineveh Shadrach has a degree in Business Administration with a focus on Public Administration. He also has a degree in Peace and Conflict Studies. The spiritual experiences of his childhood led him to the pursuit and practice of occultism. He has been studying the magic of the Middle East for close to twenty years. He is an initiate of the Beni Aur, a teacher at the Magic Society of the While Flame, and a priest of the Goddess Ishtar for close to fifteen years.

Frances Harrison practiced Golden Dawn magic for twenty-four years before leaving that tradition behind to embrace the more ancient roots of the Western Mystery Tradition. She is also an initiate of the Beni Aur and a devotee of the Goddess for close to thirty years. She is a founding member of the Magic Society of the White Flame. She is also senior editor at Ishtar Publishing.

The authors possess one of the largest libraries of ancient magic, written in Arabic and Persian, in North America. They currently dedicate their time to the translation and transmission of this ancient corpus.

For More of Magic That Works

1. Get FREE audio pronunciation for all the Arabic and Hebrew words that appear in this book. Visit: www.sacredmagic.org to download free audio clips or order a free CD (S/H still required).

2. Want to give *Magic That Works* to friends, coven or temple associates? Single copies available online at Amazon, Barnes & Noble, and may be ordered from your bookstore. Please, support your local Metaphysical bookshop by ordering through them first.

3. WIN A FREE BOOK by sending us a brief story of how you used the magic in this book successfully to change your life. Submit entries as often as you like to: fraterkm@sacredmagic.org. Best stories will win a free book. Winners chosen monthly!

THE MAGIC OF LIGHT

The magic of light is rooted in union between the heart and the mind, nature with spirit, and the pursuit of Gnostic experience of the Divine reality. Sublime in its spiritual conceptions and pursuits of human development, yet it is practical with its arsenal of earthly spells for dealing with day to day problems. It is best described as: "The spiritual art and science of a light being dwelling in the Light of all Lights." It is applicable for spiritual or mundane matters, elaborate ceremonies of initiation or nature celebrations, the path of love or the development of personal power, for helping oneself and assisting humanity and nature.

The secrets of the tradition you are about to explore in this book were previously the pursuit only of those willing to travel and seek initiation in the exotic lands of the Orient. Western history is riddled with tales of the few masters who made pilgrimages to North Africa, Turkey and the Middle East, seeking the lost pearls of those masters, whose lasting legacy continued to tantalize them. Times are changing and, with this book, this amazing corpus of knowledge has become more accessible to all sincere seekers.

Our world is facing many crises of our own making. There is a need to look beyond the barriers of language, race, and religion to rescue humanity from its descent into a clash of civilizations and its disconnection from Spirit and nature. Sacred magic provides potent tools that each one of us can use to reconnect with the eternal currents of Light and to create our small piece of paradise in this world. Magic is a path of wisdom and being. Sacred magic emphasizes the power of Spirit in our world and the essentiality of love as a cosmic force that not only connects us as human beings, but also with other living and celestial agents. Truly, it is a path of peace, knowledge, and love.

Senior Editor: Frances Harrison
Developmental Editor: Mary K. Christie
Cover Designer and Artwork: Athena Amato

Magic That Works: Practical Training for the Children of Light, Second Edition
Secrets of Ancient Magic: Path of the Goddess, First Edition
Copyright © 2001, 2005 by Nineveh Shadrach and Frances Harrison.

This book has been printed on crème white acid-free paper.

ISBN 0-9735931-2-1

Ishtar Publishing
141-6200 McKay Avenue,
Suite 716,
Burnaby, BC
Canada V5H-4M9
www.ishtarpublishing.com

MAGIC THAT WORKS

Practical Training for the Children of Light

A System of Sacred Magic and Spiritual Initiation

BY

FRANCES HARRISON
AND
NINEVEH SHADRACH

Dedication

With the greatest eternal love to these amazing magical women:

Sonya Nieman, for being a true mistress of love and life.
Karen Stankunas, for radiating so much love and innocence.
Rita Pulera, for her determination to overcome all challenges.
Prinny Stephens, for being there as a friend for so many years.

I also dedicate this work to all my wonderful students who stood by me through thick and thin as this book came to be and to the memory of our beloved brother Joseph Lacey.

Nineveh

I wish to dedicate this book to my father, Leo Fierce and to my dear sisters Dusty, Anita, Cherie, and Nonnie, who have gone before and who taught me to look for the secret nature of all things, and to my children, Kathleen and Jesse, who taught me patience and wonder.

Frances

O ancient masters of holy magic, who reside in the secret mountain of mysteries, I am
_____, a seeker
of the secrets and knowledge of the wise. I
call upon you to bring me closer to your presence and aid me with the company of those ancient beings who oversee the art of the magi.
Hear me by the name of your Queen whom you
serve and adore. I call upon you, o ancient
masters of magic, to hear my call this hour and
watch over me, and aid me with your power
and guidance. Listen to me, ye invisible radiant
ones known by many names among the ancients,
ye who are magical from birth and of flame
that doesn't burn. I call upon you, servants of
the secret and mighty name that has been kept
veiled by the sages of old. Empower this book
with a ray of magic from your world, so that
by reading it, it shall awaken in my sphere a
ray of that ancient current that has its place
at the beginning of time and keep me steady
on the path of magic. Listen to me o ancient
servants of the magic of Light, and come to me
now and empower this book without delay. Let
it be a living connection between me and the
ancient masters of sacred magic. Watch, guide
and aid me, for I am a servant of Divine Light
and it is this Light that you serve and revere.

TABLE OF CONTENTS

TABLES & ILLUSTRATIONS

★ G♁IIII#ϒ ⊞ ★ ★ G♁IIII#ϒ ⊞ ★ ★ G♁IIII#ϒ ⊞ ★ ★ G♁IIII#ϒ ⊞ ★

1
The Magical Path

agic is not what we do; it is who we are. For thousands of years our way of life has existed all over the world, and it continues to exist, even in this modern age of high-tech wizardry and industrialization. For various reasons, over the last few hundred years magic lost its glamor and became limited to fringe seekers of ancient wisdom. Things are changing and magic is slowly becoming more mainstream again and is being brought to public awareness through the modern media. There is a deep hunger for the tales of wizards of old to be true. Magicians and wizards still exist to this day, but they don't wear telling jewelry or walk around publicly in robes. They continue to practice the ancient ways silently, experiencing the miracles our ancestors talked about. The reason magic continues to exist is because it is real and it works. It is time that you experienced this for yourself.

A few hundred years ago, possession of a book like this would have been grounds for burning at the stake. Now, occult and magic books fill the shelves of many mainstream bookstores. As abundant as the books on modern magic are, there are still few magicians. In time this could also change, but that depends on whether or not people such as yourself can have valid experiences that convince you to embrace magic as a way of life. For that to happen, we need to return to the original foundation of magic as a real objective art rather than a form of ritual-psychology and mind power. The next step should be for magicians to use their magic to benefit the world around them and to help their community with their knowledge. Hillel the Elder once said, "If I am not for myself, then who will be for me? And if I am

1

only for myself, then what am I? And if not now, when?" What the future holds for magic remains a mystery, but we can try to secure it by giving you magic that works, that is safe, and that is real. We can give you magic that not only benefits you spiritually, emotionally, and physically, but also allows you to reach out to those around you and make a difference in the world. This book will challenge you and push you into new frontiers, but throughout its pages is practical magic that can change your life and, if you wish, make the world a better place. The techniques and rituals in this book will remain only words on paper until you put them into practice. Magicians don't pick up a spell book and — abracadabra — the laws of physics are suspended. They practice and live their magic year after year. As the theoretical study of religion rarely produces a profound religious experience, the theoretical study of magic rarely produces a real magical experience. You have to practice magic to truly be a magician.

If you are new to magic, you may wonder what keeps us committed to this way of life. This differs from person to person, since magicians are extremely individualistic in nature. However, we will share with you our own reasons. We have continued to practice magic over the years because it remains one of the most important spiritual disciplines available to humankind today. It provides us first and foremost with the tools to experience, on a personal level, many spiritual wonders, mystical experiences, illumination, personal awakening, spiritual encounters, and much more. The experiences of the prophets and sages of the past come to life in our own day-to-day events. Magic also provides us with tools that allow us to live in harmony with the spirit of nature, tools with which we can transcend barriers of difference and prejudice and with which we can mature on numerous levels. It gives us a system that helps us to manage many of the obstacles and issues in our material existence, from finding the right partner to healing. We practice it because we love it and it gives us joy that is hard to describe. Magic is the path of wisdom and it is the path of love. Magic is an advanced spiritual path that can bring about personal illumination and in that is a tremendous abundance of living power.

In the past, if you wanted to learn magic, you would seek out a magus. You would apprentice under this magician for a number of years and learn your craft. This is still the preferred way. People join magical orders, covens, or guilds and learn magic within an established community under the tutelage of teachers. Magicians band together in groups formed around local temples and some tend to move around in search for the perfect group. Personal disappointment bundled together with fear of group involvement have caused a recent trend toward a more solo path. This would be fine if we lived in cities with thousands of magicians and lots of social support. This is not the case and this path is lonely as it is, without our isolating ourselves from others on it. We need magical temples even more now than we did in the recent past. The world is seeing the rise of religious zealots who would like to push us back into dark times. Magical lodges are important places for magicians to band together and protect their way of life. Even though they are not perfect, such lodges continue to serve as sources of living teachers to students of the occult. As the number of books on the market increases, beginners are getting bombarded with conflicting information. It takes years to sift through the rough for the diamonds, time better served in the practice of magic. Good teachers can provide the much needed experiential guidance that few books can provide.

Still, books and magic are entwined. The linguistic origin of magic is in the root word Magus, which means wise one and stems from the ancient Persian language. It shouldn't come as a surprise then that magicians love their books. In actuality, books have been the primary means of preserving our heritage over the centuries. There are still few or no alternate sources of media that serve the needs of magicians. Books and now the Web will continue to hold that special place for the foreseeable future.

Books like this one can't make you a magician, but they can provide the tools with which you can become one. Possibly, you already are a magician and when you picked up this book, you were just searching for new information. That is fine too. This book is designed to serve as a magical reference as well as a primer. Throughout the book we will be presenting our craft from the perspective of a newcomer to magic, so if you are experienced, keep this in mind. Another difference between this book and others of a like nature is that we present a grass roots approach to our craft. Even though the ancient techniques we are presenting have been slightly modified for modern Western sensibilities, they retain their original spirit and efficacy. Our practices had to adapt to our environment, but that doesn't mean that we abandoned the ancient methods altogether. Magic has a living organic tradition, but it is a tradition.

The first step in becoming a magician is not to memorize rituals or learn spells, but to develop a new way of thinking. The practice of Tai Chi without belief in Chi will only take you so far, if far at all. Modern magicians don't all believe the same thing of course. There are those that believe in high versus low magic, and those that divide magic into white, gray, and black. There are also those who view magic through the lens of Jungian psychology or mentalism and argue that ninety percent of magic is psychology. We respect these views, even if we do not always agree with everything they purport. However, in this book we focus on the grass roots or traditional view. We do so, not because we are stuck in dogma or to push a tradition for the sake of tradition, but because after many years of searching through various occult streams, we have to come believe that these methods work the best and have worked for many people for hundreds of years. We want you to get results and have the best experience possible.

Over the years, we have talked to a multitude of people who were impressed or shocked by our magical experiences. They wondered if it was possible or if such things still happen today. It isn't that we are exceptionally powerful magicians. To be honest, we don't measure our magical development with a power meter. We look at two elements only, how much Light we are bringing into our lives and others, and how much love is generated from the work that we do. To our minds, magical experiences are due to our practising magic as it was practiced by our ancestors of long ago. They must have been doing something right, since they became the inspiration of legends and stories for centuries. Don't get us wrong, we are not claiming supernatural powers or superhuman psychic ability. But we have seen enough, that physical manifestations that others would consider as supernatural do not shock us in the least when they happen.

The more bizarre magical claims of ancient magicians, including transformation, teleportation, levitation and invisibility, were neither a product of the magician's own power nor a blind to mislead the unwary. Magicians believed in the existence of a race of beings that was both invisible and semi-physical, a magical race older than humanity. It has been known to every culture by different names: Elves, Sidhe, Jinn, Ancient Ones, and so on. By virtue of their spiritual work, magicians came into contact with these beings and enlisted their aid. For example, the Jinn would lift up the magician. Since they were invisible to most people, it became easy to think that their act of levitation was due to the power of the magician. Magical rituals enlisting the aid of these magical beings were only a minor component of the magical path. Magical practice is primarily a tool to open the doors of the Divine Mysteries.

Traditional magic focused on spirituality and spirits. The spirits described by ancient magicians were as objectively real to them as the Sun and the Moon. The forces that magicians worked with were called

4

Rouhaniah by Arab magicians, Pneuma by the Greeks and Prana by the Hindi. They are spiritual emanations or powers, embodied in all living things in nature, activated by the Divine Spirit. Working with these Rouhaniah changes not only the magician's life, but also her personality and world view. It amounts to a feeling of connection with the cosmos that is sadly lacking in our world today. The ancient magicians viewed the power of the mind and imagination as the medium, not the source. The Divine Spirit influences the soul; the soul influences the mind; the mind influences the physical form. By acknowledging the role of the Divine Spirit and then becoming a living conduit for it, magic becomes a liberating process with limitless potential. Magic views the cosmos as a living entity, interconnected on all levels, physical, mental and spiritual. It conceives of everything as having a rouhaniah that connects it to the One Divine source. This is stated beautifully in the Emerald Tablet of Hermes:

"That which is above is from that which is below, and that which is below is from that which is above, working the miracles of one, as all things were from one." (Jabir Ibn Hayyan's translation)

As with all other branches of human knowledge, magic also attempts to address the most basic needs of humanity. Our most recurring need seems to be that of change and the power to control it. We want to improve our lives or have the ability to change our situation when and how we wish. That is why magical literature is filled with techniques to change one's material status, marital status, health status, and so on.

The ancient spells call on angels and other spiritual beings by ancient and powerful holy names, to do the bidding of the magician. The archetype of the magician is thus born: standing tall in her attire, holding a wand of power, and summoning the denizens of the invisible. She isn't calling on these beings by her own authority, but by the authority of the Divine. The Divine is the source of all magical causations, directly and indirectly. The magician strives to build a reality that is in harmony with the essential reality of oneness and spiritual balance. In restructuring their internal cosmos upon a strong foundation, magicians embody the highest level of wisdom. Once having become a living agent of the Divine, transformed by the Light, the magician has the authority to call on the spiritual forces of the Cosmos to aid her. Really powerful magic happens when your will and the Divine Will are the same and act together in unison.

PRINCIPLES OF MAGICAL SUCCESS

Every craft has principles and guidelines, designed to maximize successful results. Magic is no different. As an outcome of various experiments, medieval occult scholars recorded different principles for success in each branch of occultism. Although many of the masters of our tradition insisted that these were key to their success, we are not presenting them here just to weigh you down with dogma. People who are used to more modern approaches may find these rules rigid, but experience has shown us their validity. We want you to succeed. We strongly feel that taking as many of them as possible to heart will vastly improve the results of your magical work. They are not listed in any particular order; do not worry about having to follow them all at once. Follow what you agree with, as a start, and experiment with the rest. It is better that you come to see to why they are valuable through your own experiences.

✳ **GOOD CHARACTER:** Magicians are not archetypes of perfect virtue. We are humans, with all the frailty and strength that comes with this condition. However, our work lets us stand with beings of a luminous nature and walk in the presence of angels. It is becoming of us to have a living soul, which doesn't look toward obscene things or obsess with vain or shallow materialism. Recognize who you are in relation to the world around you and focus your soul on the pursuit of Spirit and the highest virtues.

Avoid doing anything contrary to your religious beliefs. When you do magical work that, on some level, you believe is against your religion or when you behave in a way contrary to what you know deep inside to be right, it will lead to a sense of guilt, shame, and regret. We are not trying to push any specific religious or moral ethical code. Whatever your code or belief, be true to it and the magical universe will be true to you. If you plan to be a magician of the Light or what is commonly known as a white magician, shun violence and try to lead a compassionate and ethical life. When these old magical tomes talk to you about committing to righteous action, they are not just preaching the ethics of their time. They are basically saying 'like attracts like.' The more attuned you are with the principles of love, light, and life, the more attuned you will be to the spiritual realm and beings that embody those values.

❋ **PURITY:** When doing magic, you will be inviting many high level spiritual entities to your area. Cleanliness raises the vibration of your surroundings. Magicians of old would wash up to seven times a day during extended magical rites. Of course, this is unnecessary for the level of magical work we will be doing in this book. However, it should go without saying that when doing magic, your environment and clothing should be clean. This also includes all tools, such as writing instruments, ink, parchment or metal.

❋ **DIETARY OBSERVANCE:** One common hindrance to successful magical work is a heavy stomach. For daily work, try to do your work before eating, or when your food has had time to digest. Magicians traditionally fasted for extended periods when doing complex rites. You also might have heard the old saying that you are what you eat. Food is energy and animal products affect your vibration differently than do vegetables. Magicians of old would abstain from meat before and during their work. Many lived on a vegan diet. You can still do magic while eating meat. We did when we were meat eaters. However, we can honestly say that our own magical work improved when we no longer ate meat.

The magicians of old also abstained from certain vegetables. In those days, people did not have mouthwash or toothbrushes. The general philosophy was that eating highly aromatic vegetables such as garlic, leeks, shallots and onions before and during major magical operations would leave a bad smell in your mouth. If they ate a lot of them, the aroma also tended to exude from their pores in their sweat. The ancients were focused on purity and cleanliness and didn't want to reek during the chanting of names. They also believed that the smell of these vegetables would be offensive to the Jinn and make it hard to attract them.

❋ **GENERAL PERMISSION:** In doing magic, you will wield ancient currents and call on beings ranging from angels to jinn. Magicians today assume they have the right to do this at any time and for any purpose. This isn't necessarily true. Getting permission can mean the difference between a ritual that is successful and one that is not or that only appears to be. Permission can come in the form of initiation. It can result in a working agreement with an angel, before that angel is called.

It can also be the result of a divination. Divination is important, especially when your work involves influencing the lives of other people or calling upon a highly evolved spiritual being. One mode of divination used by the ancients involved a certain ritual done over a few weeks. If at the end of the operation, the magician saw a mark appear on her hand, then she knew she had permission to do it. Other methods involved doing certain prayers and meditations and looking at their emotional state afterward. If they felt dread and fear, then the rite wasn't to be, but if they felt openness and receptivity, it was acceptable to do it. Modern occultists rely on other methods, such as Tarot. You do not have to do a divination every time you want to do a ritual. The idea here is that you are attuned to the currents and have a working relationship with the beings you are charging before you do your work.

✳ CELESTIAL OBSERVANCE AND RHYTHM: Magical currents are influenced by celestial tides. The ritual that you do today with average results may prove to be extremely successful tomorrow. Some rituals are more influenced by astrological configurations than others. To keep track of these tides, magicians created occult tables and calendars such as the well-known table of planetary hours. Certain days are believed to be better for constructive operations and others more geared for destructive workings. These days are based on the lunar calendar and are related to the moon's placement in the heavens. Constructive operations are not normally done on the following days, since they are dedicated to destructive work: 3rd, 5th, 13th, 16th, 21st, 24th, and 25th.

Other important occult timing indicators are the mansions of the moon and planetary alignments near the ascendant, as well as the benign aspects of other planets to these. Each of the moon's phases also influences the kind of workings to be done. These influences depend not just on the type of work, but also on its specifics. The waxing moon is a good time to do most constructive operations and the waning moon for most destructive operations. These principles are switched in very specific cases, so they are not blanket rules to be followed blindly. Think of one phase as growth and the other as decrease and then look at the specifics of your work. You also need to consider other astrological configurations that may warrant waiting for a different time. A waxing moon that has malefic astrological aspects to it isn't conducive to constructive operations. Try to observe these tides as closely as possible to improve your chances of success.

As you can see, the magic of the ancients revolved around the stars and the heavens. They would even consecrate talismans and amulets by taking them outside and infusing them with the light and energy of the stars during certain configurations. Even today, there are eye witness accounts of female magicians in Iraq going under the light of the full moon and celebrating naked. They draw down the energy of the moon to aid them in their rites. Capturing the stellar rays is one of the principles for the success of many astrologically based magical rites.

✳ **PROPER MENTAL ATTITUDE:** There cannot be a single doubt in your mind about the magical work that you are doing. You should have confidence in yourself and in your art. If you doubt that your magic works, then it will have to work in spite of you. Doubt during or after an operation can result in failure. Carry out your magical rituals without boredom or haste. Don't expect quick or immediate results from your first try, no matter how many Hollywood movies tell you otherwise. Initially, we had to work a ritual ten or more times before we became aware of its energies. Over the years, we became more attuned to magical energies and things happened faster. Also, get into the habit of repeating a technique or an operation for an extended period and avoid jumping quickly from one method to the next. Think of those martial artists who can break wood with their hands. It takes practice and determination and, more importantly, persistence to accomplish this.

When you want to do a magical ritual, keep your mind focused on it. If you are worried about family, money, or news, or you are emotionally distracted, you will make mistakes. Mistakes have a habit of breaking your attention and the flow of your work. Ritual magic isn't a perfect theatrical performance; it stems from the heart and passion of the spirit. However, a break in focus will make you wonder if you should start again or if it is going to work, and will make it hard for you to get maximum results. To help you with your focus, try to memorize as much of each ritual as you can. The less you have to read from a piece of paper, the more you will be able to put your emotions and passions into your magic. If you need to use papers to read a long ritual or to learn a new one, make the script large. This way you can quickly glance at it without too much distraction.

The ideal place to do your magical work and to stay focused is away from the distraction of people and city life. It isn't always possible that you can cloister yourself or head out to the woods, but try to find a time when you will not be disturbed by noise.

✳ **WALK IN SILENCE:** When you have done some magic that worked, your first instinct may be to brag about it. Keep your work hermetically sealed. When you talk about the magic you are planning to do, you have just materialized that energy. Frequently, magicians who talk about what they intend to do, end up not doing it. If you also brag about the work that you have done, to impress others, you will open yourself to criticism and ridicule. Sooner or later you will begin to doubt yourself and your mind will work against your magic.

❋ **OBJECTIFICATION:** When doing magical work toward a specific goal or to affect someone, including yourself, you will notice an improvement when you create an objective link. This link can be in the form of an image or a photo. You can objectify a talisman for healing with an image of yourself surrounded with a golden aura of radiance. When your artistic abilities don't allow for this or you can't find a photo, then write down the objective clearly or use the person's full name.

❋ **DEVOTION:** Magic is a spiritual path and many of our conjurations and rites involve sacred names and calling upon entities. They are not our servants to summon at whim after work or whenever we feel like it. It is done in a sacred context, and one of the best ways to put yourself into this sacred space after a long day of struggle in the material world is prayer. Pray before and after the work to open your heart and attune your mind to the spirit. Ancient magicians actually put together a whole book of prayers that were constructed according to occult lines. In modern secular society, few modern magicians have sought out these prayers or attempted to republish them. These prayers are very powerful, but so is any prayer that comes from the heart. One other important prayer that you may want to incorporate at some point is a prayer for blessings to descend upon your guardian angel.

❋ **SPIRIT RELATIONSHIP:** Work with each spirit or being in accordance with its nature. When you ask it to do something that it doesn't believe in or is contrary to its nature, you risk offending it. This is why it is not recommended that you use elevated spiritual beings for anything destructive or injurious. It would be taken as an insult to them and a degradation of their honor.

Do not follow blindly everything you get from the spirit world, but also don't reject it arrogantly. Very rarely will the spirits volunteer information to you unless it is urgent, so most likely the advice you get will have been solicited. Show respect and listen carefully, since angels and spiritual beings will not recommend or follow any direction or advice that is not fully within the mandate of Divine.

✹ REPEATED RECITATION: People coming to this art after watching movies on magic are excused for believing that all it takes is one magical word and presto! In reality, magical names of power and conjurations are chanted many times. The most common principle is to chant names of power three times. Sometimes, though, chants are extended beyond that to a few hundred or even thousands. This depends on the length and intensity of the operation. Repeated recitation is designed to help focus the mind and raise the energy. These repetitions are usually calculated mathematically. The key is to keep your focus and not to struggle to count while keeping track of repetition. If you have to count by hand to the point of loss of focus, then stop counting and just repeat things as long as necessary to reach the desired results.

✹ USE OF INCENSE: There are three basic reasons for using incense in magical rites. One is related to the smell and its impact on the magician's consciousness. The second is related to vibration. The third is basically as an offering and as food to the rouhaniat. Magicians use incense in their working space and fumigate all magical objects. Some sages argue that specific incenses are needed for each operation; some are satisfied with planetary mixtures; others recommend a basic mixture of Benzoin and Frankincense. Commonly, incense mixtures are burned on charcoal in a censor, which may be acquired from many religious supply stores. You can also use stick incense or a diffuser. The deciding factor, in addition to magical correspondence, is your environmental situation and your sensitivity to smoke.

✹ DIRECTION: When doing magical work, magicians decide on a direction to face. They work with elements and planets and, like sailors, need a point of reference. The oldest of these was the North Pole. In time, people began to face religious spots such as Jerusalem or Mecca during their ritual work. Modern magicians now use east, the place of the rising sun, as their point of reference. Choose a point of reference that is comfortable for you and construct your operational work around it. For this book, we will be using east as the primary direction.

✹ ORDER AND BEAUTY: Magic gains much of its inspiration from nature. Rituals are constructed so that following a certain sequence yields the desired results. Therefore, it makes sense that when doing an operation, you follow it systematically. The same principle applies when you are constructing talismans or magical squares. When writing magical squares, follow the numerical order and be methodical in the remaining elements.

Our craft is also an art, and so it is natural that magicians strive to fill all their construction with beauty. This beauty can be in the form of harmony in chants and conjurations. It can also be in the quality of tool making. You don't need to be a master artist or craftsman. It is enough that you strive to do your best and achieve harmony between dimensions and lines and clarity of writing.

✳ **MAGICAL SCRIPTS:** Talismans often involve numbers. Ancient magicians wrote those numbers in specific occult scripts. They would experiment with the different scripts and then classify them, based on success and their inventors. The idea is to combine the mathematical concept of numbers, which exists throughout nature, with geometric shapes or magical glyphs. If you are unfamiliar with magical scripts, use either Arabic or Indian numerals. You can also use letters to replace numbers. Hebrew had no specific glyphs for numbers for a very long time and relied on mathematical correspondences for each of its letters.

❁ PRELIMINARY TRAINING ❁

The traditional tools of magic are the staff, pentacle, chalice and spear. These represent the will, body, heart, and mind. For any magical practices to yield results, all four of these need to be working in harmony. The mind needs to focus on the intent and different stages of a ritual. This involves visualization, focus, and clarity. The body needs to be energetic enough to endure the magical operation and physical postures. The will has to be focused and completely directed toward the success of the operation. The emotions need to be aroused, full of passion and depth of feelings, and receptive to the energies. The end result is total ecstatic inflaming of the personality and absorption into the work and results. It is very hard to do any magical work successfully if you are tired, aching, distracted, severely depressed, emotionally distanced, hesitant, lacking in confidence, uninterested, and so on. However, these physical conditions may become excuses if they are chronic. Don't wait till all the conditions are perfect. Do what you can, to the best of your ability. Often magical work helps with physical pain, emotional imbalance, and lack of focus.

The combination of mental focus and emotional intensity is used with the process of visualization during magical rites. Many readers of New Age books have come to believe that visualization and imagination are pretty much what magic is about. If you follow this principle to its extreme conclusion, you will find yourself mentally imbalanced and stuck in your head. The purpose of visualization is to help the magician with her connection to the current and to direct the magical work. Throughout this book, you will come upon many exercises that use visualization. Their intent is to improve results and aid with focus and clarity. Let us take the simple process of drawing a pentagram in the air. On two separate occasions, Nineveh has drawn the pentagram in the air and, afterward, people actually saw the pentagram hovering, plainly visible to anyone. This is because the pentagram was not just imagined in the mind. The etherial pentagram was crafted using the four tools with the aid of visualization. It was real enough to him that on two occasions, it also became real to others.

For many people, visualization doesn't come easily. It is like exercising atrophied muscles while recuperating from surgery or an accident. When we were children, these muscles of visualization were strong and resilient. As many of us were growing up, some adult authority figure told us that we had "too much imagination," or to stop behaving childishly. Fear of being thought mentally unstable may have also been a factor. Gradually, many of us stopped thinking in fully vivid pictures; we stopped seeing spirits and no longer heard their voices. This lost ability of spiritual perception is something you can retrieve. We have included a number of exercises that you may find helpful in your development. Although you may not perceive much when you begin this work, the more you do it, the more you will find your perceptions increasing. Remember, visualization skill is an important part in restoring your spiritual sight. If you find any of these exercises easy and effortless, then you may want to skip them and do the ones you need.

Before beginning, it is optional to preface your meditations and extensive ritual work with a relaxing lustral bath. This is a purifying bath with sea salt or salts soaked with essential oils. Many people like to take a shower before the bath to get physically clean first. You could also try to do some stretches or minor relaxing physical exercises instead. Don't worry if at first you don't get much – these visualization exercises are meant to stretch you back into a forgotten way of thinking and perceiving. It is all right to pretend or imagine; actually, that is the whole point! As you do them, you'll find that your abilities start to improve. You may be surprised at how much detail you get toward the end of each exercise. It is recommended that you keep a journal and write your experiences in it. As a matter of fact, we suggest that you should journalize all your magical practices, as an aid to gauging your progress.

EXERCISE ONE – Maintain a Single Image in your Mind

The first step is to learn to maintain a simple image in your mind. This is important, for in magical practice, holding an image steadily in your mind will cause you to become intuitively receptive to the essence it represents. This practice will allow it to irradiate your awareness with its subtle energy and quality. It will become easier to identify with the essence and meaning enclosed within the symbol. Let us start with a basic symbol. Take a clean white sheet of paper and draw a black oval the size of a small dish on it. Place it on the wall. Sit or stand back a few feet and begin staring at the circle. Continue to do so until it begins to strobe. Close your eyes; for a few seconds it should flash in contrasting colors in your mind. Repeat this a few times over the next few days, until the process becomes comfortable and easy to accomplish. Switch from the oval to each of the following for a week:

- Red Triangle
- Greyish-Silver Crescent
- Yellowish Square
- Green Circle
- White Crescent on black background

EXERCISE TWO – Hold a More Complex Image in Your Mind

The second step is to learn how to visualize a more complex image and hold it in your mind. Repeat the steps in exercise one, but use large printouts or hand drawn glyphs of the planets and Zodiacal signs. Make nineteen sheets using the astrological glyphs shown on the following page, one symbol per sheet, with the symbol filling half the sheet. You can stick with standard black on white or flashing colors like red and green, blue and orange, or yellow and purple. Work with each symbol at least three times for three minutes before moving on to the next one. Once you have done this, try to repeat this exercise a couple of times without the aid of the sheets. Try to picture the symbols in your mind clearly.

EXERCISE THREE – Visualize a Candle Flame

The next step is to take the visualization into the realm of imaginative sensory perception. You will have to pretend, doing so with as much feeling as possible. You will use a candle for this visualization exercise. As in the earlier exercises, begin with relaxation of some sort and then light a candle before you. Sit for a few moments staring at the candle flame. Don't blink your eyes unless they get tired. Try to think of nothing but that flame. Allow yourself to be completely focused on the flame and its flicker. Now, close your eyes and try to capture the image of that flame in your mind. Try to imagine it in any way you know how. Hold that image in your mind as steadily as you can. Don't worry about how accurate the reflection's image is. Let it be any size or shape it wants to be, but hold it tight. When the image fades or becomes difficult to maintain, repeat the preceding steps. Hold the image in your mind again and try to make it as real as possible. Concentrate on it and hold it there, just like the real candle, for a few minutes. Try not to let it waver. This will build up your visualization stamina. Repeat this phase of the exercise often for a few weeks, until it becomes easy to do.

Once it has become easy, it will be time to move to the next phase of the exercise. With the image of the candle in your mind, try to change the size of the flame. Make it bigger at first, then smaller. Next, change the color of the flame into different shades. Allow the flame to dance as if it is being hit by a breeze. Shift the focus of the visualization to the body of the candle. Watch the trickling wax as it slowly melts. Change the color of the candle itself. Keep it as vivid or real in your mind as you can. Imagine and imagine freely. Pretend all the way. Repeat this phase of the exercise, until it too becomes easy to do.

Now you can add new sensory elements into your visualization. When you hold the candle image in your mind, imagine that the candle is scented with an aroma you like, such as vanilla, rose, cinnamon, and so on. Try to imagine that smell in your nostrils as vividly as you can. Do this as many times as it takes to feel real. Try mentally running your fingers over the edges of the candle itself. Try to feel its texture and temperature. Imagine you are passing your fingers over the flame. Feel the sensation of its heat and warmth. Keep the smell of the candle strong as you play with the flame or visualize other aspects of the candle. If your mind wanders, which it will do in the beginning, return to the image again. Whenever you need to, you can open your eyes and do the same things physically to the candle as you have been imagining. Then close your eyes again and attempt to recapture those sensations in your imagination. Remember to pretend and pretend freely.

EXERCISE FOUR – Using All Your Senses

Now you can take the visualization exercises to the next level. You will need to see, feel, hear, touch and smell, all on imaginative levels. Do this next exercise over the next weeks. You may even want to go back to it as you progress further into your magical studies. In a relaxed state, imagine any of the following:

- the face of someone you know or have just seen recently
- a rose or your favorite flower
- the voice of someone you know well and with whom you have regular contact
- a cat or a dog eating from its food dish
- a room in your house with all of its furniture
- the feel of soft fur or the touch of a gentle hand
- an itch
- the taste of a lemon or your favorite fruit
- the feeling of hunger
- a sandwich being prepared
- reading the headline of a newspaper
- swimming or running
- children playing
- taking off your clothes, one piece at a time

EXERCISE FIVE – Visualizing With Eyes Open

Most people think magical visualization is done with the eyes closed. In actuality, most visualization is done with open eyes during the working process itself. You will need to be able to do this too, if you want to succeed in your magical operations. At first, this will be a game of pretend, but later on it will become a natural skill. Let us go back to the images in the first exercise. Going through each of them, stand up and, using your index finger, draw them before you as big as you can. When you draw each line, try to imagine it as if it was there in 2 or 3-D, with your eyes wide open. Pretend and pretend freely.

Begin by drawing a large oval before you in bright blue or any other color that comes easily to you. See each line as you draw it. See it as if it is there, even though part of you knows it isn't. Then step back and focus on the whole image. Keep your mind focused on the oval as if it were a three dimensional physical object. Let your mind create it and convince your eyes that it is an actual object before you. When you are successful, move on to the next symbols; draw first a triangle, then a square, a crescent and a circle. Draw them all with the color that comes easiest to you, whatever it is. Take as much time as you need to repeat this, until you achieve mastery of it. When you are comfortable with those geometric shapes, go through this process again with the astrological symbols in exercise two.

EXERCISE SIX – Visualizing Color With Open Eyes

The intent of this exercise is to teach you to see various colors with your eyes open. This is a simple exercise, but it requires practice to master. All that is required is to trace with your finger a horizontal line before you in any of the following colors: white, grey, black, blue, red, yellow, green, orange, or purple. When you draw the line, it should be bright and shiny. You should see it with your eyes open, with a combination of both mental and physical eyes. Use the power of your imagination to the fullest. Hold the line there steady before you for at least 20 seconds, before it disappears. If you know someone with good visualization ability, this can become a fun game. Choose four pre-agreed upon colors as the selection pool. Ask this person to draw a horizontal colored line in the air before your eyes, without telling you what color it is. Make sure this person keeps track of the selected color. See the color of the line as it is being drawn. Don't dwell on it; say what comes to mind. If the color is correct or very close, let your friend record a 1; if not, put a 0 on your score sheet. Then switch sides and keep score for your friend's attempts. After an agreed upon number of rounds, tally the score and the person with the most correct hits wins. Also, each person can write the colors down before they are drawn for verification afterward. You will be surprised at your success with this technique. Even if you don't score so high at first, continue until you can perceive with ease, accurately, 70% of the time.

The next combination of tools that you will need is a mixture of the spear and pentacle. Breath is the carrier of life and allows for the movement of energy throughout the body. There are two kinds of energy that can be controlled using breath: hot or solar and cold or lunar. Breathing can also be used for relaxing the body and even creating altered states of consciousness. Gaining advanced control of your breathing for relaxation is important. In this day and age of stress, strife and strain, especially in the Western culture, it is important that we have tools for combating "dis-ease". The more we are able to relax, the more open to magical energy we become. The breathing techniques in this chapter will be useful for long-term spiritual magical development. They are based on the technique of the Lunar Breath or left-nostril only. The aim of the lunar breathing is to relax your body and open you up to the infusion of Divine Light. Each of these exercises should be done until it becomes effortless. Then you can advance to the next stage. It may take a few years to reach the final stage. You don't need to reach the final stages to do magic.

EXERCISE ONE– The Lunar Breath

Sit on a chair or in a yoga posture with your spine straight. Close your eyes and attempt to calm your thoughts. Begin breathing slowly and deeply. Inhale to the count of four seconds, hold your breath for a count of either four or eight, and exhale to the count of four. This exercise uses the left nostril only, so keep your right nostril closed in some way. This is also known as the Lunar Breath. While inhaling, vibrate internally Toren, Qadosh or a similar name of Light. Repeat this cycle twenty times. You should avoid doing less or more than the allotted number of cycles. Do this exercise for at least ten weeks.

EXERCISE TWO – The Extended Lunar Breath

This is the same as the preceding one, except for the measurement of the cycle. You inhale for the count of seven seconds, then hold it for ten, then exhale for seven. The expected duration of this exercise is between ten and twenty weeks. If you find this breathing cycle hard to do, then return to the previous exercise for a bit longer.

EXERCISE FOUR – The Lunar Breath, Further Extended

This further extends the measurement of the cycle. You inhale for the count of ten seconds, hold it for twenty, then exhale for twenty. The expected duration of this exercise is between ten and twenty weeks. At this point, you may notice an increased awareness of internal sensations, or increased sensitivity. If you find this breathing cycle hard to do, then return to the previous exercise for a bit longer.

EXERCISE FIVE – The Ultimate Lunar Breath

This stage is one of the hardest and one of most important preparations for macrocosmic experiences. Try to stretch your inhalation to the count of twenty seconds, holding it for twenty and then exhaling for twenty. You may not be able to reach this stage until after many months, or even potentially years, of training. You may encounter difficulty in keeping track of breath counts, so in the beginning, just try to approximate. In time you will see your breathing becoming more at ease and natural, in this relaxed state freeing the mind to dwell on the spiritual Light or desired goal. The minimum duration for this exercise is about a year.

When you reach this stage, you should feel a clear, spiritual joy. You will have been active for about two to three years in training your breathing. You will have transformed breathing from an automatic response to a spiritual experience and sensation. This produces a state of joy, excitement and happiness, as if you have a new lease on life. Continual practice will center you in a profound state of peace. It must be noted that there is no need to increase the length of the held breath beyond twenty seconds, and you must only do twenty seconds when you are comfortable with it. Anything further will exhaust the physical body and the lungs. Lengthy practices will not enhance the experience beyond a plateau level; it is best merely to do the exercises as often during the day as your individual schedule permits.

Another method to help you to relax is guided body relaxation scripts. You may want to put them on CD with your own voice and listen to them. You can also have someone guide you through them. Choose the method that works best for you and use it. The script is a bit repetitive, but that is solely to make it easy to read out loud.

METHOD ONE

Breathing: Inhale for a count of three: one, two, three. Hold your breath for a count of three. Exhale for a count of three.

Procedure: Keep up this breathing in a steady rhythm. Allow all the stress of your daily life to leave with your breath. Focus on your left big toe. Tense up your left big toe. Release. Focus on the sole of your left foot. Tense up the sole of your left foot. Release. Focus on your left ankle. Tense up your left ankle. Release. Focus on your left knee. Tense up your left knee. Release. Focus on your left hip. Tense up your left hip. Release. Focus on your right big toe. Tense up your right big toe. Release. Focus on the sole of your right foot. Tense up the sole of your right foot. Release. Focus on your right ankle. Tense up your right ankle. Release. Focus on your right knee. Tense up your right knee. Release. Focus on your right hip. Tense up your right hip. Release. Focus on your buttocks. Tense up your buttocks. Release. Focus on your pelvis. Tense up your pelvis. Release. Focus on your navel. Tense up your navel. Release. Focus on your solar plexus. Tense up your solar plexus. Release. Focus on your chest. Tense up your chest. Release. Focus on your left shoulder. Tense up your left shoulder. Release. Focus on your left elbow. Tense up your left elbow. Release. Focus on the palm of your left hand. Tense up the palm of your left hand. Release. Focus on your left fingers. Tense up your left fingers. Release. Focus on your right shoulder. Tense up your right shoulder. Release. Focus on your right elbow. Tense up your right elbow. Release. Focus on the palm of your right hand. Tense up the palm of your right hand. Release. Focus on your right fingers. Tense up your right fingers. Release. Focus on your throat and neck. Tense up your throat and neck. Release. Focus on the back of your head. Tense up the back of your head. Release. Focus on your brow and eyes. Tense up your brow and eyes. Release. Feel all the stress in your body leaving you. Imagine yourself drifting deeper into a relaxed state. Continue to repeat to yourself: I am very relaxed and calm.

When doing the preceding section, allow your breathing to dictate when you are ready for the next step. For example, if you are inhaling while focusing on your right ankle, keep your focus to the count of three. Next, while holding to the count of three, tense. Then, while exhaling to the count of three, relax.

METHOD TWO

Breathing: Inhale for a count of three: one, two, three. Hold your breath for a count of three. Exhale for a count of three. In this method, a steady breath is important, but keeping track of the count isn't that vital.

Procedure: Imagine a beautiful and warm ball of golden light surrounding your feet. Let your feet feel like they are being massaged in a bubbling and warm Jacuzzi. Feel your feet very relaxed and calm, more relaxed and calm than ever before. Repeat in your mind a number of times "I am very relaxed and calm. I am drifting deeper into a relaxed state." Imagine a beautiful and warm ball of golden light surrounding your lower legs. Let your lower legs feel like they are being massaged in a bubbling and warm Jacuzzi. Feel your legs very relaxed and calm, more relaxed and calm than ever before. Repeat in your mind a number of times "I am very relaxed and calm. I am drifting deeper into a relaxed state." Imagine a beautiful and warm ball of golden light surrounding your thighs. Let your thighs feel like they are being massaged in a bubbling and warm Jacuzzi. Feel your thighs very relaxed and calm, more relaxed and calm than ever before. Repeat in your mind a number of times "I am very relaxed and calm. I am drifting deeper into a relaxed state." Imagine a beautiful and warm ball of golden light surrounding your buttocks and pelvic area. Let your buttocks and pelvis feel like they are being massaged in a bubbling and warm Jacuzzi. Feel your buttocks and pelvis very relaxed and calm, more relaxed and calm than ever before. Repeat in your mind a number of times "I am very relaxed and calm. I am drifting deeper into a relaxed state." Imagine a beautiful and warm ball of golden light surrounding your stomach area. Let your stomach feel like it is being massaged in a bubbling and warm Jacuzzi. Feel your stomach very relaxed and calm, more relaxed and calm than ever before. Repeat in your mind a number of times "I am very relaxed and calm. I am drifting deeper into a relaxed state." Imagine a beautiful and warm ball of golden light surrounding your lower back. Let your lower back feel like it is being massaged in a bubbling and warm Jacuzzi. Feel your lower back very relaxed and calm, more relaxed and calm than ever before. Repeat in your mind a number of times "I am very relaxed and calm. I am drifting deeper into a relaxed state." Imagine a beautiful and warm ball of golden light surrounding your solar plexus and mid back. Let your solar plexus and mid back feel like they are being massaged in a bubbling and warm Jacuzzi. Feel your solar plexus and mid back very relaxed and calm, more relaxed and calm than ever before. Repeat in your mind a number of times "I am very relaxed and calm. I am drifting deeper into a relaxed state." Imagine a beautiful and warm ball of golden light surrounding your chest and upper back. Let your chest and upper back feel like they are being massaged in a bubbling and warm Jacuzzi. Feel your chest and upper back very relaxed and calm, more relaxed and calm than ever before. Repeat in your mind a number of times "I am very relaxed and calm. I am drifting deeper into a relaxed state." Imagine a beautiful and warm ball of golden light surrounding your shoulders. Let your shoulders feel like they are being massaged in a bubbling and warm Jacuzzi. Feel your shoulders very relaxed and calm, more relaxed and calm than ever before. Repeat in your mind a number of times "I am very relaxed and calm. I am drifting deeper into a relaxed state." Imagine a beautiful and warm ball of golden light surrounding your arms and hands. Let your arms and hands feel like they are being massaged in a bubbling and warm Jacuzzi. Feel your arms and hands very relaxed and calm, more relaxed and calm than ever before. Repeat in your mind a number of times "I am very relaxed and calm. I am drifting deeper into a relaxed state." Imagine a beautiful and warm ball of golden light surrounding your neck and head. Let your neck and head feel like they are being massaged in a bubbling and warm Jacuzzi. Feel your neck and head very relaxed and calm, more relaxed and calm than ever before. Repeat in your mind a number of times "I am very relaxed and calm. I am drifting deeper into a relaxed state." Feel the golden ball of light surrounding your body. Focus on feeling good. Repeat to yourself: "I feel very good. I am very relaxed. My mind feels calm."

METHOD THREE

Breathing: Inhale for a count of three: one, two, three. Hold your breath for a count of three. Exhale for a count of three. In this method a steady breath is important, but keeping track of the count isn't that vital.

Procedure: Imagine a white ball of light above your head. This ball is made of glowing white substance. It grows stronger as you become more and more relaxed. Count down in your mind: 100-99-98. Inhale deeply and let the light fill your nostrils. Say in your mind, "I am very relaxed and very calm. I am drifting deeper into a relaxed and aware state. My mind is very calm and my body feels good." Let the golden ball of light keep your body warm and relaxed. Count down another three numbers, in your mind: 97-96-95. After each three numbers, inhale deeply, letting the light fill your nostrils, and repeat in your mind, "I am very relaxed and very calm. I am drifting even deeper into a relaxed and aware state. My mind is very calm and my body feels good." Let the golden ball of light keep your body warm and relaxed. Continue doing this until you have counted in your mind: 4-3-2-1, then repeat one last time, " I am very relaxed and very calm. I am drifting even deeper into a relaxed and aware state. My mind is very calm and my body feels good." Know that you can always return here. Repeat in your mind: "My mind and emotions are sources of awareness and pleasure to me. My body is regenerating and is healthier with every breath I take. I am at peace and my body is in a state of ecstasy. I am relaxed and my body is tapping into the unlimited source of energy. I am one with the primal essence of life and every cell in my body is plugged into it. I am love, light and life in the flesh. I am relaxed. I am one. I am at peace."

From the preceding exercises, use what you need to get comfortable with your magical work. If you feel confident with your visualization, breathing, and relaxation abilities, you can skip them altogether. If you feel you are weak in these areas, spend a few weeks working with them, before moving to direct magical work.

MAGICAL MEDITATIONS

Meditations are key to the transformation process. Many of our negative spiritual and psychological patterns have their roots in mental habits and experiences. Using meditation's mental transformation can be an excellent vehicle for our spiritual and magical alteration. The first meditation is unique and can be used in any setting that you choose. Its intent is to help you understand another person's point of view, especially their spiritual essence. It is very helpful when working with other magicians to build a strong bond between you and to strengthen the magical circle. It can be used between friends, lovers or even total strangers. The second set of meditations are daily meditations that focus on mundane benefits, such as health and prosperity, and spiritual benefits, such as closeness to the Divine and magical development.

For the first meditation, you and another participant need to find a room free of noise or distractions. It is better if you dim the lights or rely on candlelight. You can also have gentle incense burning. Sit down cross-legged, facing each other, on the floor. If you can't sit cross-legged, then sit in any other comfortable position. The only requirement is that you are comfortable and that each other's knees are touching. You both should extend your palms before you. Place your palms on top of each other's. Gently bend your heads forward so that your foreheads are also touching, especially at the third eye (right between the eyebrows, slightly above the eyes). Once your knees, hands and foreheads are touching, begin to relax using any of the relaxation exercises. Once you are very relaxed, indicate with a finger movement that the mental transfer is to begin. Focus all your consciousness and awareness into your third eye. Shrink your awareness of everything else but that. Feel as if both your third eyes have become one. Imagine yourself standing before a door and that door is the other person's third eye. Feel your consciousness going through that door. Focus all of your awareness of being on the third eye, as if you exist in the third eye, as if all your consciousness of being is there. Focus, not on your own third eye, but on your partner's. Now slowly spread your consciousness to your new body, new hands, new torso, new legs, new feet. Don't force it; let the feeling come to you naturally. Feel as if this new body is your body and you have no other body but this one. The body you came from isn't you anymore. Let the thoughts and memories of this new body flood through your mind as if they were your own memory. Use all the mental senses that you developed in previous exercises. Let the feelings overwhelm you, for they are now your feelings. This is who you are now without a single doubt. You have always been this person. You have always had this body. You have always had these memories and feelings.

Once you are ready, gently begin to return to your body in the same way that you left it. The two of you should have a method of signalling that the return transfer is about to occur. Refocus your consciousness of being on your third eye, in the body you now inhabit, and begin to move to your older body. Feel the move and shift occur. Once you have returned to your body, begin to take control of it again as you did with your visited host. When that happens, begin to slowly separate your third eyes. It should feel like they were glued together and are being torn apart. Do it slowly and gently and don't jerk during the separation. Once you have fully separated, do a gentle breathing meditation. Let yourself integrate the soul essence that you have brought with you or may have been left with. You may want to share your thoughts, feelings and experiences with your partner. The more you do this exercise, the stronger it will get.

The next set of meditations is divided among the days of the week. Each of them will take about half an hour of your time, and the best results come from regular extended use. They are designed to manifest beauty, health, prosperity, joy and intelligence in your life. Each of these is attributed to a single day. The sixth day is that of internal focus. The focus is on your magical energy body, inner development and so forth. The seventh should always be dedicated to Divine contemplation, where you are immersed in the Light and feelings of love. It is recommended that beauty be given to Sunday, prosperity to Monday, health to Tuesday, intelligence to Wednesday, and joy to Thursday. Thus, internal contemplation is done on Friday and Divine contemplation on Saturday.

These meditations differ from other popular methods in that they integrate various techniques. They work primarily on focusing your mind on the spiritual body. You will need to use your breathing exercises, relaxation exercises, visualization ability and the mental development of focusing without wavering on an idea. Each daily meditation should be done at least twice a day for a minimum of a month and, for maximum benefits, four times a day. An effective length for the meditation is between half an hour to an hour, not including the duration of the breathing exercises.

Let us take health as an example. Sit in a comfortable position and begin doing your breathing exercises. After completing your breathing exercises, continue to say silently, in a loud, clear, and stable inner voice, "I am health." While focusing the mind on the affirmation, begin to visualize your body in the desired state of health. Focus on every part of your body, beginning with the face. Feel and know that your body is changing to its new, desired state. Now, with your eyes closed, visualize an image of your body standing before you in a state of utter and perfect health, shining brightly as the sun in its radiance. Every time your mind wanders, without feeling frustrated, just say "I am health," and reinvigorate the visualization with conviction.

The same procedure can be applied to the other five general points of focus. For example, in beauty you should not only see your body in the form that you seek, but also in good health. You should focus on an ideal image of yourself, standing before you in its amazing beauty. Make all the details count and make it very vivid. While breathing, continue to repeat, "I am beauty," non-stop. Don't permit your mind to wander from dwelling on the image and its reality. Know for a fact that this is how you do look, without question or doubt. This positive message of reinforcement will trigger the mechanism of change. Some may doubt the ability of spiritual beauty to influence physical beauty. Let us share a personal experience we have had with this. Frances is in her mid fifties. She describes in wonder being approached by young men in their early twenties. Traditionally, we muse on this but do not give it much thought. However, since she committed herself to practice, Nineveh has noted a mysterious occurrence on several different occasions. They would be sitting talking indoors or walking outdoors. He would glance her way and he would see physically the beautiful and gentle face of a woman in her early twenties superimposed on her features. This beauty and light emanating from her face would enchant him for a few minutes, then as he gave his head a shake, he recognized her normal features again. This is not only a product of her magical work, but also of a youthful spiritual body. Beauty is in the eye of the beholder and there are two things the eye sees, the physical features and the emanation of the spiritual body. The same method applies for the focuses of the meditations.

Practice of the preceding visualizations for a period of two to three years will result in tremendous changes in your psychology and nature. It is common for people to attend expensive prosperity seminars, and yet, afterward, still spend many hours worrying about bills, income, and so forth. It is important that your mind be focused on prosperity rather than poverty. This state of being generally materializes your needs. Worry about money only serves to negate this state and create the opposite of prosperity. This is where mental magic is at its best and most effective. Don't let the simplicity of these exercises fool you, so far as their effectiveness is concerned. Also, don't forget persistence is an important key for success in this art. Magic doesn't always happen in a flash! Two years invested in this practice is of more value than twenty invested in 'could have been' or worries, depression, sadness and such.

When it comes to the Divine Contemplation, this part of the meditation is different. No complex visualization is involved. You spend two and a half minutes every day, without wavering focus, meditating on the love of the Divine, experiencing this love and feeling yourself made of pure Light and surrounded by it. On the allotted day, this meditation is stretched to the normal half an hour. After a year of this visualization regime, you can, if you wish, increase the meditation on the Light and on the Divine presence to half an hour, three times a day. Then after a few months, you can change it to twice a day for an hour each time. Once the second year is complete, do this at your convenience during the day. When you visualize the Light, don't just think of candlelight or merely white light. The Light must be accompanied by a sense of Holiness or an awareness of the presence of the Divine all around and within you. Feel the sacredness and sanctity. This may be difficult for those who have had few experiences with mystical states. Focus your entire being on the Divine and on the love you feel, so that no other emotion or thought enters for at least two and a half minutes at a stretch. You will find it easier to sense this state with practice. The intent of this exercise is to lift us up from a physical state to a more spiritual one. Divine Love is the cornerstone of this transformation and of all spiritual operations. With time and practice, people will begin to comment that the Light in your face is shining strongly, and your spiritual abilities will have increased considerably.

It may seem you that these meditations require too much time per day. However, it is a limited program and after about a year or two the duration can be shortened considerably. With the spiritual muscles having been exercised, it takes much less time to maintain and reach these states. But, even if it looks daunting, consider how much time you spend doing everything else. The lifelong physical and spiritual benefits are tremendous. Without the proper foundation, spirituality becomes a matter of intellectualism. With these exercises, you can soar in the Light and change your life for the better. These are the keys not only to spiritual development, but also to life mastery. The magical techniques you will learn later in the book will augment this. The first step is to implant the seed of a new you in the world of images. You will find the benefits to be priceless.

In this chapter, we have covered the principles of the art. These are by no mean conclusive or exclusive, but they are enough to get you started. In the next step in your journey, we will discuss the sacred names used in our art as well as the spiritual beings and hierarchies that you will be working with in this book. We will be coming back to those materials repeatedly, so we advise you not to skip the next two chapters. Read them carefully and refer to them on a regular basis until they become familiar to you.

Works Referenced

al-Ghalani, Mohammed (D. 1740 C.E.), *al-Der al-Mantzoom wa Khilasat al-Sir al-Maktoom fi Al-Sihr wa al-Talasem wa al-Nojoom*. al-Maktaba al-Tahqafia, Beirut, Lebanon: 1992.

al-Marzooqi, Ali Abu Hai Allah, *al-Jawaher al-Lama'a fi Isthadhar Muluk al-Jinn fi al-Waqet wa al-Sa'a*. Maktabat Iqbal Haj Ibrahim. Siragh Bantan: 1962.

al-Toukhi, A'adu al-Fatah. *al-Bidaya wa al-Nihayah fi A'aloom al-Haref wa al-Awfaq wa al-Arsad al-Rouhani*. al-Maktabah al-Thaqafiah. Beirut, Lebanon:1991

al-Toukhi, A'adu al-Fatah. *Mudhish al-Albab fi Asrar al-Haroof wa A'ajab al-Hissab*. al-Maktabah al-Thaqafiah. Beirut, Lebanon: 1991

2
Magical Divine Names

We want you to get the maximum benefits from the rituals and the magical development program in this book. It is hard to do that if the language is unfamiliar to you or the names of the Divine and other spiritual entities appear distant and archaic. Through the ages, magical rituals and rites contained many names of power. The language and names, as well as the approach to the relation between the magician and the spiritual realm, are some of the things that differentiate systems of magic. In our system, we hold to the truthful reality of the various spiritual names and the sacredness of the Divine's attributes. We don't see those beings as human constructs. We use the sacred names, both for their spiritual essence and as a way to improve our connection with the Divine. They are more than a means to a material end or a label to various energies in the universe. They are a way to infuse ourselves with the Divine rouhaniah and inflame ourselves with illuminating Light. Before we delve into the list of the Divine names used in this book, we should discuss the view of the Divine within this tradition.

In our magical philosophy, the Divine is that ever living creative spirit and is experienced as spiritual Light, within magical currents. Magic depends on this Light. Magic flows when the spark of the Divine within the mage becomes aware of or connects with its all-pervading Divine source. The flow of the Divine Light into the magician charges her with an ecstatic and empowering feeling unlike anything she may have felt before. The conception of the Divine as Light isn't primarily an outgrowth of modern New Age thinking, but has been inherent in the writings of ancient mages and mystics for thousands of years. It can be found in the religious and philosophical writings of the ancient Persians and in neo-Platonist and Islamic mysticism. The concept of God as Light is almost universal. The Divine is the Light of Lights, the Real beyond illusions and the Principle before the first principle.

The Divine has infinite facets. Since each facet in and of itself is absolute and infinite, it becomes akin to a deity in and of itself. However, all the facets form a singular whole representing both a personal and impersonal nature of the Creator. This is similar to each one of us having different roles or states in life. You can be a father or mother, a son or daughter, a brother or sister, joyous or sad, and so forth. In this case, we are talking about a God of War, a God of Magic, a Strong God, Gods, a Goddess of Love, a God of Thunder, and so on. These can be seen either as facets of one Divine principle or each a powerful being in its own right, and both are correct to a great extent.

Keep in mind though, that the Divine as the Ever Living isn't a supernatural being that lives in some imaginary place. The Ever Living is a being that is the essence of life in and of itself. Therefore, every thing that lives is an expression of the Ever Living. To understand the Ever Living would be to understand the meaning of life in the cosmos itself. The Divine is All Existing with no end, nearness, farness, will, wish, time, above, below or place. There is no universe as a separate existence. While we call the Divine by many names, the Divine is the self-named one and none other than the Divine is named. The Divine is the First without anything before and the Last without anything after. The Divine is visible in all that is seen, and known clearly in all that is hidden. The Divine is in all forms and images without any relation to any appearance.

It is easy to fall into the trap of thinking then that the Divine is infused in us in some way. You hear that a lot in New Age circles, that God is within me. The Divine is never in anything, neither is anything in the Divine. Only the Divine can see the Divine; only the Divine can know the Divine by the Divine; only the Divine can conceive the Divine by the Divine. The Divine is hidden in oneness and is veiled by the Divine being. When the magician is said to be guided by the Divine or sent by the Divine, what we are saying is that the Divine has sent Herself, from Herself, for Herself and without any cause or means beside Herself. She sent Her essence, from Her essence, by Her essence, to Her essence. There is no difference between the One who sent and Her magician who was sent. You are not you, and you – without being you – are She. She is not within you; nor are you in Her. You don't exist, with an essence and qualities and attributes, for you never existed, neither do you exist, nor will you ever exist. Without being, your essence is with Her and in Her. You are not even temporal. Without having any identity, you are Her and She is you.

Magicians didn't know the Divine by making themselves nothing or destroying their egos or trying to rid themselves of their selves. How could a thing that doesn't exist try to get rid of its own existence? The key is to know that the Divine exists and none other exists with Her. She is now as She has always been. Ultimate magical realization is to see your attributes as the Divine's attributes, your essence as the Divine's essence, without your attributes and essence being either in the Divine or out of Her. Your self is only the Divine's being. You are eternal. You never ceased to be, for you never were, since there is only the Divine self and essence.

Therefore, these Divine Names or deities of old were to the magicians holy sacred names by which magic happened and their awakening, gnosis, or illumination of Divine states occurred. Initially, the magicians worshipped the Divine in a balanced fashion, as a God and Goddess. This balance began to fade with the rise of the Levite priesthood. The Goddess became an esoteric doctrine to which the initiated were introduced. Even though few of the occult texts of the 13th century C.E. mention the Goddess at all, She is hinted at. We noticed that, in these magical tomes, the name Gilgamesh appears as a Divine name or a word of power right next to Hebrew Elohim. However, Gilgamesh was not a deity in the ancient world. He was a human hero and a historical king of Uruk in Babylonia. The Arabian magicians would not have worshipped him or equated him with other names of the Divine. They knew the history of cultures that came before them, for it was that of their ancestors. The important clue to this mystery is that Gilgamesh's fame comes from his epic, the epic of Gilgamesh and Ishtar. Ishtar was an important, if not the most important, Goddess of the ancient world. Hence, in Arabic occult texts Gilgamesh was in actuality a code word alluding to Ishtar. This is further supported by the flower symbols, eight pointed star, and many other symbols of the Goddess that adorn those texts. While some modern magicians may find this objectionable, we firmly believe that magic in its grass roots was a gender balanced system of spirituality. It was not the privilege of learned patriarchal scholarly men, while women turned more to earth-based religions, as is today. Magic appealed to men and women equally, for its cosmology was balanced and natural.

From our perspective, the mythology of the Gods and Goddess is

31

designed as a vehicle for understanding the essence of their names and facets. The myths give us insight into what energy to expect, but by no means are they always factual. It is the same as the symbolic depictions in the ancient world. The Goddess Ishtar is portrayed as standing over a lion with the scepter of authority in Her hand. This doesn't mean that an entity that looks like this or in this posture exists. It is a symbolic way for us to identify that the feminine facet of the Divine has power and dominion, that this kind of power and authority isn't the sole domain of the male or positive facet of the Divine. The same goes for many of the myths of the ancient world. This doesn't negate the power inherent in a name as a source of awakening to the Divine reality in our lives.

In studying the Divine names throughout the old texts of our tradition, we have also found common linguistic and spiritual roots reflected in the magical rituals and practises. The three common streams are Syriac or Assyrian, Hebrew and Arabic. In occult texts belonging to the 9th-13th centuries C.E., it was common to mix an assortment of names of the Divine from diverse Semitic sources. The conjurations would contain names of power, such as Ba'al and Gilgamesh, with the various ninety-nine names of Allah and Hebrew Divine names, such as Elohim, and even Greek names, such as Metatron. The combination and mixture of the different names of the Divine or gods and goddess of the old world isn't a mixing of religious dogma. In its philosophy, magic transcends the limitations and barriers of religious thought. This is one of the biggest challenges for newcomers to magic to understand. In the Middle Ages, ancient magicians considered those systems to be a conjoined whole that worked well together. Today, seeing the political and social turmoil between Arabs and Jews in the Middle East, people may find the combining of Arabic and Hebrew hard to accept. This is a modern state of affairs and more political than anything. The ancients saw the streams as all coming from a single source.

To illustrate this, let's look at a medieval ritual from al-Buni's Sun of Knowledge. This is a prayer for calling on the angel Kehial. The ritual requires the seeker to chant the Divine name Allah sixty-six times after each mandatory Islamic prayer for sixty-six days. The number of repetitions is because the numerical value of the word Allah is sixty-six. The name Kehial also has the value of sixty-six. The repeated chanting matches the oral and numerical harmonies of the name. It also awakens the rouhaniah of the name, which, by the end of the cycle, will infuse the reciter with its own inherent power. This would be a good example of an Islamic Sufi magical rite. Interestingly enough, al-Buni states that the when the angel of the word Allah appears it would chant "Yah [x2], El [x2], Elohim [x2]." Yah is a Hebrew name of the Divine that is the first two letters of Yahweh. El is a Caananite name of God that was also used in the Bible. Elohim is Hebrew name, which translate as Gods. From a modern Western perspective, the mixing of Divine names from a diversity of languages and religions may seem strange, but it was natural for the occultists of his time and a very common occurrence in Arabic esoteric manuscripts.

How the Divine name is used in ritual manner should reflect on the relationship between the magician and the Divine. Should you verbally summon, conjure, or bind the various names of the Divine, that would reflect and reinforce a belief that the God and Goddess are merely human constructs or limited entities, similar to angels, spirits, and demons. It declares your superiority as an entity that can summon God to serve your will and bidding. Should the names of the Divine appear on your lips only within the rites in the context of using them to command other beings, that reflects a means to an end approach. The only reason for using those names is to get what you want and beyond that the names are replaceable and meaningless. There is no transcendental spiritual relationship at play here. You are literally using the names of the Divine for vain and selfish ends. This would make you a sorcerer rather than a magi. On the other hand, if you aspire to get closer to the Divine presence, then your usage of the names should be like the lover to the beloved. At least, you should also use those names in a non-magical setting as part of your devotional and spiritual work.

The key thing is to make sure your ritual style represents your spiritual beliefs and what you hope to get. You should take the time to consider this well, as over time, performing spiritual and magical rites have a profound impact on your own development. In our tradition, the Divine names are the cornerstone of all magical effectiveness. Magicians spend their time in the vast sea of Holy Names. While it is true that in their rituals those names are used to command other beings, that is only one of the many functions. Let's take a look at al-Buni's conjuration for the angel Kehial as an example of the attitude inherent in our own tradition.

"I ask You, O Allah, [x3] O Ever Living Eternal Being, make me live a good life that I may exist on the shore of the ocean of Your love. Adorn me with charisma and awe before the upper worlds. Open the eye of my heart and my vision with Your Light, so that my heart is open to the reception of the mysteries and that it may utter the inner jewels of Your protection. Radiate upon me from the ocean of Your holy emanations and make it easy for me that I may reach the coast of gentleness. Take me with a gentle taking, that I may find its sweetness the day I meet You, O Lateef [x3]. O Divine One, I ask You this with the discharging of the living breath of the breezes of the fragrant exhalations of Your mysteries and the revelation of the mystery of Your name that You have recited for the reception by the thirsty centers. I wish to delve in Your reverence and seek to swim in Your mysteries.

O Thou who has the Greatest Name and He is the Greatest, O Thou who has no known limits and He is the Most Knowing. O Ancient One, I ask You by the mystery of Your name and with what Your pen has flowed, with what You have inspired Jesus son of Mary, with what You have confided to Moses upon Mount Sinai and cried with tongue of ability: I am Allah El, [x3] Elohim El, [x3] By what You have descended upon Your prophet Mohammed, peace be upon him, hurry with the success of my pursuits and facilitation of my aim and reveal to me from the world of the kingship and kingdom. Recompense my aim from what is satisfactory to You from ordinations. Reveal to me from the hidden spirits of the kingdom that are endowed from the mystery of Your name that unites all names and attributes and by which You have called Yourself in all languages. Praising you are all creatures, O Allah, [x3] O Ever Living Ever Being, O Best Guardian and Best Champion. O Divine One, I ask You to enlist to me the servant of this name, Kehial, for You are capable of all things."

The preceding conjuration's emphasis is on the magician's personal unity, love, and direct experience of the Divine and the Holy Presence. The lines between magic and mysticism, conjuration and prayer, evocation and adoration, all become blurred in the aspiration to both achieve enlightenment and gain the aid of spiritual beings along the path. The Divine names act as a vehicle by which the magician hopes to lift the veil within our world and behold the unseen. The known names are used with acknowledgment of the existence of even more powerful, unknown names. Getting to know the great names of the Divine is one of the main aims of the magician. There is no separation made between the Islamic and Hebrew Divine names. They are all seen as part of one stream. There is also reference to emanations similar to those found in Jewish mysticism, for example we see references to the World of the Kingdom that is filled with many spirits and mysteries. From further reading of al-Buni, it is evident that Jewish mystical thought and the Neo-Platonic world view were part of the magical teachings of his time. To understand how it all come together in this way, we will need to discuss a brief history of the magical system of our tradition. In the ancient world, people belonged to tribes instead of states with borders, and inhabited a very small geographic area in comparison with today. Their sages travelled from city to city and exchanged knowledge openly and freely. The cradle of civilization was also a melting pot of the heritage and philosophy of various peoples who shared common roots. This continual borrowing made it difficult to even know who wrote a given book or developed a certain technique. It didn't matter that much to them, for they were concerned less with intellectual property rights and more with transmitting a working, effective system of magical development and ritual practice. The primary written magical sources are in both Arabic and Hebrew, dating from the 9th-13th centuries C.E. The sources may have been written in a combination of Arabic and Hebrew, but the tradition itself goes back to the even older civilizations of the Middle East.

The story begins in the cradle of civilization itself. Magic owes its heritage and even its name to a class of priests known as the Magi. Historically, there were two types of Magi, those associated with the Zoroastrian faith and those who lived in Chaldea, which today is part of Iraq. It is the Chaldean Magi that are of interest to us in this book. The Chaldeans in the Bible are called Kasdiym, a word derived from Arpakhsadiym. The Chaldeans were descendents of Arpachsad, son of Shem, son of Noah. The word Chaldee also means 'Servants of God'. Abraham was an Arpachsadite and he set out in his travels from the Chaldean city of Ur. He moved to a city named Harran. Harran was one of the most important centers for celestial occultism. The people that lived there later were called the Sabians. At some point, the Chaldeans and Sabians met and from their union rose the Nabateans, who left us a large amount of occult lore they had inherited from their ancestors. The Nabatean language gave rise to Arabic and they transmitted as much of their knowledge as they could to the Arabs. Many of the original sources have been destroyed or are hard to find and decipher, but the Arabic copies remain.

In these old magical texts, the names of certain masters of our tradition appear frequently. These names are Agathodaimon and Hermes. They occur in the Arabic texts because they were viewed as prophets by the Sabians. One other important figure that also gets much mention is Enoch, known in Arabic as Idris. The Sabians were known among Muslims as the 'hunefa', which is derived from the Aramaic 'hanefo' or star-worshipper. This may be the reason behind the Quran's description of Abraham as 'hanif'. While the Quran has many references to stories from the Bible, the actual ritual practices and theology of the Arabs before and after Islam had strong Sabian influences.

The Sabian beliefs were stellar-based to a great extent, but also had room for spirits and other celestial hierarchies. During the early time of the Chaldeans, the primary deity of Harran was Sin, a cosmic being whose symbol was the moon. During later periods, other Chaldean facets of the Divine were included, primarily Ishtar and Shamash. These were symbolized by a crescent with two stars above it. Later on, the crescent with the three stars above it became a major symbol in ancient Arabic magical and mystical texts, hinting at their connection with the ancient mystery schools of the Sabians.

The Chaldean magi and many Sabians were thus priests of the Goddess Ishtar, one of the oldest names of deity symbolizing the female generative side of nature. Ishtar is the Goddess of Love and Her mysteries reflect this. The Chaldean rites were held in towers known as Ziggurat - a type of stepped pyramid. The top of the Ziggurat had a chapel that was oriented to align with certain astronomical configurations. Common religious service was held in the bottom of the Ziggurat, but only the initiated priests entered the top. The top of the chapel had no statues or idols, and none were allowed. This chapel was their holy of holies, where sacred and secret rites were held. Herodotus tells us that in this chapel there was an altar of gold. The only one allowed to remain there at night was a maiden, selected by God from the whole nation. She was chosen to undertake the hierogamos or sacred marriage (marriage to the Divine). This sacred marriage concluded a year-long celibacy. It was accompanied by a sacramental supper-feast shared by the king and the whole population of the city, who were united in prayer and shared communion.

The ancient Chaldean faith and stellar magic were so widespread in the Middle East that the renowned Islamic historian Abul Hasan Ali Ibn Husain Ibn Ali Al-Mas'audi (d. 957) mentions seven planetary temples. One of those temples is the famous Ka'aba in Mecca. Others were in San'a in Yemen, in India, in China and three in Isfahan and Khorsan. Al-Mas'audi says that these were shaped to carry a planetary geometry. The temple of Saturn was hexagonal, the temple of Jupiter was triangular, the temple of Mars was rectangular, the temple of the Sun was a square, the temple of Venus was a triangle inside a square and the temple of Mercury was a triangle inside a rectangle. The square formed into a cube would match the shape of the Ka'aba, making it the Sabian temple of the Sun.

Islamic and Jewish prayer practices also shared bowing and prostration with the Sabian rituals. Islamic prayer times match the three Sabian periods, with an additional two more. Like the Sabians, Islamic prayers involve ablutions, declaration of intent and a call to prayer. Like Sabians, Muslims also fast for 30 days a year, based on seeing the moon.

We mentioned that the Sabians recognized Hermes as one of their prophets and that they translated many of their texts into Arabic. One such important Sabian was Thabit ibn Qurra, who was born C.E. 835, and died C.E. 901. He moved from Harran to Baghdad, where he gained great favour with the Caliph. He wrote and translated close to one hundred and fifty works in Arabic and sixteen in Syriac. He translated such titles as Proclus's commentary on the Aurea Carmina of Pythagoras and texts belonging to Aristotle, as well as other important Hermetic texts. He also paid attention to astrology and wrote a commentary on the Book of Hermes, a treatise dealing with the cryptic significance or magical efficacy of letters of the alphabet. Many other important Sabians were responsible for translation of occult and Hermetic texts into Arabic, some of which were later translated into Latin, as well as many others awaiting translation. A hundred or so years later, an intolerant and puritanical interpretation of Islam arose. The Sabians were forced to flee and their writing was absorbed into the Brotherhood of Purity or Ikhwan Al-Sifah.

The cycle of occult transmission peaked during this period and came to an end around the 13th century, C.E. Ahmed Al-Boni, the famous medieval Arab occultist, mentions an exploration under the great pyramid where he uncovered 300 tracts hidden by the early Greeks. He claimed to have incorporated their teachings into his books, and he made regular references to Aristotle, Plato and Hermes. Similar translations of this golden age include the Emerald Tablet (Tabula Smaragdina), attributed to Hermes Trismegistus, and the alchemical writing of Jabir Ibn Hayyan. There is also the Book of Images by Pseudo-Ptolemy, the Picatrix, the Turba Philosophorum, the Flower of Gold, Liber De Compositione Alchemiae, and the Book of the Moon.

This intellectual and oral transmission continued with the earliest work of the Brotherhood of Purity, the Ismaili, the Assassins and the emanationist neo-platonic schools of Sharawardi and Ibn Arabi. It is evident in the mathematical formulae of the Arabs that were transformed into the 'Barbarous Names' in the Western tradition. There are other links, such as the Green Man, who appears in the ancient Arabian tradition as al-Khudur (the Green One). The astrology of the Chaldean and ancient Greeks lives on in the work of Arabic astrologers such as Al-Biruni and Abu Ma'asher and later European medieval astrologers. Geomancy, the ancient method of divination attributed to Enoch, was transmitted by the Arabs to Europeans such as Agrippa. These ancient occult traditions exist, preserved in the following three languages: old Ottoman, medieval Arabic and Persian. These contain the wisdom collected from the Sabians, Hermetists and Jews, intermixed with mystical Islam and Gnostic Christianity. At the same time that the Arabic contribution tapered off, we saw the continuity of the tradition in Europe during the Renaissance and on to modern times.

This vast reservoir of ancient wisdom isn't readily available to modern Western seekers. In modern New Age and Occult books, there is a disconnect from much of the older aspects of the tradition, which remain largely untranslated in Arabic, Ottoman and Persian. Although many of those modern books talk about ancient mystery schools or connection to antiquity, much of the last fifty years of development in Western occultism has not been rooted in the ancient magical traditions of the Sabians and Chaldeans, due to lack of access to original sources. This disconnect isn't as bad when it comes to ancient Egyptian or Greek writing, where archeological and historical research has uncovered a substantial amount of information. This is why many modern occult schools mix the Jewish occult tradition with the Egyptian, with some minor adaptations from the Greek. In this book, we will skip the Egyptian line of transmission and go back to the Chaldean.

THE DIVINE NAMES OF MAGIC

There were simply thousands of Divine names in the ancient world, in numerous languages. We will focus here on only a small fraction of them. These names occur in many magical contexts and systems, some known and others more ancient and obscure. We will go through the basic Chaldean names, then Hebrew and Arabic, and then move to more obscure names of power used primarily by magicians.

Anu and Antu (Anoo and An-too): These are the Sumerian names for the cosmic creator aspect of the Divine. The Milky Way galaxy is known as Tariq Anu or the path in which Anu travels. Anu is the masculine and Antu is the feminine. The Babylonian myth tells us that Anu was the sky god and Antu was the earth goddess. They produced the underworld gods or Anunnaki (Jinn / Sidhe) and the utukki or the seven evil demons. His second consort was Ishtar, under the name Innana. Anu is also the King of the Igigi or heavenly host. The shooting stars belong to him and have awesome strength. Anything that he puts into words becomes reality.

Ellil / Enlil (El-Leel / En-Leel): This is the name of the Divine facet that created mankind and is associated with wind and storms and the floods. He represents a wrathful and jealous king. He can determine the fate of all things, animate or inanimate, through the tablets of destiny. He is lord and king of the Annunaki and his symbol is seven small circles representing the Pleiades.

Ea / Enki (Eaa / En-kee): This is the facet of the Divine associated with water or spirituality and consciousness. Thus, He is said to know everything and be the Lord of Wisdom and Incantations. He and his consort Damkina produced Bel Marduk. He is also associated with the creation of man and instructs humanity in all crafts, writing, building, and magic.

Ishtar (Ee-sh-taa-r): As we mentioned earlier, the Magi were priests and priestesses of the Goddess Ishtar, one of the oldest names of the Divine, who symbolized the manifestation of Light in nature. She is the 'Queen of Heaven', the Supreme Creator through the power of begetting of life. She aids Bel-Merodach in begetting man. She is Arurur and Nin. The Divine was worshipped by the name Ishtar by ancient people living in Nineveh, Erech, and Arbela. The name and cosmology spread far and wide across Asia. It entered India as Lakshmi, the consort of Vishnu, the Preserver; She represented the continuation of life. Ishtar passed to Phoenicia and become Astarte. The word Astarte gave us the word 'star'. Astarte was considered the queen of the entire Phoenician pantheon. She entered the Jewish faith as Asherah, where the populace flocked to Her shrines, burned incense and sacrificed their chastity before Her image. The Goddess as Ishtar enticed the hearts of the faithful, like an intoxicating liquor, in Sidon, Tyre, Carthage, Babylon, Judah, and even Rome. Ishtar represents different things to different people, because the Divine is conceived differently by different people. She is Ishtar Ashsuritu, the

39

Lady of the World. She is Ishtar Zerbani, the Seed Producing. She is Ishtar Mama, the Mother. She is Ishtar Mariama, always fecund. She is Ishtar Zanaru, the Goddess of the Lands. She is Ishtar Karadun, the Goddess of the Strong. She is Ishtar Ulsiga, the Goddess of the Heavens. She is Ishtar of the Stars. The Goddess is the parent of all things, the Mistress of the elements, the one Divinity whom the entire world worships in many ways, with varied rites and under a multitude of names. What makes the name Ishtar so special, other than its celestial connotation, is that it represents the Divine emanations of love, life, light, and beauty. Thus, it has the ability to bring the faithful to a state of unity through love and rapture, which is one of the highest of mystical states. She is also the Goddess of Magic and hence represents the principle underlying the Chaldean currents.

Shamash (Sha-mash): This is the Divine facet associated with life-giving light and with the rulership over the Sun. In the mythology, he is depicted as rising from the mountains with rays of light emanating from his shoulders, and entering and exiting the underworld through a set of gates in Mountain Mashu guarded by scorpion-people. He upholds the principles of truth and justice. He is also the lawgiver and oracle informer.

Marduk (Mar-dook): This name is of the savior facet of the Divine and is associated with being King of the Igigi. Marduk has fifty names, each of which is actually considered as another deity. This principle later emerged in Islam as Allah with ninety-nine names. Like Ishtar, Marduk is the God of Magic and in mythological depictions has four eyes and four ears and fire flowing from his mouth. His principle role is bringing order out of chaos, vanquishing evil, and raising the principle of good.

There are many more names of Gods and Goddess among the Sumerian and Babylonians. Those we have given here form a brief summary of some of the most important names used regularly in ancient Chaldean magic. Among the Hebrews, another list of names appeared with regular frequency. These names can be found in the Bible and other religious writing. Some of these names were based on other cultures and some were extracted through the mathematical process of letter permutation or Temurah.

El: Other than the name Yahweh, El is the most commonly appearing name of God in the Bible. It is also one of the most important Hebrew names in ancient magical texts. Yahweh was originally worshipped as a God of war from the deserts of southern Palestine. El was worshipped as the God of Israel from Mesopotamia. The importance of the name El in occultism stems from being the primary suffix for angelic names, even among Muslims. It is also the name associated with the ancient master of the mysteries Melchizedek, who not only initiated Abraham, but to whose line of priests Jesus was said to belong. The most commonly appearing titles are El Elyon (God most high), El Shaddi (God the Strong), and El Chai (Ever Living God). The feminine form of El is Elat.

Yahweh (Ya-ho-eh): This is the most common name of God among the Jew and Christians. The proper pronunciation of the name has a mystery surrounding it, since the vowels were omitted at some point. The four letters that form the name were attributed to four of the five Elements and thus became the basis of much of the mystical Jewish writing and philosophy. It is the most commonly used name in modern ceremonial magic in the West, although there have been attempts by pagan occultists to sideline its usage. A shorter version of this name, which also appears regularly, is Yah.

Elohim (El-oo-heem): This is the plural of El and translates as Gods. It could be a reference to the concept that the creator is both a masculine and feminine facet, the Elohim being the union of El and Elat. The possessive form of the name is Elohai (My God).

Adonoi (Ad-on-oi): This is also a name of the Divine with a crossover to pagan culture. Its meaning in Hebrew is Lord. A variation of this name is Adonis, the Greek lover of Aphrodite. In occult literature, the name also appears combined in the form of Adonoi Tzebaoth or My Lord of Armies.

Shekinah (Shek-ee-nah): This name literally mean the Dwelling of God or the Divine presence. The Shekinah is the feminine facet of the Divine in Hebrew mystical and occult lore.

From the Arabic corpus comes a rich number of Divine names. The most commonly known are the ninety-nine names of Allah. The literal meaning of Allah is the Divine. The word Allah has both feminine and masculine form, but is written almost exactly the same. In the Quran, the most commonly used reference is the masculine, but quite often the plural preposition we is used in its verses. This is very similar to the plurality that exists in the Old Testament in conjunction with Elohim. The feminine facet was denied by clerical authority, due to a verse in the Quran that stipulates that Allah has no wife. Indeed, the masculine and feminine facet of the Divine neither implies a husband and wife in the human sense at all, nor does it imply male and female in the human biological sense. Each of the ninety-nine attributes of the Divine has a masculine and feminine form. A good number of them, however, carry both masculine and feminine form equally. Like many other names of the Divine, these names are rooted in pre-Islamic times and are by no means limited to those who adhere to the modern incarnation of Islamic practices. In this book, we introduce only a small number of them, as used for magical workings.

Al-Nur (El-Noor): This translates literally as the Light and is completely gender neutral.

Al-Wadud (El-Wa-dood): This translates into the Loving God who wishes the best for all of creation. Through the act of Divine Love, spiritual blessings and magical gifts occur. This love is unconditional in nature. The feminine form of this name is Al-Wadudah

Al-Salam (El-Sa-Laam): This translates into Infinite Peace and is an important facet for those seeking a state of peace profound through their occult work. This name is also gender neutral.

Al-Hhai (El-Hhaa-yy): This is the equivalent of El Chai and means the Ever Living God. The feminine facet is Al-Hhaiah.

Al-Bassir (El-Ba-ss-eer): This translates into the All-Seeing One and represents the Divine facet which watches and observes all things. This sight involves awareness of things physical and non-physical and isn't limited to things visible by physical eye sight. The feminine facet is Al-Bassirah.

Al-Ahad (El-Ah-aad): This translates literally as the Single One. This is the Divine's attribute of unity in multiplicity. There is no division in attributes, traits, essence, and so on, and there is no duplicate. Nothing exists but this singularity. There is nothing that competes with the Divine's unique existence. This is a gender neutral name.

Al-Qayum (El-Qa-yoom): This literally translates as the Self-Existing One. This is a reference to the first cause or principle, since everything depends to some degree on another thing to exist. This is a gender neutral name.

Al-Fattâh (El-Fat-taa-hh): This name literally translates as the Opener. This is the opener not only of obstacles and blocks in one's life, but also gateways. This is a name used as a precursor to many magical rites, to open the veil between us and the other worlds. It can also be called upon to open our spiritual centers and perceptions to the heavenly realms. This is a gender neutral name.

Al-Qudus (El-Qa-doo-ss): This name translates literally as the Holy One. It is an attribute that is beyond human perception and imagination. When manifested, this noble trait can cause the dead to be raised to life, as in the story of Jesus. It reflects a Divine state without any blemish or weakness. This name is usually added to other names to further exalt the spiritual state reached by reciting them. This is a gender neutral name.

Al-Latif (El-La-teef): This name translates as the Subtle One. It represents a Divine attribute that combines gentleness in action with delicacy of perception. Regular calling on this name will open the hidden as well as the manifest to the magician's knowledge. The feminine form of this name is Al-Latifah.

Al-Rahman (El-Rah-hman): This name translates literally as the Most Merciful One and is based on the linguistic root Rahem or Womb. The mercy of the Merciful is perfect in every sense for the Divine doesn't just meet the needs of the needy, but satisfies them completely. There is an oral saying that the Divine has one hundred portions of Mercy and that only one portion was given to the Universe and that was divided among all of its creation. Divine mercy embraces everything and is on a cosmic scale beyond our human potential or ability to perceive. It is a gender neutral name.

Al-Shafi (El-Sha-fee): This name means the Curer and is connected with establishing health by removing imbalances. This represents both physical and spiritual imbalances and you can call on this name magically to recenter yourself in times of crisis. The female version of this name is Al-Shafeeiah.

Al-Hadi (El-Ha-dee): This name translates literally as the Guide and is connected with initiation and enlightenment. This guidance can be in the form of spiritual and magical knowledge, as well as to one's true purpose in this world. It can also be more basic guidance, providing solutions to problems that you may face in your daily life. This is a name to call upon when you are doing a divination or when you are trying to find your bearings. It is also an excellent name for those teaching others and helping them on their magical journey to use frequently. The feminine form of this name is Al-Hadeeah.

Al-Haq (El-Hha-qq): This name means the Truth or the Real. It is a Divine facet that is valid in and of itself and causes the existence of everything else. The Truth is self-evident and exists without external influence. It is magically used to remove the veil of illusion that is the result of perceptions. It is a gender neutral name.

In addition, there are also names of power that belong to the Syriac or Suryani tongue. The Suryani is the language of the Assyrians and was believed by ancient occultists to be the language of the prophets and the angels. A substantial set of Suryani names appear in the old magical texts and in old Sufi books such "Al-Ibreez."

Al-Manhhamana (El-Mahn-hah-mah-nah): This is the Suryani name of the prophet Mohammed. It is composed of two words. The first one is Al-Man, which means 'grace' or 'boon.' This grace has an inner and outer beneficence. The external beneficence refers to what is for beings in the world of ghosts. The inner beneficence refers to what is for the spirits in the world of spirits, which is a grace that quenches the thirst of all creatures and all worlds. The second word, Hhamana, means, like the first, 'a grace' or 'a boon.' However, it is a grace or a boon that reaches the extreme and is raised to the end. It is as if it is being said that the prophet Mohammed is the grace that reaches the extreme, without any equal before or after.

Ahhma (Ahh-mah): This is also Suryani, and it translates to 'O King.' Its occult meaning is 'King of the Kingdom, the Majestic, the most Magnificent, the Ever Living and Omniscient.'

Hhmaytha (Hh-may-thah): This Suryani name is a reference to the Divine kingdom. It is the equivalent of saying: "O Owner of the Mysteries, O Owner of the Lights, O Owner of the night and day, O

Owner of the clouds that roll, O Owner of the suns and the moons, O Owner of giving and withholding, O Owner of exaltation and abasement, O Owner of all that is living, O Owner of everything." According to a number of ancient occult authors, this name is a great mystery that no pen can stand to write, or any example can convey.

Atmah (Aht-mah): This Suryani name is equivalent of describing the Divine with magnificence, greatness, dominion, victory, glory, and as distinct in all those traits. It is as if you are saying: "O knower of all things, O capable of all things, O determiner of all things, O director of all things, O compeller of all things, O He who is never afflicted with an inability, and doesn't imagine a shortcoming in His directives."

Tamaytha (Ta-may-thah): This Suryani name is a reference to all things that the Divine directs and into the possibilities through which He does everything and judges what He wants.

Marazaho (Mah-rah-zah-hoo): This Suryani name is spoken by the angels to the spirit of the dead upon its return to the realm of spirits. The first letter's placement corresponds to all of cosmos, and the totality of creation. The second letter's placement corresponds to all goodness that exists in all the cosmos. The third letter's placement corresponds to all the evil that exists in all the cosmos. The fourth letter's placement represents the Holy Being that created all the worlds. The intended meaning of the entire word, based on the rule of the Suryani language, is: "All of the cosmos and the prophets, angels, scriptures, and all goodness, including the demons and all evil, are they created by God or not?"

Marada'zirho (Mah-rahd-a'-zeer-hoo): This Suryani name is what a faithful and believing spirit would answer to the question posed by the previous name. As in the previous word, the first letter's placement corresponds to the totality of creation. The second letter's placement corresponds to all the lights that branch from the Light, such as the light of the spirit of prophets, angels, the light of the Tablet, the light of the Pen and the light of the Bardo. The third letter represents the truth and reality of all that is encompassed by the previous letter, as if saying: the prophets are true, the angels are true, the Pen is truth and so on. The fourth letter represents what comes after it, as if saying: "this is." The fifth letter represents idolatry, division, and partnership or the primordial darkness and all other forms of darkness that emanate from it. This is the exact opposite of the second letter in the word, and enters into it Gehenna, or hell, and all that is dark or evil. The eighth letter represents the reality of all that is represented by the sixth letter, which is nurtured by the seventh. The ninth letter, connected with the tenth, represents the Exalted Being that created all things and influences it. The meaning of the answer is: "All the Universe and all the prophets who are real, all the angels who are real, all the lights which are true and real, hell, which is real, evil, which is real, all - the Glorious One is its creator, its King and the sole authority and controller of it, without an equal or challenger."

There are also sacred names of the Divine believed to have potent spiritual and magical power, that were constructed using guarded formulae. Their construction comes from an understanding of the occult mystery of sounds and letters, as well as through guidance from the heavenly host. One such name of importance is composed from the fourteen Arabic letters known as the letters of Light. These form a secret and guarded Divine name known as the Name of the Mysteries or the Secret Name of Light. The letters are divided between the five ancient Elements: Spirit, Fire, Air, Water, and Earth. The name, in part and in whole, is used to connect the magician with the Elemental currents. It can awaken these Elemental forces, in a highly concentrated and balanced way, in the magician's essence and spiritual body. This mighty and sacred name is **Aham Saqak Hhala'a Yass Taren (Ah-am Sa-qak Hha-la-a'a Ya-ss Tah-ren)**. Some manuscripts have the second name as Sakaq instead of Saqak.

The second constructed name is associated with the power of love. It is used heavily in ancient magical texts in all workings of love, unity, harmony, and benevolence. It is constructed by combining letters whose numerical values correspond to 2-4-6-8. This name is also believed to have great power over the spiritual Jinn. It is pronounced **Baduh (Ba-doo-hh)**. This name appears regularly in talismanic magic and will be used later in this book in a technique that opens the heart center.

In addition, there are also sacred and mighty names of unknown origin or meaning. They were recorded and transmitted by different occultists over hundreds of years. They continue to prove their efficacy and potency, but over time their full symbolism and translation was lost to us. Even though we don't fully know what these names mean today, we do know what they can do and that they are safe and important

46

names of power for any magician of our tradition. One such important set of names are known in Arabic as the Ta'at (Arabic) or Tethim (Hebrew), due to the abundance of that letter in the names. However, they are more commonly known as the Tahateel Names. The ancient magical teachers of our tradition say explicitly that in these names is a mystery from the mysteries of God, that gives them potency over the angels and the jinn, who can't resist them ever. There are many recorded and oral legends surrounding them, from various masters of ancient magic. One such legend belongs to Abu Bakir Al-Turyzi, who said that these famous seven names were found preserved on a tablet of seven metals in a white marble chest in the belongings of Abi Al-Qa-sem Al-Qurtabi. He in turn said that it was taught to him by a student of the wise philosopher Handrius. He claimed that with them he did marvellous and strange magic, both indoors and outdoors. Concerning them, he mentioned a retreat and a certain sequence and order in removing occult wards. They can be used for spiritual magic with nei-ther a retreat nor extended periods of practice, as long as the proper planetary days are observed. Their occult applications are extensive, such as curing women stalked by spirits at any time or discharging spirits that guard places. They are used effectively as a vehicle to con-tact the spirits of the planetary spheres. These seven names are each made of seven letters, making the total number of letters forty-nine. They are as follows: 1) **Leltahteel (Lel-tah-teel)**, which is associated with the planet Saturn, 2) **Mahtahteel (Mah-tah-teel)**, which is asso-ciated with the planet Jupiter, 3) **Qahteeteel (Qah-tee-teel)**, which is associated with the planet Mars, 4) **Fahtobteel (Fah-tob-teel)**, which is associated with the Sun, 5) **Nahahtateel (Na-hah-ta-teel)** , which is associated with the planet Venus, 6) **Jahlahtateel (Jah-lah-ta-teel)**, which is associated with the planet Mercury, and 7) **Lachhatoteel (Lach-ha-tot-eel)**, which is associated with the Moon.

There are also secret and mighty Divine names of power that can't be pronounced by any human. These names are written in the form of glyphs or symbols. The combination of those symbols presents a pen-etrating and powerful vibration that causes magic to happen. If you have been raised in modern complex society, it is easy to dismiss them as scribbles. We would encourage you to try their potency for yourself and be prepared to be surprised. One such mighty and secret name is composed of seven glyphs. They are associated with the seven seals of King Solomon and were used by Jewish mystics to ascend to the seven heavens in their vision of the chariot. They also appeared on magical amulets and vases in Babylon. They are believed to symbolize the sacred and ineffable, unpronounceable name of God. The deep esoteric lore identifies them with the symbols on the Circle of Dominion and Kingship, which contains nineteen symbols. It is believed that King Solomon had only seven symbols from that circle, by which he was given power and authority. His authority extended to the realm of the Jinn and the winds. He was also able to understand the language of animals. Whoever possessed them all would have dominion over many aspects of creation. It is doubtful that anyone knows more than seven or eight of those symbols. The seven glyphs are as follows:

$$ G \ominus \text{IIII} \# \Upsilon \, \overline{\text{III}} \, ☆ $$

Finally, there are ancient secret names of power that were preserved through the ages, with minor variations of spelling between manuscripts. The proper spelling was considered a great treasure by seekers, due to the potency of those names in magical context. They were powerful enough that those who worked with them for a while could call forth all kinds of spirits by reciting them a few times. All that remains is the approximate phonetic spelling, with their deeper secrets available to less than a handful of magicians worldwide. What is known is that these names are to magic what a switch is to a light bulb. These names are organized into categories. One of the most famous of these categories is the Berhatiah names or the Ancient Oath, also known as the Red Sulphur.

The master Al-Boni said in his book, Sharhu Al-Barhatiah, *"Know o seeker, God aided me and you with a spirit from Him, that the names of Barhatiah are the dependable conjuration from the ancient of times. The ancients used to refer to it as the Ancient Conjuration, Powerful Binding, Guarded Mystery, Vaulted Secret and the Red Sulphur. It was spoken of by the original wise men, then by our master Solomon Ben David, peace be upon them, then by Assif Ben Barkhiah, then by the wise man Klaphitrius and whoever apprentices with it to our current day. This is a powerful conjuration, which no Angel can turn from, and which can't be refused by any Jinn, Ifreet, Mared or Shitan. Any seeker's knowledge of the arts is handicapped, who doesn't possess it or doesn't know of it."*

While there is no way to authenticate the historical claim of this conjuration to a pre-Solomonic era or to Solomon himself, no Arabic book on occultism worth its mettle, dating as far back as we could get (7th-8th centuries C.E.), was without a copy of these names. The medieval astrologer Abu Ma'asher says these names have great power over the Elements and the spirits of the six directions. They are used heavily in our magical tradition and their applications are extensive. One of their most important applications is in the calling forth of jinn and other spirits.

Berhatyah (Ber-hat-yah): This name approximately translates into holy, and, in some accounts, praise. The name on its own has been used magically to help woman with giving birth, to ease financial hardships, and to improve memory, among many other applications.

Kareer (Ka-reer): This name translates approximately to God of all things. It has been used magically to help the magician see Jinn, protect themselves from theft, increase sales, and find love.

Tatleeyah (Tat-lee-yah): This name translates approximately to God that answers all things. It has been used by ancient magicians for rituals of protection of the home, prosperity, establishing harmony between people and to call upon the spirits.

Tohran (Toh-ran): This name translates approximately to Ever Living, and in some accounts to the Giver of Life. It was used by ancient magicians for freedom from tyrants, escape from captivity, success in any pursuit, and to improve spiritual vision.

Mazjal (Maz-jal): This name translates approximately to 'Ever Being'. It was used by ancient magicians for purification and spiritual elevation and clarity.

Bazjal (Baz-jal): This name translates approximately to the Beloved One, and in some accounts to the Giver of Peace. It was used by ancient magicians for manifestations of needs for protection from harmful magic and hexes .

Tarqab (Tahr-qab): This name translates approximately to Giver of Peace, and in some accounts, the Capable One. It was used magically for prosperity.

Barhash (Bar-hash): This name translates approximately to O God this is your servant so answer him, and, in some accounts to the Capable One. It is believed to be the praise of the archangel Michael.

Ghalmash (Ghal-mash): This name translates approximately to the King.

Choteer (Cho-teer): This name translates approximately to the Powerful One.

Qalinhod (Qal-in-hod): This name translates approximately to All Encompassing, and in some accounts to the All Hearing or the Glory.

Barshan (Bar-shan): This name translates approximately to pure tranquility. This is the state of absolute perfection and absolute peace. The ancient master Ibn Arabi states that the name means the Merciful One, and the master Al-Boni identifies the name as the Majestic God.

Katzheer (Katz-heer): This name translates approximately to praise to God, and in some accounts to the Merciful One. It is believed to be the praise of Jonah.

Namoh Shelech (Na-moh Shelech): This name translates approximately to God is He, and in some accounts to I am God, the haven of those who are afraid.

Barheeyola (Bar-hee-yoh-la): This name translates approximately to O Sufficiency, and in some accounts to God, my spirit to Your Spirit is ascended upon Your will. It is believed to have been used as praise by Abraham.

Bashkeelach (Bash-kee-lach): This name translates approximately to O Giver of Faith.

Qaz Maz or Qazmaz (Qaz-maz): This name translates approximately to my spirit to Your Spirit toils for Your Kingly will, and in some accounts, it is two words: Qaz, the ever living, and Maz, the eternal being.

Anghalaleet (An-ghala-leet): It translates approximately to O Wise One.

Qabarat (Qa-ba-rat): It translates approximately to the Guardian.

Ghayaha (Gha-ya-ha): It translates approximately to the Majestic, and in some accounts to the Generous One.

Kayedhola (Kayed-ho-la): It translates approximately to O Ancient One that is capable of everything.

Shemchaher (Shem-cha-her): It translates approximately to O Elevated One.

Shemchaheer (Shem-cha-heer): It translates approximately to O Eternal Judge.

Shemhaheer (Shem-ha-heer): It translates approximately to He is God. It was used by ancient magicians to test the presence of spirits through signs of manifestations and spiritual sight.

Bakhathonyah (Bak-hat-hon-yah): It translates approximately to the Ancient One and the Eternal. Another spelling variation on this name is Bakhathathonyah (Bak-hat-hat-hon-yah).

Basharesh (Ba-sha-resh): It translates approximately to the Capable of Everything.

Tonesh (To-nesh): It translates approximately to the Object of Praise.

Shemcha Baroch (Shem-cha Ba-roch): It translates approximately to He is God the Blessed.

The preceding list is far from exhaustive, but it will be sufficient to set you on your way to intense magical experiences. We will be using them extensively in this book in the practice of white magic. The more comfortable you are with them, the more likely it is that you will get success from following any of the techniques in this book. If you are totally new to our art, this list may seem daunting. We recommend you take it one step at a time and open mindedly begin to work with them. You will see for yourself why these names have survived the test of time and why thousands of magicians over the ages have relied on them in their practice.

Works Referenced

Anonymous. *Kitab al-Dir al-Manzoom fi A'aloom al-Talasim wa al-Nojoom*. Maktabat al-A'alem wa al-Iman. Egypt.

Arabi, Muhi al-Deen (D. 1238 C.E.). *al-Kibreet al-Ahmar wa al-Sir al-Afkhar wa al-Dir al-Jawhar*. Maktabat Jamhuriat Massar. Egypt.

Mubarak, Ahmed. *Al-Ibriz fi Manaqib Sayyidi `Abd al-`Aziz al-Dabbagh*. Maktabat Mohammed Ali Sabeeh. al-Azhar, Egypt. (Composed 1716 C. E.)

al-Buni, Ahmed (D. 1225 C.E.). *Shamsu al-Ma'aref al-Kubrah*. Maktabat Isha'at al-Islam. Delhi, India.

al-Buni, Ahmed (D. 1225 C.E.). *Manba'a Ussol al-Hikmah*. Maktabat al-Hidayah. Surabaya, Indonesia.

3
Angels and Jinn

Magicians feel strong kinship to all living things and a bond with animals, which they view as companions rather than pets or lesser species. They also feel and know that they are surrounded by the realm of the unseen. The inhabitants of this invisible realm are seen some of the time and felt most of the time. They have been given different names by different cultures and religions. This doesn't change their nature or identity, or the fact that much magic involves interaction with these beings and enlisting their aid. Modern magicians view the inhabitants of this realm as archetypes or aspects of the astral realm, accessible through the subconscious and visualization. The traditional view is that these beings are objectively real, even if they are not always visible to us. You may be sceptical of their reality and this is fine, given our modern, worldly, thinking and upbringing. Do the work with conviction and you will get the evidence you need. Many of us have experienced it repeatedly, which gave us was the inner support to remain true to our convictions when faced with opposition from people trying to tear down our craft, or to mock us for our position.

Whether you believe in objective spiritual beings or not, most likely it is your experiences, or lack of them, that have shaped your views. This is why, no matter how many magic books you read, theory will only do you so much good. You need to have magical experiences for yourself, so that you know and not just believe. You need to know to the core of your being, for it is in that core that your magical self resides.

Of the inhabitants of the unseen, angels are the first group with which you will work. You may think that by working with angels, you will be adhering to a Christian or Jewish worldview. The reality is that angels transcend any single religion. One of the oldest references to them exists as part of the Magian Zoroastrian theology. They also appeared in ancient Chaldean temples in Babylon, and a number of the names given to angels in Hebrew were once worshipped as gods in Babylon. Most angelic names end with El, a Caananite name of God.

Angels are part of the spiritual tradition of many cultures, from the Divas of the Hindus to that of modern day Islam, Christianity and Judaism. Even now, their images permeate our culture, many of our homes, places of worship, and greeting cards. The traditional word for Angel is Malach, which means messenger of the Divine King. Scriptural texts are filled with stories of these messengers appearing to selected prophets in some human form. However, they are also described as winged, luminous beings of light, filled with pure holiness and devotion. Angelic lore and names have been preserved through the spiritual and occult heritage of Judaism, Christianity, and Islam. This is because it was through angelic contact with the old prophets that these faiths originally came to be. They laid the first stones and man built edifices upon them.

Magicians work with angels on different levels. Only in rare situations do they communicate with them directly, since that isn't necessary to achieve results. The exceptions to this are communicating with the guardian angel or if there is a pressing matter. Communicating with angels presents an interesting dilemma to magicians. Angels appear on their own terms and leave on their own terms. They can't be bound or forced, except by Divine commandment. Fortunately, communicating your intent to the angel is not difficult. They are messengers of the Divine, so they are engaged back and forth between all facets of the creation. Whenever you communicate your request directly to the Divine, an angel is involved. Communicating your intent to the angel doesn't guarantee that it will come to pass, and you can't force the issue.

The second part of the dilemma is our difficulty in understanding the angelic response or in getting them to appear. They are so different from us and so celestial that we have to break away from the illusion, or penetrate through the veil. When appearing, angels can also choose to be physical, but for the most part they remain invisible. They are like watchers who interact with our lives indirectly or silently. Fortunately, there are a number of ways of communicating with the angels, when and if they choose to visit. The first way is to communicate with the angel in a dream. The angel might appear as a being of light or a person all draped in white. You will get a clear or symbolic message that you understand. This usually happens only in cases where you ask very important questions or if you need to be told something very vital. Many times, the messages foretell birth or death or warn against something. It is very uncommon to have an angel in your dreams nightly.

The second way of receiving a response is through the angel's appearing physically. This shouldn't come as a shock, as many of the old accounts of angelic encounters are of that kind. They appear as people who are very beautiful and radiant, with uncanny knowledge of their host's life. Their mission is usually urgent and highly spiritual in nature. The tales of physical contact with angels have dwindled over time, but the mages of old kept records of such encounters and the methods by which they experienced them. Physical encounter, even with one's own guardian angel, is possible, but highly difficult to arrange. The magician of old would go into a cloister for months on end and dedicate her time to such a contact. Finally, after many physical signs and occurrences, humanoid beings clad in white with a powerful glow around them would appear. They would talk briefly with the magician to hear what she had to say and usually make a promise to help, if she promised to follow the spiritual message given. The physical encounter was seldom repeated, but the magician maintained a connection with the angel(s) for the rest of her life.

The third way of receiving a response is through intuitive revelation. This occurs when the angel lightly touches or 'hugs' the spiritual body of the magician. This brief touch floods the magician's body with light, almost orgasmic in nature, and her mind with a clear and profound knowing of what the message is. This is akin to a brief gnosis experience. There is no doubt or guess afterward about the intent of what is being delivered. It is as clear to the consciousness as the sun at noon in a desert. The message tends to be brief and to the point. Once the message is delivered, the angel usually departs or severs the connection. This kind of connection is not privy to the imagination, as it is not a result of mental imaging or mind-talk in a normal way. This was the method most commonly experienced by the ancients .

The fourth way of receiving a response is through the imaginative spiritual sense, using a magical device, such as a mirror or an ink cup. This method is usually used by beginners, as it allows back and forth dialog and can be done any time. Basically, the magician feels she can summon an angel forth and communicate with him about any issues or questions she may have. The response tends to be in the form of imagination and mind-speak. This form has been used repeatedly and requires a minor state of auto-hypnosis to achieve proper reception. Even then, the magician needs to be aware that half of all messages received in this fashion will be corrupted by reception noise.

Most likely your relationship with angels and your reception of messages will entail a combination of various methods. Any angelic experience will be real, sensory, experiential, awakening, peaceful and orgasmic, to say the least. Whatever form it may take, in the end it will be personal and valid. However you may communicate with an angel, take the advice given and follow it through. This is the least you can do after such a blessing as being touched by an angel.

The first step in working with angels magically and having such intense experiences is knowing their names and their function. Popular angelic names found in the Hebrew scriptures have their roots in the theology of the Chaldean or Persian Magi, or are a result of the visions of saints. Generally, they are written in the Hebraic tongue, even though they have appeared in other religions and languages. Angelic names are either descriptive or vibratory. For example, the Archangel Raphael translates into 'God has healed', or 'God's Physician'. Raphael's name is descriptive in nature, giving us insight into the angel's character and attributes. Not all angelic names can be translated, for some are vibrational in nature to represent the vibratory tone of a mathematical concept.

In angelic lore, each angel or group of angels has its own role or classification. In our craft, these are used to understand which messenger to enlist for help with our needs and in our rituals. For example, an angel governing water represents the spiritual essence that dictates the functionality of water in the Divine Order. The angel of water oversees its function, but doesn't necessarily share its characteristics. In a similar fashion, a letter carrier delivers the mail to you, but doesn't share any of the characteristics of your mail or packages. This may seem like an obvious statement, but it is surprising how much confusion has crept into modern occult iconography. Modern magic uses occult iconography as part of a system of hermetic correspondences with which to adorn angels represented in human form. These images are then used in ritual and magical work. Ancient iconography focused more on conveying the cosmic and magnificent state of angels. This reliance on more human based iconography is due to the difficulty of capturing the written description visually. It is easier to create an image of Uriel (Light of God), who among other things is said to rule over the abyss and earth, as draped in black, with earthy tones, holding a sheaf of wheat, than to try to behold the dazzling presence of the Fire and Light of God. This is an important point to remember, because the use of such iconography magically, as a basis for your visualization and rituals, will act as psychic barrier to a more geniune experience.

The list of angels available to work with us is extensive and covers every conceivable area and numerous traditions. There are a few who have appeared again and again over the years and have a special place in our art. We will list them here and provide some basic background information on each. These selected angels are listed due to their importance within our tradition and because they are used in the rituals of this book.

Melchizedek: This figure appears in old Jewish, Christian and Islamic writings. However, he existed before Abraham as a priest of the most high God or El Elyon. He also appears in the Dead Sea scrolls as the redeemer of angels, with similar attributes to those of the archangel Michael. He appears in the final jubilee of world history, to rescue the men of the lot of Melchizedek and to do battle with Belial and the children of darkness. This connects this figure with the ancient priestly mysteries, for the lot of Melchizedek are those of his line of initiation. In the fourth book of Pistis Sophia, he plays a key role in the process of purifying human souls for entry into the Treasury of Light. He is in many ways an important ancient figure for the development and growth of mysteries and may represent a spiritual and earthly office and not just a single being. Even though Melchizedek isn't an angel, he is an important figure in angelic magic.

Metatron: This angel is the Prince of the Countenance. In the Soncino Zohar glossary, Metatron is said to be the head of the world of creation and is also called the servant or body of the Shekinah. He is the chief of the Chieftains that reside beside the Divine Throne, and is charged with the sustenance of mankind. The name appears in both Jewish and Arabic occult texts. Metatron is said to be the master to whom many faithful Jinn bow and they regard him as their guide to the Divine.

Carriers of the Throne: The Divine Throne is described in the book of Revelations, as the result of a magical spirit vision. The seer mentions the throne with someone sitting on it with the appearance of jasper and carnelian. The seer appears ambiguous about the form of the entity on the throne. This is curious, considering how in Jewish tales, God is described with a beard and long flowing hair. Jasper and carnelian were known in ancient Egypt as the blood of Isis, creating a powerful link between their symbology and the Goddess. This is further enhanced by the reference to an emerald rainbow encircling the throne. The emerald color is associated with the green crescent, Venus, and the Queen of the Heavens. The Cherubim are the angels that bear the throne and they come from the Chaldean vision of angels. Images of the Cherubim adorn Babylonian temples and stone tablets.

These angels are esteemed and most honored before the Divine. Other angels seek their closeness and greet them in their coming and going, due to their placement near the Divine. Each of the four Cherubim angels has a different image. One angel is in the image of an eagle, who will intercede for birds. One is in the image of a bull, who will intercede for cattle. One is in the image of a lion, who will intercede for predators. One is in a human image, who will intercede for humanity. At the end of time, they will be aided with another four. This is alluded to in the Quranic verse: "And carriers of the Throne of your Lord over them, that day, eight."

The Cherubim angels are focused on the Holy presence, with no diversion from their attention to the Divine. They are immersed in the beauty of the presence of Divinity, praising, day and night, without stop. In the Islamic angelic tradition, it was said that God had created a white land, equal in size to the movement of the Sun in thirty days, filled with all kinds of creatures that don't know that God can be disobeyed, even for a split second. These creatures are said to be of the order of the Cherubim.

Gabriel: This is the angel known as the Faithful Spirit and is allegorically referred to as a column of light, before whom all other angels are like rows. This angel was named a spirit, because every breath from him becomes a spirit to an animal. He was assigned by the Divine to the management of the constellations, the movement of the planets, and all things under the sphere of the Moon. This angel's power is greater than the Zodiac. Gabriel is among the favorites of the angels, with six wings, from each of which springs another hundred. Two of these wings are folded except when he is sent on a mission of uprooting evil. His aides are assigned over all affairs of the world; their station deals with affairs of vengeance and protection from evil and injury.

Israfel: This angel is the herald of the commandments and the blower of spirits into the bodies. He is the carrier of the trumpet, which he holds while listening for the command to blow. The head of the trumpet is said to be the width of the heavens and the earth. When he blows, all that is in the cosmos, except those for whom the Divine has chosen otherwise, will be stunned. This most likely refers to the shock of the illusion unravelling and awareness of the reality of being. Israfel is a mighty angel with four wings. The first wing covers the east. The second covers the west. The third covers the distance from heaven to earth. The fourth covers Israfel out of respect for the Divine Majesty. His feet are below the seven earths, and his head ends at the corners of the pillars of the Throne. Between his eyes is a tablet of gemstones. Whenever the Divine ordained an event to occur in creation, the Pen would be ordered to write it on the Tablet. The tablet would then be brought close to Israfel, so it ended up between his eyes. From there it reached the angel Michael. These angels are Divine aides in the cosmos. They breathe the spirits into the angels residing over birth and creation and these become metals, plants or animals. They are the vital spiritual power by which these function and exist.

Michael: This angel is assigned over sustenance for bodies, and wisdom and knowledge for the souls. In the seven heavens is a sea filled with uncounted numbers of angels. Michael resides over that sea and no one knows his description or his wings except the Divine. The heavens would be like a pebble in the sea compared with the size of his open mouth. The hosts of the heaven and earth can't stand his presence, for the intensity of his light will burn them. He has aides set over the affairs of the world. Their duties are the initiating of the power of movement in the sources of manifestation, and overseeing what is necessary to achieve the purpose and perfection of things in creation.

Azrael: This is one of the most powerful and, at times, most misunderstood of the angels. This angel is the quieter of movements and the separator of bodies from their host spirits. Azrael is in the heaven of the world. God created his legs to be under the earth and his head in the highest heaven, facing the preserved Tablet. He has as many aides as those that die. All of creation is between his eyes and he doesn't grab the soul of a creature till it has fully received its inheritance and completed its time. It doesn't matter where the soul is, for he simply calls over and they all end up in his hands.

There is an old and interesting story about the angel Azrael. The angel of death entered unto Solomon's court and he began to stare at one of the people seated there and kept on staring. When the angel of death departed, the man approached Solomon and said, "O prophet of God, who was that?" He replied to him, "The angel of death." The man said, "I saw him looking at me as if he wanted something. I want you to save me from him. Command the winds to carry me to the farthest reaches of India." Solomon ordered the winds to do this. When the angel returned, Solomon said to him, "I saw you staring at one of my guests." The angel replied, "I was amazed by him, because I was ordered to snatch his soul in the farthest reaches of India in an hour and I saw him here with you."

Nahanael: This angel is the prince of insight.

Rahael: This angel is the prince of the secret of the Shekinah and in the book of Tobit, he is the healing angel.

Ashmoyeli: This angel is the prince of the scriptures.

Raphael: This angel is of Chaldean origin and is considered to be the guardian of the Tree of Life in the Garden of Eden. He is associated with healing, understanding, and medicine.

Suriel: This angel is associated with delivering knowledge to the prophet Moses and is called Surial the Releaser. He is also one of the twelve angels of the Divine presence and one of the seven angels that rule over the earth.

Tzadkiel: This is the angel of Divine justice.

Sartiel: In modern occultism, this is one of the angels that presides over the sign of Saggitarius. In ancient writing, he appears in a number of prayers for protection.

Nanial: This angel is associated with the seventy-two fold mystical name of God and is said to be a caster of the proud. He exercises dominion over the great sciences and influences philosophers. This angel also appears in medieval rites of protection.

Sharantiel: This is an angel that appears regularly in ancient medieval Arabic grimoires, and is said to be a stern and feared angel before whom all the spirits tremble.

Kehial: This is the angel of the Divine Being and thus, according to Al-Boni, is the servant angel of the word Allah.

Tamhiel: This is the angel of the Divine facet, the Opener, according to al-Buni.

Raziel: This is the angel of the mysteries and is said to be the author of the magical text, the Book of the Angel Raziel. He is believed to have handed his book to Adam and Eve after the fall, so that they could find their way back to the garden of Eden.

Safafiel: This angel is the prince of reason.

Afafiel: This angel is the prince of knowledge and stands guard in the halls of the seventh heaven.

Katatiel: This angel is the prince of understanding.

Aramiel: This angel is the prince of the crown.

Yahuel: This angel is the prince of testimony and his name literally means Yahweh is El. He is thus the mediator of the ineffable name and is one of the angelic princes of the Divine presence.

Ghassdaiel: This is the angel that governs the letters of Fire.

Ghathssaiel: This is the angel that governs the letters of Air.

Ghadha'aaiel: This is the angel that governs the letters of Water.

Ghasheezaiel: This is the angel that governs the letters of Earth.

Munkar and Nakeer: These are two strong and stern angels associated with the grave or afterlife. They ask questions of each individual in the grave or station of bardo, concerning the person's faith, which God the person worshipped, and which prophet the person believed in. Those who are true to their faith are rewarded by being shown their station in heaven. Those who are hypocrites or those who reply that they believed only what others believed are immediately struck down in punishment.

Shedechiel: This is an angel who governs all those in the celestial or upper worlds and those in the underworld.

Derdiel: This is an angel with a thousand heads and on each head a thousand faces, and on each face a thousand mouths, and in each mouth a thousand tongues, praising the Divine in a thousand different languages.

Haroot and Maroot: These two angels share much with the angels known as the watchers in the old biblical tales. They appear frequently in magical tomes and are used in ancient spells. The reason for this is that they are said to have taught people the art of magic, with a warning that there is a test for humanity in its use. They are also said to have fallen from grace. Arabic lore states that these two angels are being punished in the land of Babylon or modern day Iraq. One version of the story goes like this:

When Adam left paradise naked, the angels looked at him and said: "Our God, this Adam, the marvel of your awareness, lift him and don't let him be debased." When Adam later approached a host of angels, Haroot and Maroot were among them. They chastised him for his betrayal of his oath to God. Adam said to them: "O angels of my Lord, be merciful and don't chastise me, for what happened to me was the ordinance of my Lord." After that, God ill fated them till they disobeyed and were barred from rising up to heaven. During the time of Enoch, they approached him and told him their story. They asked him if he could pray for them, so that God might forgive them. Enoch asked how he would know that they were forgiven. They told him that if he saw them afterward, the prayer was accepted, but if he didn't see them, then they were doomed. Enoch purified himself and prayed; then he looked and they were gone and he knew punishment had befallen them. They were taken to the heart of Babylon, where they were given a choice - punishment in this world or the hereafter - upon which, they chose this world. It is widely believed that they remain to this day, hanging upside down from chains in a well, in the land of Iraq. This well is said to magically change locations in the desert and, if anyone was to find it, he would be taught the most powerful of angelic magic by these two angels.

Angels of the Seven Heavens: Amongst the most esteemed angels are also those that reside in the seven heavens. These angels are consistent in their adoration of the Divine in rising, sitting, kneeling and prostrating. They praise during the night and day and will not stop till the end of time. These angels appear in different forms in various tales among Semitic angelic lore. In one ancient occult version, the angel named Ishmael presides over the angels of the heaven of our world. The ministering angels are in the image of a calf. The angels of the second heaven are in the form of a scorpion, and an angel named Michael presides over them. The angels of the third heaven are in the form of an eagle, and the presiding angel over them is Saa'adiel. The angels of the fourth heaven are in the image of horses and the angel residing over them is Salsael. The angels of the fifth heaven are in the image of nymphs, and the angel residing over them is Kalkael. The angels of the sixth heaven are in the image of cupids, like cherubic boys, and the angel residing over them is Semchael. The angels of the seventh heaven are in the image of the children of Adam and the angel residing over them is Ruqiel.

Lieutenants of the 1st Heaven: According to the ancient occult book the Sepher Razial, these have a close link with our world and the seven planets. The angels of the first heaven are governed by seven archangels or angelic lords with great clout. These seven lieutenants reside over seven thrones. They are seated, surrounded by angelic soldiers in every direction. They listen to the people when they address them. Each of the lieutenants should be addressed individually and with piety. These seven lieutenants are called: Aorphenial, Ayigeda, Dohal, Phelmiya, Asimor, Phesker and Phoal. They are created as if from Divine Fire and from their eyes burst flames. Their soldiers are likewise fiery and are willing to listen and move forth into the world in all they are commanded from constructive and destructive work.

HEBREW ANGELS OF 1ST HEAVEN

Lieutenant	Angel (English)	Angel (Hebrew)
1st	Aorphenial	אורפניאל
2nd	Ayigeda	אינדא
3rd	Dohal	דוהל
4th	Phelmiya	פלמיא
5th	Asimor	אסימור
6th	Phesker	פסכר
7th	Phoal	פואל

The angelic prince Aorphenial and all the angels in his company are dedicated to listening to the needs of people all year long. They are also called upon to help cure illnesses.

The angelic prince Ayigeda and all the angels in his company are stern and quick to wrath. There is no mercy in their service and they are always ready to way-lay destruction in war, on cities, upon the seas, in calamities and in fires. Few escape their swords.

The third angelic prince Dohal and all the angels in his company are the ones who know all that occurs on the earth. They know what happens in this world in every month and year, and they will reveal what is veiled from you.

The fourth angelic prince Phelmiya and all the angels in his company are responsible for the administration of the hearts of kings, rulers, judges and the nobles in good and bad. They will bring about respect, greatness and glamor unto whomever they are asked.

The fifth angelic prince Asimor and all the angels in his company are the governors in the day and night. They are the guides of the movements of the Sun, Moon and rest of the planets. They also guide the spirits and the dead to their places and stations.

The sixth angelic prince Phesker and all the angels in his company are angels of war. They act by power and wile. They move from place to place and fly to all the corners of the world, seeking every fleeting scoundrel. The ancient books gave a ritual utilizing these angels for throwing fear on sight into the heart of one's enemy of war. This was for a time when soldiers fought in close quarters and engaged with melee weapons. This ancient ritual may be outdated today, since wars generally are no longer fought in this way.

The seventh angelic prince Phoal and all the angels in his company are knowledgeable about dreams. They guide and instruct the dreamers and explain their dreams to them.

The Angels of the Seven Planets: These angels appear differently named from grimoire to grimoire, and are considered very important for magical work. In our craft, the work observes the days and involves the seven planets of the ancients. It should come as no surprise, then, that the angels of the seven planets have an important position. The information about them has been standarized in our tradition. We have relied on the work of Al-Boni for this information.

The first angel is Ruqiel. This angel descends within a green dome with a green banner. The door of the dome is open and he is attended by five aides, all of whom are also in green garments. When the angel descends to the seeker, he will remain in the dome for a period and then will exit from the door. As he exits, a chair of light will be erected for him. This angel is best invited on Sunday.

The second angel is Gabriel, who descends within a dome of pure light. On top of the dome is a yellow banner. Gabriel will not exit from the dome till the seeker directs her speech to the angel. She has ten angels aiding her. The best time to call on Gabriel is Monday.

The third angel is Semsamiel,and in some manuscripts Shemesha-miel, who descends within a dome of pure light. On top of the dome are two red banners. With him are three aides, who stand beside the door of the dome. The best time to invite Semsamael is Tuesday.

The fourth angel is Michael, who descends within a dome of pure light. On the right of the dome is a white banner. Under the banner are four aides. The best time to invite Michael is Wednesday.

The fifth angel is Sarfiel, who descends within a green and white dome. The dome has two doors, and ten aides stand beside each door, with four banners in green and white. To the left of the dome stands a very tall angel known as Salsiael; she is the leader of Sarfiael's aides. The best time to invite this angel is Thursday.

The sixth angel is A'aniel, who descends within a dome of pure light with six aides and three banners. The best time to invite this angel is Friday.

The seventh angel is Kasfiel, who descends within a dome of black light, with thirty aides and ten black banners. The best time to invite this angel is Saturday.

The eighth angel is their governor, Tahitmeghilial. When this angel descends, two domes of radiant and blinding light descend first, shooting forth brilliant sparks. Then his dome descends between them with a thousand aides. Some of them stand around the dome and others stand outside the perimeter. This angel has fifty white banners and whenever he descends, the other seven descend behind him and none can approach the perimeter.

Those angels are associated with the Great Name symbolized with seven glyphs. They are also associated with traditional planetary correspondences such as colors, plants, incenses, rocks, days and nights of the week, and so forth. The one unique set of attributions is the association with seven Arabic letters known as 'Sawaqet'. Those seven letters are the only letters of the alphabet not used in the seven-versed chapter known as al-Fateha or Opener in the Quran. This makes them unique in Arabic esoteric lore and as such each was associated with one of the glyphs and the angels. Each of those letters starts a Divine name that is equally became associated with one of the glyphs. We have presented the accurate attribution as listed in al-Buni's work; however, it would make more sense for some of the letters to be switched. For example, the letter Shyn is associated with Mars and with it the Divine attributes, the Witness and Thankful, none of which appear suited for Martian energies. Nevertheless, we kept the attributes as they are, since we found no alternate arrangement in any other work.

SEVEN HOLY SYMBOLS AND THE PLANETARY ANGELS

Day, Planet, Sign	Symbol	Angel	Letter	Metal	Robe, Ink Color
Sunday Sun Leo	✪	Ruqiel רוקיאל	ف	Gold	Yellow
Monday Moon Cancer	ⴸ	Gabriel גבריאל	ج	Silver	White
Tuesday Mars Scorpio	٢	Semsamiel סמסמיאל	ش	Iron	Red
Wednesday Mercury Gemini	⚯	Michael מכאל	ث	Mercury	Blue
Thursday Jupiter Sagittarius	‖‖	Sarfiel צרפיאל	ظ	Tin	Blue & White
Friday Venus Libra	ⴇ	A'aniel עניאל	خ	Copper	Green
Saturday Saturn Aquarius	௬	Kasfiel כספיאל	ز	Lead	Black

✸ THE JINN ✸

The second most important group of unseen beings that you will come across is the jinn. They are responsible for many wondrous tales of ancient magicians. The word Jinn is their Arabic name, although they have other names as well in other cultures. While the lore has slight differences from region to region, they appear to share many of the same characteristics as the Sidhe, the Elves, the Fairy folk of Europe, and the Rakshaha. These are what modern magicians call the Elementals: salamanders, gnomes, undines, and sylphs. These beings are not elemental in the sense that they are of a given element, but rather in that they inhabit or take residence in various elements. The oldest of the jinn reside in caves under the ocean. Some of the jinn have the power of flight. Many of the jinn have a potent fiery nature, with strong electrical characteristics, and prefer to stay near sources of fire. The legends of yore called them, en masse, the inhabitants of the underworld or underearth. They also live among us in our homes, cities, grave sites, and in the wild areas near our dwellings. They see us as we go around our daily lives, staying mostly unseen. When one of us sees them even for a brief moment, that person assumes a paranormal experience has occured.

Knowing where the jinn live doesn't tell you who they are or what they are like. We don't really know much concerning the origins of the jinn. The tales of old tell of a race of beings, created before man from primordial fire. This race interacts with people or co-inhabits the world with humans. Their general attitude toward humans is that of aloofness and pride. This race is believed to be magical in nature or to be possessed of great spiritual powers and to be attuned to nature. They are sentient, with the moral capacity of telling the difference between good and bad. They have free will and share many of their own religious beliefs with humans. Overall, jinn populate the world with their own offspring, live in communities, and raise families. Evil jinn are considered renegades and outlaws in their own communities and are classified by us as demons. This race is invisible to us, unless it chooses to be seen. It is speculated that the reason they choose not to be visible or to take on a physical form is to avoid being spotted and killed by humans. Jinn also have been known to abduct humans and even to mate with them. Powerful jinn tribes who follow Iblis, a fallen jinn king, are enemies of humankind and are at war with us. This is mostly a spiritual war, but it also can be a physical one. In scriptures, the leader of this enemy jinn tribe is called Shitan, which means adversary. Shitan or Satan isn't the antithesis of God, but he is the sworn enemy of the human race from the jinn race.

We only have speculations and theories about the appearance of the jinn. We are referring, of course, to their actual state and not to how we encounter them. There are many old tales that describe their appearance, ranging from like a Cyclops to lizard-like people, but we haven't been able to verify these with any confidence. One of the most accurate depictions of a jinni, based on consensus of accounts, resembles that of the god Pan. Even if we can't see them, we can tell with almost absolute certainty when one of them has dropped by for a visit. We do know certain things about them that have been confirmed by the various accounts through the ages, as well as from our own experiences. As we mentioned, we know that they are generally invisible to us. The word jinn itself encompasses all that is hidden and veiled. It is common to say in Arabic, 'Jinnah Al-Layel', or the cover of the night. Children in the womb are called Janeen, because they are hidden from their mothers. The medieval Arab philosophers classified jinn as being made mostly from an ethereal body, yet still possessing reason, understanding, and even a capability for hard work. This idea that jinn are made of ethereal matter corresponds with the tales about the faeries. The faeries were called Sleagh Maith or the Good People. They were believed to be intelligent, studious and made from light, changeable bodies, like that of a condensed cloud. They could make their bodies appear or disappear at will. Some were believed to have mixed bodies, including some that were porous and thin, that fed by sucking on some oil or liquid.

Our experience is that jinn have two different bodies depending on their spiritual status. Upper jinn have a body that is translucent and shiny. Lower jinn have a body that is like a shadow. This may fit in with the stories of high elves and dark elves. You may spot one of the lower jinn, out of the corner of your eye, as a quickly moving shadow. You may think someone is there and when you turn, there is no one. They are very fast. You may at first consider this imagination or what some modern authors have referred to as astral nasties, but it is neither. If they get comfortable around you, they may not move for a while and you will find yourself staring for a few seconds to a minute at a shadow-form of a humanoid, before it quickly darts by you.

It is very possible that you will do jinn magic for a long time before you see one, and that your first encounter with a visible jinni may not be in a magical setting. They can appear and disappear at will and they don't need to be evoked to come. Indeed, there is a specific class of jinn referred to as residents. One of the rules in our tradition is that you release the resident jinn before you do any serious magical operation. This is important, as resident jinn may well interfere with the operation in any way they can. You may feel like you are tugging through a wall of resistance or that something is blocking full success. This is usually the work of resident jinn, who may object to having other beings invited into their area. Certain jinn and all angelic beings can be too much for the residents to handle, causing them unwarranted discomfort, based on their own alignment. You should release the residents to limit potential conflict and as a courtesy to them. Additionally, the release will force negative or hostile residents out from your sphere. You should almost feel like the room got empty beyond empty, as if something that you were used to being there is now gone.

In the end, the best way to know to get to know a jinni is to encounter one. It is a natural progression for those who practice our art, since they constitute one of the causes behind magical phenomena. Old grimoires tell of many tales of spirits teleporting the magician, causing invisiblity, delivering all kinds of fortunes and performing so many wonders. These tales are neither exaggerated nor are they blinds. Accomplishing those results doesn't depend on psychic powers or on the personal power of the magician, but on the aid and assistance of the Jinn and their own technology. Due to their semi-physical reality, they can cause direct physical effect even if normally unseen. This is why they constitute a good portion of our ancestors' lore and stories. They captivate us to this day. We write and tell stories about them, such as the magical creatures in *The Lord of the Rings*, and keep their lore alive through our entertainment media. Many people may be content to keep those experiences on the big screen, but very few of us who follow this path do.

It would be impossible to teach you all you need to do to gain mastery in the art of magical summoning in this book. The one lesson we can impart to you at this stage is that those who seek to dominate the spirits of nature and bind the jinn to their will, do so at their own peril. These beings are not created to be servants of people, magicians or otherwise; they only have one master. They follow the Divine and in ancient lore, this was the Queen of Heaven and Earth, who was also the Queen of the Underworld. Therefore, if you want to be a successful summoner, serve the Divine, the Queen of Heaven, Earth, and the Underworld. She will aid you with the armies of the jinn, just as She aided Solomon, who built a temple for Her using the ring of dominion, and enlisted the jinn to his service.

Also, keep the following points in mind: a) when the jinn kings arrive, you must ask them to enter into a pact of service to you; b) if you think you have managed to constrain them into a triangle of the art, then it isn't the kings that are present; c) if there are no physical signs of manifestations that can't be explained by your being in a trance, then your work isn't finished; d) don't be distracted by initial signs of physical manifestation into thinking your work is finished; e) if you see physical manifestations of jinn, be careful lest this be a distraction by their aides; f) don't summon them to prove their existence to yourself; g) don't go into this thinking to rely on traditional generic banishing methods, as their magic is superior to anything we possess, so only by the grace of the Goddess and Her angels will you be protected; h) don't ask them to do something against their nature, such as asking the servants of the jinn king of Saturn to aid you in a love spell, for they will do it and then punish you. We are sharing these points based on direct firsthand experience.

We have mentioned the kinds of assistance that the jinn gave our ancestors. These days we have many human inventions that make this kind of assistance unnecessary. You may be wondering how else jinn can help you now, or how they have been helping us over the last hundred years. Jinn serve in areas such as communication. Many cases of ouija board contact, channeling, and spirit guide communication are induced by the jinn. They are powerfully telepathic and, if they so choose, can be heard audibly. Jinn telepathy can be positive. There are tales of people who can tell, almost with certainty, many things about events and people. These people don't tend claim to be psychic, but rather that they are guided. This guidance is sometimes angelic, but most often it is a spiritual jinni assisting them. Such guiding jinn can communicate all sorts of information to you that can help you to understand people's motives better and to make good choices. This ability of the jinn can be very useful, but it can also be harmful. It is important to keep this in mind.

Jinn are also called upon to bring things to the magician. This can range from a person to an object. Many of the spells that fill the old Arabic texts are dedicated to this purpose alone. The same jinni called upon to bring something can also be sent to someone to deliver a message or to accomplish a specific task.

The question that may arise in the minds of many people who

are new to our craft is, can jinn really do what has been claimed? In our experience, the answer is yes, and much more. Here is a brief example: A few years ago, after watching the movie Independence Day, Nineveh and a friend got into her car to go home. A discussion began over whether or not aliens are another name for jinn and their potential power. The friend half-jokingly pointed out that she was too tired to drive and wouldn't mind being teleported. Nineveh jokingly obliged and said aloud: "If you want to play, let's play." The matter was dropped and they talked about jinn and aliens for a bit and then switched to another subject, while driving home. During the trip, they saw the normal signs of an upcoming bridge signalling they were close to crossing over water and driving through the next city. Nineveh felt strange, as if things were moving too slowly and things were flickering in and out or as if there was an overlay of images. He asked his friend if she was feeling something strange and she replied that she was and that things didn't feel or look normal. A few seconds later, as they were crossing an intersection, the road vanished and suddenly, they were driving toward the ocean front, overlooked by large buildings. To their dismay, that road also vanished as the car came to a full stop in an underground parking lot at the exact opposite end of town. It took them five minutes to come to terms with what had happened and where they were. They were about a thirty minute drive in the other direction from where they had been and, what's more, it took them a few minutes to even find a main road heading toward the theater and begin the journey back home, back toward the place where things got transformed. Driving along in a state of shock, their trip was interrupted halfway back by the sudden flash of an entity flying toward and then through the windshield. This being was draped in a bluish purple hooded robe and his body was pure shadow with piercing reddish eyes. He sat behind the driver. Nineveh enquired of his friend whether she saw or felt anything, and she confirmed the same image he saw and the feeling that someone was sitting behind them. The jinni delivered a simple message: that they had witnessed the power of the jinn, and they shouldn't reveal their secrets or names to the public. Amazingly enough, upon arrival home, they found out that the whole journey took less time than it would have taken to drive from the theater to the house directly, let alone half way there, teleported the opposite direction from the theater and then driving back! This wasn't the only story of teleportation either. A few years later, we held a class at our local study center. During the event, Nineveh suddenly felt the presence of an underworld jinni. He enquired if anyone was feeling different. Everyone at once complained of a feeling of heat, pressure on the head and strange psychic tension. He informed them that it was a jinni dropping by for a visit. The students left and afterward, we couldn't locate our black cat. We enquired from the last student to leave whether, on her way out, she might have let the cat out by accident. She wasn't sure, so an exhaustive search was conducted. After an hour or so, we abandoned the search inside and outside, and Frances went to bed grieving over the loss of her cat. Nineveh, feeling somewhat distraught as well, contacted a friend of his in California. His friend informed him that he had just had a dream about receiving a phone call from him about a missing cat and that, in the dream, she was taken by these strange looking creatures and that they would bring her back later. They were using some kind of unfamiliar device. He was shocked at this coincidence. Two hours later, they heard a meow that came as though from far away. Frances got up and began calling for the cat. She stood in the kitchen calling her name. The meowing increased, but she couldn't see her. Suddenly, as if from out of nowhere, the cat materialized before her, terrified and shaken. She behaved strangely for the next few days, as if she had experienced a horrifying ordeal, but she was unharmed.

There are many such tales and our magical colleagues have had their own share of encounters, ranging from one with a resident jinni that disliked company and threw objects at the human residents, to a woman who, asking for proof, had objects around her levitated and fell unconscious out of shock! This is why it is important not to be surprised or frightened if such things happen. The more committed you are to this path, the more likely it is that the jinn will visit you. This visit can be friendly or hostile or a combination of both, depending on who is visiting and how you react to them. The more attuned you are to the Divine and to your magical identity and craft, the more you will be able to get rid of hostile jinn and befriend wonderful spiritual jinn that will help you spiritually and even, when in desperate need, materially. There are stories of holy men who had spiritual jinn aiding them with monthly payments of gold under their prayer rugs, so that they need not disrupt their devotional efforts, or of spiritual jinn teleporting them so they could teach at seminars across the globe. They are more likely to do this for you, if they feel a spiritual affinity to you and consider you a friend.

Knowing the names of those friendly jinn is one of the treasures most guarded by the old masters of our craft. The reason for this is that most jinn don't want to be summoned by people with ulterior or unfriendly motives. Names have power in our art and the same principle applies to the names of jinn. Even though teachers in our craft guarded the names of most of the jinn with whom they worked, they did record some of the most important ones. These were commonly found in magical summoning textbooks as far back as the 9th century C.E. Some of those names appeared in minorly modified fashion in later European grimoires. They were left in print because without them, a newcomer to our art would be handicapped or would end up struggling for many years.

Seven Jinn Kings: These seven are associated with the planets and each resides over many tribes. Some consider these specific jinn kings to be enemies of mankind, but others feel that they are good and helpful. Our experience is that they are more neutral in their inclinations and not to be taken lightly. The names we have for them are more titles than actual names. Their real names are unknown and most likely unpronounceable to us. They are mentioned throughout history and by many cultures under various aliases.

The old magical texts refer to them as the mighty children of the realm of Tartarus and rulers over his domain. According to the Greeks, Tartarus was first born a god that personified the great stormy pit beneath the earth where the Titans were imprisoned. This pit was surrounded by a wall of bronze. Beyond that wall was a three-fold layer of night. Tartarus's name was often used as a synonym of Hades and later became a place of punishment for sinners. Tartarus gave birth to Typhon, a frightening creature of immense size with a hundred dragon heads springing from his shoulders. Tartarus is the underworld and the seven jinn kings may very well be the imprisoned Titans. They were also known in Sumeria as the Anunnaki or the seven judges of the underworld. The Sumerians believed that they were the children of Anu and rested in the underworld before the throne of its dark queen, Ereshkigal.

Therefore, while these seven Jinn kings correspond to the planets, they are more in tune with the netherworld energy. This is the reason many fear them, or feel that they are dangerous or harmful. This attitude is exaggerated, for they are not malignant demons by any means. There are other jinn of a more elevated or celestial energy. Unfortunately, no such planetary alternatives are mentioned in the old Arabic texts, only that these seven Jinn Kings have been replaced with faithful jinn of the same names.

Each of these kings have many children and each one is called after their most prominent child. This is a common Semitic practice. If the eldest son of John is Tob, then they would call you John, Father of Tob. The word for father in Hebrew and Arabic is Abba and the name for son is Ben. Maymon is known as Maymon Abba Nuch, which means that his son is Nuch Ben Maymon. This is important to know, since there are many jinn with the name Maymon. So, when calling the jinn king of Saturn, we have to identify him specifically with his full title Maymon Abba Nuch.

☉ The jinn king of the Sun is Al-Mazhab Abba Deebaj (the Golden One, father of Silk Brocade).

☽ The jinn king of the Moon is Al-Abeyadh Abba Al-Nur (the White One, father of the Light).

♂ The jinn king of Mars is Al-Ahmar Abbu Muhrez (The Red One, father of the Attainer).

☿ The jinn king of Mercury is Burqan Abbu Al-A'aja'eb (Two Thunders, father of Wonders).

♃ The jinn king of Jupiter is Shemhuresh Abbu Al-Waleed (Shemhuresh, father of the New Born).

♀ The jinn king of Venus is Zawba'ah Abba Al-Hhasan (Cyclone, father of the Handsome).

♄ The jinn king of Saturn is Maymon Abba Nuch (Prosperous, father of Rest)

Each of these jinn kings also has numerous aides or assistants from their tribes and many other offspring. Listing them all is beyond the scope of this book. As a matter of general principle, the kings should always be called under the auspices of angels. At no point should you call them forth to run any kind of errands personally. If you need their aid for something, always ask them to send a jinn from their tribe to assist you. This point of not asking the kings directly has been emphasized repeatedly by many of the accomplished masters in our craft.

Qaryn: The other jinni that you will most likely encounter is the Qaryn or consort, known in some traditions as the familiar or the personal genius. The Qaryn is a jinni that shadows people through their lives. Some say a person has only one and others believe a person has two, one male and one female. The Qaryn is believed to be responsible for assisting our spirits to integrate with our bodies and physical environment. The Qaryn also can influence on many of our decisions. If you are born and raised a Christian and find yourself inexplicably or strangely surrounded by and exposed to constant Jewish influences, then most likely your Qaryn is Jewish. The same can be said of other religions, ideologies, or even lack of faith. The Qaryn respects your ability to make free and informed choices, attempting to influence you in the way a friend would, by exposing you to situations and people.

It is also said that the Qaryn plays a role in relationship harmony. If you are in a relationship with someone that your Qaryn despises, or if your Qaryn dislikes their Qaryn, then it will try to cause as much trouble as possible between you. The Qaryn can also be affected by your own choices. If you lead a spiritually unhealthy lifestyle, then you are bound to attract to your home jinn from the underworld that would enjoy your company. These jinn tend to be too strong for the Qaryn to resist and in many cases, they tend to beat up the Qaryn and abuse it. The Qaryn may retaliate by whispering in your mind all kinds of suicidal thoughts or by leading you into situations where harm could befall you.

This has led many an ancient magician to seek protection from the Qaryn and its possible influences, especially if the Qaryn was unspiritual or malicious by nature. On the other hand, if your Qaryn is spiritual, then it will guide and assist you along your spiritual path. A spiritual jinni that guides you along the path is considered a higher, or upper world, genius. The prophet Mohammed mentioned that he had converted his Qaryn to his own faith and that his Qaryn continued to advise him and encourage him along his spiritual and devotional path. Many people's contacts with spirit guides are really communions with their Qaryns, who present themselves in a way acceptable to them.

The Four Elders: These elders are equivalent to the Elemental kings of the faeries. They preside over thousands of thousands of tribes including the powerful and magical Beni Ghilan, which pays them homage. The Beni Ghilan are the children of Ghol, known in the West as Ghoul. Folklore tells of the Ghilan taking on various forms, such as seductive women, to lure travelers off the path, and hideous monstrosities that feed on dead human flesh in catacombs and graves. We have no confirmation of these legends, but we do know from experience that this is a powerful and magical jinn tribe. The four elders govern them and most of the Ifreets. The Ifreets are the jinn aristocracy, known for their cunning and great strength. Ifreets can also deliver many magical artifacts to the magician. The jinn that teleported the car in our story was an Ifreet. Actually, it was one of the four Ifreets that advised King Solomon. Therefore, as they govern even the seven jinn kings, it is important that you establish a good relationship with those four jinn elders first.

The first elder, Mazer, is described as wearing a turban covered with pearls and rubies. He oversees the direction of east and has for an aid the king Al-Ahmar. The second elder is Kamtam and he is known as the elder with the golden pen and silver inkwell. He oversees the direction of the west and has for an aid the king Al-Mazhab. The third elder is Qaswarah who, if he moves or talks, all rulership, dominions, corners and hills tremble and shake. He oversees the direction of the south and has for an aid the king Shemhuresh. Taykal is the elder whose speech burns all veils and evil jinn. He oversees the direction of the north and his aid is Al-Abeyadh. These four elders are governed by a number of powerful and potent angels. The first is the angel and master Metatron, known as the angel with the whip, that the thunder praises and the angels fear. The second is the angel Shedechiel and the third is the angel Derdiel.

FOUR JINN ELDERS

Elder's Name	Arabic Spelling	Aid	Day	Direction
Mazer	مازر	Al-Ahmar	Tuesday	East
Kamtam	كمطم	Al-Mazhab	Sunday	West
Qaswarah	قسورة	Shemhuresh	Thursday	South
Taykal	طيكل	Al-Abeyadh	Monday	North

Shadow Creatures: For hundreds of years, there have been many reports around the world of people seeing what looked like shadow people or folk. They tend to appear as dark silhouettes of humanoid form. They rarely have details of any kind, and tend to run or go invisible once spotted. This isn't always the case, as some tend to linger and even stare down the observer. Some observers have recounted seeing them as columns of dark smoke or shapeless, wispy black blobs, some even having odors associated with them. A number of our magical associates have witnessed them and each one of them sensed that they personified pure evil and hate. It was no chance fleeting encounter also. In one case, the shadow creature was running down the street hunched over and fully visible to the naked eye, before disappearing.

It appeared as an embodiment of a shadow and had no facial features, and caused Frances's little dog to tremble in terror of its evil emanations, and her to murmur prayers making it disappear into thin air.

What exactly are these creatures? If you listen to a popular radio show, you have probably heard many theories ranging from ghosts to elementals. The shadow creatures are no great mystery at all; they are a specific class of underworld jinn. Underworld Jinn, in general, appear as shadow creatures when they manifest in the physical and even when they visit in dreams. Possibly, you may have spotted one or two of them, but only from the corners of your eyes, because they are very fast. Generally, those spotted by sensitive people have been the neutral or observing types. Those that do appear and tend to be very hostile and evil are the servants of Shaitan, and his earthly magical viceroy, the Dark One (Belial).

Their identity is no mystery to those experienced with jinn. What is mystifying is why they are now choosing to appear in such frequency and increased visibility in the West. We can honestly say that we have no idea why this is happening. It could be anything from a rift or portal that is open, to a sense of security in being visible among us. It could also be a prelude to something more sinister. According to the *Codex of Love*, as faith diminishes in the world, these creatures become more comfortable in showing themselves among us. "The fires of faith hold the shades and shadows at bay." They wouldn't appear to simply frighten, for as a rule they shy away from being seen by humans. The increasing frequency, visibility and the type of visitors are a serious concern. We simply don't know for a fact what the underlying causes are. What we do know is that, for those who have had run-ins with them, there is a growing need for protection. General methods of protection may not be sufficient against these foot soldiers of the Dark One. Here is a method that we have tested, that works against them with a good deal of success:

The method we present here is based on a Quranic chapter. This is a special chapter, whose spiritual servant is fierce and mighty. It also corresponds to the Source River or river basin of Paradise, from which the four rivers emerge. The name of the chapter is Al-Kawther, and we highly recommend that you say it in Arabic. Al-Kawther is the shortest chapter of the Quran, consisting of just three verses. It is the chapter of a challenge or duel, a chapter for blessings, a chapter for great prosperity, and a chapter for victory over one's enemies.

STEP ONE: Hold your cupped hands open before you. Say the following three verses seven times in Arabic:

(1) We have given you Al-Kawther. (**In-na A'- a'a -tie-nak-a Al-kaow-thar.**)
(2) So pray to your Lord and sacrifice. (**Fa-ssal-lee Le-rub-bi-ka Wa An-hhar,**)
(3) That your hater be the one amputated. (**In-na Sha-nee-a'-ka Hua Al-ab-tar.**)

STEP TWO: Spit into your palms three times and then move your hands over and around your body front and back from head to toe as if you were washing it.

STEP THREE: While doing this, say repeatedly: "**O Rouhaniah of Al-Kawther, protect me from the touch and presence of shadow creatures and the children of Iblis and the Dark One.**"

So far, we have covered the sacred names of our art, the angels, and the jinn. In the next stage, we will be looking at the magical letters that form many of those sacred names of power and angelic names. We will start doing some practical magic intended to illuminate and connect you with the Divine emanations. You want to be connected with the Source at all times and one good way to accomplish this magically is through working the Tree of Life.

Works Referenced

al-Buni, Ahmed (D. 1225 C.E.). *Shamsu al-Ma'aref al-Kubrah*. Maktabat Isha'at al-Islam. Delhi, India.

al-Buni, Ahmed (D. 1225 C.E.). *Manba'a Ussol al-Hikmah*. Maktabat al-Hidayah. Surabaya, Indonesia.

al-Toukhi, A'adu al-Fatah. *al-Siher al-Azeem (v1-3)*. al-Maktabah al-Thaqafiah. Beirut:1991

l-Falki, Mahmood al-A'askari. *al-Muntkhab al-Nafees fi A'alem Nabi Allah Idris*. Beirut, Lebanon.

4

The Magical Tree

"She is more precious than pearls; and all the things you value are not equal unto her. Length of days in her right hand; in her left are riches and honor. Her ways are ways of pleasantness, and all her paths are peace. A tree of life is she to those that lay hold of her; and every one that firmly grasps her will be made happy." (Book of Proverbs)

The Tree of Life is one of the most popular concepts in the occult world today. It has a long and rich history that dates back thousands of years. Although it is popular today, it isn't truly given its due. Many modern magical systems and groups see it as road map for their journey. It is also used as the blueprint by which their entire system of correspondences is organized. As with many aspects of our craft, the modern and ancient views don't always match. We can't possibly cover the mysteries of the Tree of Life in a single chapter of a book, but we can give you a tool by which you can experience it on your own.

Experiencing the Tree of Life is an interesting challenge. On one hand, you will hear occultists talk about the Tree of Life as a living breathing force and on the other, they will center most of their discourse on a diagram that is crafted by humans to represent spiritual concepts. The two views tend to overlap in interesting ways that more often confuse than bring clarity to beginners in our art. The confusion happens when the experience is measured by the various points of the diagram. We consider it confusion, because it gives the impression that the Tree of Life is a ladder that you can climb, stopping at different stages. This confusion grows even more when you start piling everything from Tarot cards to metals and herbs on the diagram. What we are seeing here is a mixture of two distinct approaches. The idea of correspondence is an authentic occult methodology. Old writing shows that many aspects of the universe were attributed to the planets. When you attribute the planets to the Divine emanations of the Tree

of Life, it becomes an easy jump to attribute all those same correspondences of the planets to the emanations too. The Tree of Life metamor-
phoses from a spiritual concept, a holy object, to an occult filing cabi-
net. It becomes customary to ask questions like, "Where on the Tree
of Life do you fit Innana?" Historically Innana, the Sumerian Queen
of Heaven, was considered larger than the Tree of Life. Furthermore,
the Tree of Life was considered an object growing in Innana's Garden.
From a psycho magical point of view, those are semantics, but from a
traditional point of view, what they do is muddy the water and limit
the student's ability to appreciate the full meaning of each concept.

The Tree of Life has its oldest mention in the lore of the Sumerians
and the Chaldean magi. It was associated with the Goddess of Love
and Queen of Heaven, to symbolize the primeval mother at the central place of the earth. The roots reached down into the underworld,
while the branches ascended to the heavens with the stars as fruits.
This association with the tree continued when the Goddess was openly
accepted by the tribes of Israel and Judah as Asherah. Asherah's symbol was the Tree of Life in the form of the female palm tree. Female
palm trees provide much needed food in the desert; they grow near a
source of water and provide shelter from the sun. The rituals honoring the Goddess were held in sacred groves. Since the Jews were in
exile in Babylon, it was only normal that their mysticism or Qabalah
was influenced by the Chaldean magi. The Qabalah owes its heritage
not only to the Jewish mystical lore, but to the entire philosophy that
spawned it, which has its roots in Chaldea, Neo-Platonic thinking and
the Illuminati movement of the Middle east (Ishraqia). Even though
the Goddess appears to be absent in Jewish writings, evidence of Her
mysteries can still be found in the Tree of Life itself.

In the Qabalah, the Tree of Life is depicted as a diagram of ten
spheres and twenty-two connecting lines. The ten spheres, known as
emanations, are like fruits. The connecting lines between them are like
branches. The ten emanations are facets of the Divine. They are emanations of light. The totality of the emanations contains the essence of
life itself. Each emanation shares of itself in perfect love. Each of these
emanations represents an infinite spectrum or a world of its own. We
experience each of these as a state of being or a level of reality all unto
itself. Naturally, our grasp is of but a fraction of the totality of the
Limitless Light. These emanations actually overlap with each other
since they are all aspects of the singular Divine facet. When we talk
about the facet of Wisdom, we mean this in a more cosmic and Divine
element. By meditating on each of these emanations, through names

and symbols, you will be able to raise your spiritual awareness to a new level. The Tree of Life diagram is the key knot tying together the relationship between traditional Jewish mystical writing of the Qabalah and modern magic. Many modern magicians view it as a road map or a grid for correspondences. But another way to look at it is that at its heart, it is a reminder that magic is both the path of wisdom and the path of love. Love is the highest spiritual expression and is the twin of wisdom. It isn't the unique domain of mysticism. Both the heart and mind approaches are needed for a balanced journey along the path of the mysteries. You might probably be used to magic being expressed as the path of power and causing things to bend to your will. The idea of love may appear weak and sentimental to some, but the initiate knows that love is a powerful force on its own. In the hands of a master, love-based magic can be one of the most powerful kinds of magic for manifesting forces and even consecrating talismans. It goes back to the fact that the three primary natures of the Goddess are Light, Life and Love. These facets are therefore expressed and celebrated in the Tree of Life and brought to life in our magical craft by the rites and ceremonies we perform and our attitudes to the world around us.

HEBREW TREE OF LIFE

Emanation's Name English	Emanation's Name Hebrew	Translation
1) Kether	כתר	Supreme Crown
2) Chokmah	חכמה	Wisdom
3) Binah	בינה	Understanding
4) Chesed	חסד	Mercy
5) Geburah	גבורה	Strength
6) Tiphareth	תפארת	Beauty
7) Netzach	נצח	Victory
8) Hod	הוד	Splendor
9) Yesod	יסוד	Foundation
10) Malkuth	מלכות	Kingdom

We will look at each of those emanations beginning at the bottom of the diagram and moving upward. The Kingdom is the tenth emanation and represents all that lies under the Divine's dominion. It is the dwelling of the Shekinah, or the feminine facet of the Divine One. The world of Kingship is both the Revealed World (expression of Understanding) and Hidden World (expression of Wisdom). Modern occultists have attributed the four Elements and Earth to the Kingdom. The beginning and end of all things are in the dwelling of the Divine, for without the Goddess, the continuity of creation and process of transformation would be impossible. This means that the Kingdom represents all that rests under the Divine's physical and spiritual dominion, so the entire physical and spiritual universe and all its inhabitant would be part of it. The physical universe dwells in the Goddess's spiritual kingdom. The spiritual kingdom dwells in the bosom of the Goddess, She is ever the pregnant Mother.

The Foundation is the ninth emanation and is the point of balance from which the entire trunk of the tree grows. The foundation of spiritual emanations is a complete focus of Divine Will, coupling with it both Divine Mind and Emotions. For our lives to have a Foundation in Light, we must have a complete focused intention in our spiritual aspirations toward the Divine. This is what is known in the Quran as the 'Straight Way' or the narrow way, straight path, path of the arrow and other such titles. For most people today, this arrow is inverted and their intentions are focused toward feeding their animalistic souls. Those whose foundations are in Godly Soul are marked by the never-ending awareness of the Divine in every aspect of their lives, from consumption of food to business transactions. That there isn't a secular activity in the Godly Soul doesn't mean that religious institutions play a dominant role in all human affairs. It merely indicates that spirituality and our connection and awareness of the Divine's presence are not allocated a separate division of our consciousness.

Hod is the eighth emanation and signifies the Divine splendor in our lives. The Divine splendor manifests in nature and the beautiful world around us. It ignites within us the power to feel connected with all life and to appreciate the beauty that surrounds us. This is the active form of the Divine Word. The Divine Word contains what the Greeks called Ethos (character and relationship), Pathos (feelings), and Logos (logic). The empathic nature of this emanation is best understood through the Semitic greeting in Arabic as 'Assallam Allaikum' and its Hebrew counterpart, 'Shalom Aleichem.' Both phrases carry the same meaning: 'May you enter, or may there be upon you, a state of perfect peace.' The greeting is spoken, develops positive relationships, healthy feelings of peace and is the most logical thing to say to let someone know you are a friend and not a foe. By permitting our minds to contemplate the glory of the Divine Word and allowing it to fill us and radiate out from us, we are able to enter into this state of peace and communicate the splendor of Divine presence. This greeting is extended further in the philosophy and greeting of the Magi of the Magic Society of the White Flame. We initialize our greetings with 'Peace Profound.' This represents the elevation of initial human contact and entry into perfect state of peace. It is met with 'Love Sincere' from the point of empathy and spiritual connection with the eternal essence of the Goddess. Then, in a state of union, both individuals declare their aspiration and reaffirmation of their role in the magical path through 'In Service of Divine Light.'

Netzach is the seventh emanation and represents the Divine's active grace in the world. Through its essence, we are driven by a desire to break down barriers between individuals. The ability to establish love-to-love connection between us is spiritual victory. As Chesed is the emanation of giving, so is Netzach the emanation of reaching out. Even though many people associate this emanation with love, this is a misunderstanding of its nature. It doesn't deal with love in the sense of romance, in falling in love per se, but rather true love, where you feel for others as much as you feel for yourself. It is the concept of Agape rather than Eros. It is a necessary tool that allows us to experience spirit outside the limitations of our ego boundaries and, hence, spiritual victory.

Tiphareth is the sixth Divine emanation. Beauty is associated with the Goddess. Aphrodite is the Goddess of love and beauty. Love is in the heart and the heart is the center. Tiphareth is the center of the Tree of Life and its cosmic eternal love radiates in utter beauty. In the Quran, it says that the Divine is beautiful and loves beauty. This love is manifested in making the creation as beautiful as possible. This emanation provides a harmonizing influence within the Tree of Life. One of its other titles is Rachamim (the Compassionate One). The term Rachamim is related to the word Rechem or womb. Tiphareth is not only the heart, but also the womb of the Tree. Its compassion and nurturing qualities bestow its beauty and majesty. Through its energy, the aspirant can develop and grow a wise heart. According to the Hassidic Jewish teachings, Tiphareth also carries with it the quality of truth. The concept of the Divine as the Truth predominates the Arabic occult literature. Truth is the antithesis not only of falsehood, but of illusion; as such, the Divine is the Truth or the Real. Through the relationship of love between us and the Divine, we are surrounded with beautiful light and we experience the union of the womb. This is the union of the Real, beyond the illusion.

Geburah is the fifth emanation and it means strength. Other titles for Geburah are Din (Judgment) and Pachad (Fear). The Goddess Ishtar is depicted standing with one foot on the back of a fierce lion. The strength and dominion of the Goddess shapes and directs spiritual energies so that they can achieve their goals. Geburah deals with discipline and self-mastery on all levels. The idea of the Great Work, or Avoido in Hebrew, comes from proper application of this emanation. Avoido is based on the process of self-containment or self-effacement. It permits us to outgrow our animal soul, replacing it with the Divine soul. Animal soul is our inert drive for lustful pleasure and self-fulfillment, even at the expense of others. This pursuit of pleasure is devoid of love. According to Al-Boni, Behamit (the Beast) is the reflection of God's Throne in the Underworld (its antithesis). The Godly Soul allows the magician to be other-centered, rather than being self-centered. The pursuit of pleasure is tempered with spirit and love. It is not denied or ignored, but simply transmuted. When people manifest Dominion without loving spirit, it becomes a gateway to the demonic Evil. The first act of Satan was to tempt Adam and Eve to disobey the Divine, an act of falsehood as they violated their promise. Once this pattern of disobedience was established, it was easy to tempt man with the first real sin, murder.

Chesed is the fourth emanation and is the first form of what is manifest. Mercy is inherent in the first act of manifestation. It is a veil for the love involved in every part of the process of light bringing to fruit the seed of life in its bosom. Another title for Chesed is Gedulah or greatness. This greatness led Al-Boni to draw a parallel or a relationship between this world and the Seat of the Divine Throne. The Seat is said to be incomprehensible, for it is absolute greatness of which, due to the limits of the mind, we can't conceive. Rabbi Yitzhak of Troyes identified Chesed with the Divine's motivation to create the Universe. It is a flow, which propels us toward unity with the Creator via the holy attributes of bestowal.

Binah is the aspect that gave the manifesting Light form and function. It is the Cosmic Womb of Life and Creation. It is generally conceptualized as the feminine form or the Shekinah, the Holy Queen or the Mother. The Zohar states that Chokmah deposited its seed in Binah. This union gave birth to the remaining seven emanations. Chokmah is eternal Divine Wisdom and is considered to be the primordial spiritual inspiration for the evolution of the Cosmos. Al-Boni wrote that Wisdom is a form of knowledge, and there is really nothing better than knowledge of Divine. Wisdom is an attribute of being that is revealed by the Mind. It is divided into six categories: secret wisdom, declared wisdom, wisdom in spirit, wisdom in soul, wisdom in heart, and wisdom in body. The occult is the first manifestation, which was awarded by The Real, in His brilliance, to those in the worlds whom He desired from His knowledge to guide to knowing Him. For none can know Him, except by the occult measure, which was placed in you before manifestation.

Kether is the Divine Light in the point between non-manifestation and manifestation, or the point of first existence of being. Some of its titles are: the Ancient One, the Most Holy Ancient One, the Ancient of the Ancient Ones, the Ancient of Days, the Concealed of the Concealed, the Primordial Point, the Smooth Point, the White Head, the Inscrutable Height and the Vast Countenance. Al-Boni had this to say about the Inscrutable Height: "Know that the Exalted One (the High One) is He whose station has no station above it. The exaltation (height) is either sensory as in degrees or as elevation in the level of the comprehensible, such as in the interface between the cause and the total or incomplete causality. If you understood this mental process, you would know that manifestation couldn't be divided into degrees with variations of mental phases." Of His name the Concealed, Al-Boni wrote that "indeed God is the concealed One, for if you contemplated Him from the point of sensory comprehension, He would be concealed from this." The concealment is a declaration of the Divine's wisdom. Certain traditions ascribe to Kether six hundred and twenty pillars of light. In conceptual terms, it represents the Divine Head.

There are of course more than ten aspects to the Divine. However, the Tree of Life is one manifestation of the Holy Light. It is the movement and manifestation of Divine Light within the various levels of spiritual and material reality. Any study and exploration of the Tree of Life should be focused on this Divine experience. The aforementioned muddying occurs because the seeker begins to see the Tree of Life in interpersonal or mundane terms, due to mundane correspondences and extensive human-centered psychological analysis.

Being a holy symbol passed on from culture to culture, the Tree of Life also appears in Arabic occult work. The actual lore surrounding the Tree of Life and Four Worlds is covered in the writings of the Brotherhood of Purity and the Ismaili. The ten emanations and Four Worlds are covered in their esoteric lore, but are illustrated in concentric circles rather than a tree diagram. In the Arabic writing, the Tree of Life retains its original tree form. The Divine facets are represented as leaves, because they are easier to symbolize on a diagram when dealing with so many names and facets. It is also keeping with the older Sumerian concept since Palm trees have distinct leaves. Unlike the Hebrew version, the Arabic Tree of Life contains more than ten leaves to represent a wider array of emanations and is portrayed as being part of the Garden of the Eden.

Old Arabic Diagram of the Tree of Life

This diagram of the Tree of Life contains many layers of symbolism. First of all, we have the two pillars with an arch. The arch represents the heavens. Even though it isn't etched on the image, a possible fitting decoration would be the seven planets or zodiacal signs, or simply the stars themselves. The arch is resting on two pillars that represent the duality of all things in nature. There are five mini-windows at the top of each of those pillars. They represent the perfect ten. It is stated in the writing of the Ismaili and the Brothers of Purity that: "By the ten ordinations, the world was created. Upon ten words is the world fixed. The Divine to you is the treasures of the world." Upon each pillar are eight plaques. The sixteen total represent the movement of the four Elements and their manifestation. The four Elements flow from the four rivers within the gardens of Paradise. Between each plaque there are smaller pillars for a total of 42 pillars, representing the establishment of the 42-fold name of the Creative Innovative Divine One.

Upon each pillar is written the name of four of the gardens. They are written so that by tracing the movement from plaque to plaque between the pillars, we would have the movement of the flaming sword. They depict the barrier of entry into this state without first experiencing the pronouncement of the Divine name and its action through the four Elements in our temporal world. This is the mystery of the Cherubim guarding the garden of Eden from the return of the fallen or descending spiritual man, yet the guard who keeps us out is also the guard that lets us in. Through working the spirit of the Elements and the Divine names of the world of formation, we slowly begin to experience the facets of the various gardens. The experience in and of itself is a matter of ascension from one heavenly state of bliss to the next.

Upon the foundation of the pillars are a seven and eight pointed star, both of which are symbols of the Goddess of Love and Queen of Heaven. This indicates that the foundation of the pillars and the gardens rests on the presence of the Divine Queen of Heaven. This is further alluded to on the bottom of the building in the center of the diagram, where is written, the 'Holy Presence', which is a reference to the Shekinah or Divine Feminine in the Jewish Mysticism. On top of the building, just underneath the tree, is written "The Doors of the Gardens", indicating again that the doors of the gardens, like the gardens, are only accessible through the experience of the Divine Presence, the Queen of Heaven. This is also understood in the Jewish tradition as the Queen of Heaven is known as Malkah, and Malkuth, the tenth emanation, is considered the emanation of not only the manifest world, but also the garden from which flow the four rivers of paradise. Therefore, the tenth emanation symbolizes how the perfect ten is in essence the gate of the garden of Eden.

The name on the plaque nearest to the base is House of the Peace. Unlike the other seven, it isn't a garden per se, but a spiritual abode in which peace profound reigns. This is achievable in this world by those who follow the path of the priest and king of the city of peace, Melchizedek. Those children of Light, through walking the path of magic and service of the Queen of Heaven, attain an inner sense of peace and reside in its abode in total safety. The next seven are various gardens that are suitable for different stages of spiritual attainment and closeness to the Divine. These seven gardens are as follows, in ascending order:

- Garden of the Sanctuary
- Garden of Immortality
- Garden of Bliss
- Garden of Paradise
- Garden of the Dwelling
- Garden of Eden
- Garden of Intercession

Shifting our analysis to the building in between the pillars, we observe that it is carried by a three-layered platform lifted upon six pillars. Six is the number of perfection and the gateways to the garden are lifted through perfection that results from union with the Light. Between these pillars pervades the Holy Presence of the Divine. The building contains eight gates to the eight heavenly abodes. Each gateway has eight mini-bricks, totalling sixty-four bricks in all. There are twelve windows at top of the doors, representing the zodiacal signs. Above the gates rests the Tree of Life. On the bottom of the tree is written, the Divine, meaning it is the Divine One who nourishes the tree and gives life to its many leaves (sacred attributes). Above the word Divine is written "Beatified Tree." On each leaf is written an attribute of the Divine such as Ever Living, the Light, the Truth, the Compassionate One, and so on. Those correspond with the 99 names used in Sufi work. Above the Tree of Life rests once again the star of the Queen of Heaven, but this time with six leaves. Above that star is written: "Divine Throne."

In the writing of the Ismaili and the Brotherhood of Purity, when discussing the Tree of Life, they quote the Quranic verse which states that: "the example of a good word is like a good tree." They say that the example of the word, which is the first limit charged with action in the world of creation is like a good tree, that is, the logos that is active with action in the world of nature in teaching, leading to the manifestation and guiding to the containment of happiness and expansion of the Divine way. For every being, the Divine has placed a path from among the paths and a will from the wills, so that it will be a guide to what is higher from the limits in the Divine faith. The first mind is the center of the world of minds to the acting mind. The acting mind comprehends everything and it is center of to the world of bodies, from the fixed celestial bodies to the volatile bodies in the world of being and decay. The world of bodies contains the emanations of the minds and is central to the existence of the pure self, which is the soul of the orators to the self-existing. The self-existing contains everything that has reached to him that has flown from the blessing of innovation. This center gives birth to three others of nine divisions, all feeding from the same center.

THE PERFECT TEN IN ACTION

This same illustration can be understood as the four levels of manifestation, two of which represent the upper celestial worlds and the other two, the lower world. The lower world manifestation occurs in various spiritual stations and levels of awakening. This table shows an understanding of the emanations and the four worlds that is slightly different from, but parallel to, what is commonly found in modern Qabalah literature.

Upper Limits		Lower Limits	
First Being is the First Innovator	Upper Celestial	First Being is the Logos	The Station of Revelation
Second Being is First Arisen	2nd Celestial	2nd is the Foundation	Station of Recital
3rd Being	3rd Celestial (Saturn)	3rd is the Guide	Station of Will
4th Being	4th Celestial (Jupiter)	4th is the Door	Station of Detailed Oration
5th Being	5th Celestial (Mars)	5th is the Proof	Station of Deciding between truth and falsehood
6th Being	6th Celestial (Sun)	6th is the Caller to Edicts	Station of Protest and Passing Knowledge of the Return
7th Being	7th Celestial (Venus)	7th is the Limitless Caller	Station of Teaching the Upper Limits and Inner Worship
8th Being	8th Celestial (Mercury)	8th is the Limited Caller	Station of Teaching the Lower Limits and External Worship
9th Being	9th Celestial (Moon)	9th is the Limitless Notified	Station of Taking the Oath and the Covenant
10th Being	10th The Four Elements	10th is the Limited Notified	Attraction of Responsive Souls

❂ LETTERS OF LIGHT ❂

We have looked at the fruits of the Tree of Life; let us take a look at the branches. These branches are the letters that act as gateways or portals between these Divine facets. In essence, each gateway is another dimension of reality or a universe on its own. Myths and stories tell us of the Divine origins of many alphabets and how they contain keys to Creation or the Spiritual Realms. The runes of ancient Europe are the magical symbols given by Odin himself; similarly, according to the Jewish lore, the Hebrew letters are cosmic glyphs containing Divine Truth. People believed these letters to be capable of changing the order of Creation. The Arabic language was perceived as the language of people in heaven. Angels also were believed to speak their own language; this belief has been the source of extensive lore. The magi of old viewed each letter as a world of its own, with its own sets of traits and attributes. Every letter in these magical alphabets was awarded numerous correspondences, ranging from Elemental properties to plants and spirits. Some alphabets were accompanied by mystical mantras and beautiful ornate designs to activate their power. The ancient people wove a rich mosaic of occult lore and practices around their languages. Many of these practices lend themselves easily to other languages.

It is important to keep in mind that the letter images that form the alphabet are not the same as the spoken language. A language renowned for its magical or spiritual properties can be written in many different letter designs. Letter designs also change through time, so what may be considered a magical alphabet today may have looked drastically different a few hundred or thousand years prior to its current form. Therefore, it is important to take cultural self-promoting mythology with a grain of salt, no matter how widely accepted it may be. Understanding the basic historical roots of these alphabets is an important precursor to delving into their hidden occult lore.

One of the earliest-known alphabets, Proto-Canaanite, was developed around 2000 B.C.E. among the people of the East Mediterranean. The Proto-Canaanite alphabet was made of twenty-two consonant letters. There is evidence to show that it was influenced by Egyptian pictograms, since some of the hieroglyphics adopted included an ox, a house, and so forth. They were based along the lines of the acrophonic principle, which states that the phonetic value of a symbol is the first letter of the name of that symbol. From the Proto-Canaanite alphabet

emerged the Phoenician and South Arabian alphabets. The Phoenician alphabet was almost identical to the Proto-Canaanite, but with
more linear symbols. The Phoenician script was adapted into Greek,
Hebrew and Aramaic. In turn, the Greek became the model for the
Etruscan, from which the Roman alphabet and, ultimately, all Western alphabets derived.

The Old Hebrew alphabet was the alphabet in which most of the
Old Testament of the Bible was originally written. It was the script
of the old prophets of the Bible and closely resembled the Phoenician. When the Jews returned from their Babylonian exile, they had
become accustomed to the Aramaic speech and alphabet. Many no
longer understood Hebrew script. When Ezra the Scribe read the Hebrew scripture to them, he translated it into Aramaic (Nehemiah 8:8).
Old Aramaic was also the language of Jesus and the Apostles, and
dates back to the second millennium B.C.E. The adapted Aramaic script
was known as the Jewish script. It was characterized by its square
form and remains in use today as modern Hebrew script.

The original Hebrew alphabet may have had up to twenty-eight
letters, as some researchers on ancient Hebrew believe. In his book
'How the Hebrew Language Grew,' Edward Horowitz mentions one of those
missing letters as Ghayin, merged with the Hebrew Ayin. Currently,
the Hebrew alphabet is composed of twenty-two consonants, with no
vowels. Some of these letters change shape when they are at the end of
a word and become known as final letters. Three of the Hebrew letters
are known as mothers, twelve as singles and seven as doubles. These
correspond to three of the five basic Elements (Fire, Air, Water), the
twelve Zodiacal signs and the seven planets.

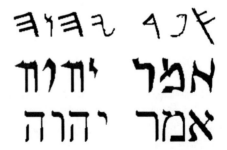

First line - Old Hebrew;
Second Line - Aramaic Hebrew;
Third Line - Modern Hebrew

The extensive occult lore surrounding the Hebrew alphabet was documented within medieval Jewish mystical texts, such as the *Sepher Yetzirah*, *Zohar* and *Bahir*. As a primary source for understanding the mysteries of the Hebrew alphabet, we have relied on the Sepher Yetzirah, as provided in its oldest known copy, written in Arabic with commentary, by Saadia ben Joseph Al-Fayyumi.

The lore surrounding each Hebrew letter derives from four areas. The first is the meaning of the letters and the mystical or symbolic analysis stemming from that. The second is from analyzing the various shapes of the letters, as far as some letters contain other letters within them. The third is from analyzing the location of letters within important words in Hebrew scripture, such as Beth being the first letter of the Bible. The fourth is through the study of the numerical values of the letters and the words they form.

Contemplating the shapes of the letters is an important tool for unveiling their deeper and concealed spiritual mysteries. The letter Aleph א, for example, is conceived as being made of two Yuds י with the letter Vav ו between them. The two Yuds י are symbolic of the upper and lower waters and the Vav ו represents the firmament between them. Water is a metaphor for spiritual states of being; the upper water is the state of bliss arising from contact with the Divine's presence and the lower is that which is experienced by most people as the state of separation.

The meaning of each letter also presents a symbolic clue to its spiritual nature. The letter Aleph means ox, which symbolizes spiritual stability as well as strength. The letter Lamed means shepherd's staff and represents authority, both spiritual and material. When the letter Lamed follows the letter Aleph, it forms 'AL', which symbolizes strong authority. The word AL is also the Divine name EL, which translates into 'Strong One of Authority'. When the letter Tav is added to El, it becomes Elath or Goddess. The letter Aleph is the first letter of the Hebrew alphabet, Lamed is in the middle, and Tav is the last. The Goddess is the beginning, the middle and the end of creation. Further occult meanings for the letters are also extrapolated based upon the words they start or end. As an example, the letter Aleph forms the word Phala פלא, which translates into wonder and miracle. Mathematical symbolisms are also considered within the Qabalah of letters. The numerical range of Aleph is one, symbolizing the Divine Oneness and unity of all things.

CORRESPONDENCES OF THE HEBREW LETTERS

Ancient & Modern Letter		Old & New Name	Polar Sphere of Influence	Meaning	Type
ひ	א	Al Aleph	Air, Spirit-Wind	Bull, Strong, Leader	Mother
⨅	ב	Bet	Life, Death	House, Tent, Into	Double
Ⴑ	ג	Gam Gimmel	Peace, Harm	Camel, Walk	Double
ㅜ	ד	Dal Dalet	Wisdom, Foolishness	Door, Enter	Double
⥾	ה	Hey	Vision, Blindness	Look, Breath	Single
Y	ו	Waw Vav	Hearing, Deafness	Nail, Hook, Secure	Single
⊏	ז	Zan Zain	Odor, Odorlessness	Cut, Nourish	Single
⊞	ח	Hhet Chet	Word, Silence	External Divide	Single
⊗	ט	Thet	Eating, Hunger	Surround, Snake	Single
⨼	י	Yad Yod	Copulating, Castration	Closed Hand, Worship	Single
⨊	כ	Kaph	Wealth, Poverty	Open Hand	Double
Ɉ	ל	Lam Lamed	Acting, Impotence	Ox Goad, Shepherd's Staff	Single

94

Ancient & Modern Letter		Old & New Name	Polar Sphere of Influence	Meaning	Type
ᴡᴡ	מ	Mah Mem	Water, the Earth	Water	Mother
ᔨ	נ	Nun	Walking, Limping	Darting Fish, Seed	Single
⧘	ס	Sin Samech	Rage, Loss of Faith	Prop, Thorn	Single
◉	ע	Ghan Ayin	Laughing, Loss of spleen	Eye	Single
⊂	פ	Pey	Fertility, Desolation	Mouth	Double
ℴᴧ	צ	Tsad Tzade	Thinking, Loss of Heart	Fish Hook, Man on His Side	Single
⊸	ק	Quph Qoph	Sleeping, Languor	Ear, Back of Head	Single
ᖰ	ר	Resh	Grace, Ugliness	Head of a Man	Double
ᴜᴜ	ש	Shin	Heaven, Fire	Teeth	Mother
†	ת	Taw Tav	Dominion, Slavery	Cross	Double

In magical work, the other important Semitic language is the Arabic. The Modern Standard Arabic language was derived from the Aramaic, and is unique in that it has preserved a large majority of the original Proto-Semitic features. The Arabic script was derived from the Nabatian script, which in turn was derived from the Aramaic. The Arabic script still shares with the Aramaic the names of the alphabet letters, similar graphic representations for phonetically similar letters, connections of letters in the same word and several forms for each letter depending on its location in a word. The Arabic alphabet contains eighteen letter shapes. By adding one, two or three dots to ten of these shapes, other letters are derived. This brings the total letters in the Arabic alphabet to twenty-eight. There is overlap between the Arabic and the Hebrew. The Arabic contains all of the twenty-two consonants used in Hebrew. Because of the cultural proximity of the various Semitic tribes, in old magical books it is customary to find prayers and conjurations in Hebrew, Aramaic and Nabatian, mixed in with Arabic. The Arabic alphabet contains twenty-eight letters, which at first glance makes it incompatible with the Tree of Life diagram. However, there are ten basic geometric shapes that can be used to form any of the Arabic letters. These ten shapes fit well with the mathematics and polarities of the tree.

The first shape is the single dot. It is the simplest and most basic of all figures. It is representative of the potential of every figure possible; it is the embodiment of the first principle of Being. All the other shapes have their roots in it and can not be drawn without it.

From the potential of this Unity emanate the two dots. The two dots are representative of the masculine and the feminine. They represent the polarity present in all things, in a sense, the one having divided itself to form the two. It can be likened to the beginning of life and the process of meiosis that occurs when the sperm and egg join to create the zygote that will eventually become a person. It represents a definitive starting point and ending point, but also demonstrates the inherent continuity of life.

By the same token, the triad emerges from the duad. The triangle itself symbolizes the trinity acting as a single form. There are two opposing forces and one reconciler acting between them to create a fourth force, or emanation, of the Divine. It can be likened to the universal womb from which Life was born, or the vacuum of creation, with a strand of Divine Light piercing to allow for the Divine to manifest in physical form. The first three shapes contain the non-manifest aspect or the essence of all things. They remain in their unadulterated essence, the dot. They represent the state that exists immediately before manifestation occurs. Once the process of manifestation begins, the essence of each shape takes on a form with solid lines. This parallels the creation of humanity, from the non-manifest essence of God, to physical manifestation that occurs in the womb and finally, fully in the world.

In the fourth shape, the two dots manifest as a single horizontal line. The line is ever expanding and ever extending. It is highly representative of the projective Divine attribute.

In the fifth shape, the three dots manifest as a circle, which represents infinity, containment and restriction. The circle is a symbol of the womb from which we were all created and born. It is Ouroboros, or the winged serpent, biting its own tail.

The sixth shape is linked directly to the single dot. If the dot were allowed to flow down the page, like a drop from the Pen on the Cosmic Tablet, it would flow as a vertical line. The line is vertical to denote ascent and descent from and to Spirit and the Divine Essence.

The seventh shape is the unification of the vertical and horizontal line. Interestingly enough, whether the horizontal line is on top or bottom, the result is almost the same - two different forms of the letter Dal (Daleth), one in Arabic (د) and the other in Hebrew (ד). It is the door through which manifestation occurs. It is the doorway of the womb.

The eighth shape is a result of the division or subtraction of the fifth and sixth shapes, which forms a half-circle. Subtraction is akin to the force of restriction.

The ninth shape is similar to the vertical line of Tiphareth, (the sixth shape described), but more convex, forming a lunar crescent. As the sixth shape is associated with the Sun in its reflection, the ninth is associated with the Moon. It is representative of the flux and reflux of the stream of energies in the Universe.

The tenth and last shape is the lunar crescent shaped into a cup. This shape rests in the last emanation, Malkuth (Kingdom). This is the receptive end of all the energy of the preceding shapes. This is the container of the final manifestation of the process that began in Kether or in the dot.

These ten shapes, in different combinations, form all the Arabic letters. Some of the shapes constitute the top and some the bottom of each letter. It is our theory that if a letter has a top and a bottom, it has more than one facet to its energy. We believe the top shape is that of its manifested or outer influence, while the bottom is that of its inner influence. This means that every Arabic letter would correspond in some form to one or more of the emanations. This permits a deeper analysis of the energy of the letter based on shape.

TEN SHAPES ON THE TREE OF LIFE

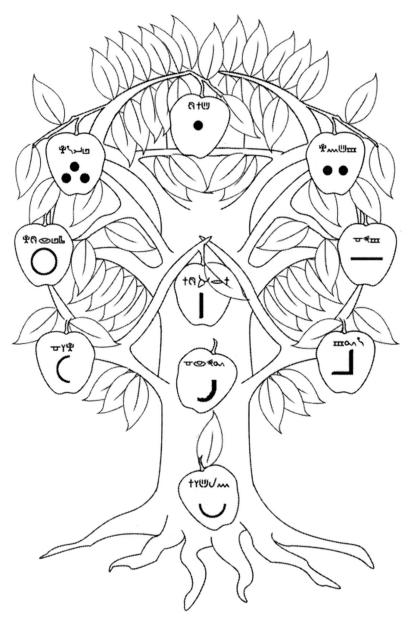

ARABIC LETTERS AND THE TREE OF LIFE

Arabic	English Name	Outer Energy	Inner Energy
ا	Alef	Tiphareth	Tiphareth
ب	Ba	Malkuth	Kether
ج	Jym	Chesed	Hod Kether
د	Dal	Netzach	Netzach
ه	Ha	Geburah	Geburah
و	Waw	Geburah	Yesod
ز	Zyin	Kether	Yesod
ح	Ha (guttural H)	Chesed	Hod
ط	Tah (guttural T)	Tiphareth	Geburah
ي	Yah	Hod	Malkuth Chokmah
ك	Kaf	Tiphareth (Hod Chesed)	Malkuth
ل	Lam	Tiphareth	Malkuth
م	Mym	Geburah	Tiphareth
ن	Nun	Kether	Malkuth
س	Syin	Malkuth	Malkuth

Arabic	English Name	Outer Energy	Inner Energy
ع	Ayin (gutteral growled A)	Hod	Hod
ف	Fa	Kether Geburah	Malkuth
ص	Sad (deep gutteral S)	Geburah	Malkuth
ق	Qaf	Chokmah Geburah	Malkuth
ر	Ra	Yesod	Yesod
ش	Shyin	Binah Malkuth	Malkuth
ت	Ta	Chokmah	Malkuth
ث	Tha	Binah	Malkuth
خ	Kha	Kether Chesed	Hod
ذ	Zah (bite your tongue at Z)	Kether	Netzach
ض	Dhad (deep gutteral dh)	Kether Geburah	Malkuth
ظ	Tzah (bite your tongue at Z)	Kether Tiphareth	Geburah
غ	Ghyin (baby talk gh..gh)	Kether Hod	Hod

✿ THE GARMENT OF LIGHT ✿

PURPOSE: The Garment of Light is based on Jewish mysticism and the Tree of Life. This is a good technique to do if you need to focus yourself spiritually when you are feeling scattered.

The premise of this exercise is to realign the individual's spiritual vessel and personal attributes of the Divine Emanations with the more cosmic ones. These emanations correspond in the human soul with many inner forces. For example, if our reflection of Geburah is unbalanced, we are likely to exhibit anger, resentment or worse - apathy and lack of the will to live. Overindulgence can unbalance the connection of our Yesod or inner spiritual foundation with the Divine influx. Rebalancing these spheres helps us to maintain the pure connection and allows us to overcome negative impulses such as anger, depression and so forth.

TIMING: This is a good exercise to do three times a week for ten weeks. It can be done any time, but it may work best before you do other major rites or early in your day.

STEP ONE: Say: "**Elohai, the soul You have placed within me is pure. You created it, fashioned it and breathed it into me. You constantly safeguard it for me and eventually You will take it from me and restore it to me in the hereafter. Yet, as long as it is within me I will gratefully give thanks to you, O Adonoi, in whose hands are the souls of all the living.**"

STEP TWO: Stand in the form of a cross, that is, stand upright with your arms spread out at shoulder height. Draw the symbol of Venus or Ankh aroundyou mentally or physically. The symbol for Venus or Ankh is the only known symbol to fully encompass the entire Tree of Life. Chant internally '**Elat Ha-Aur**' as you do so.

STEP THREE: After taking this position, visualize the spheres of the Tree of Life forming around your body. When visualizing the spheres, do not exert a lot of energy trying to create them. Instead, just be aware of them as if they have always been there. Kether should be above your head, Chokmah at your right temple, Binah at your left temple, Chesed at your right shoulder, and Geburah at your left shoulder. Tiphareth will be in the center of your chest, Netzach at your right hip, Hod at your left hip, Yesod at your groin and Malkuth will be at your feet. As each Sphere forms, vibrate its name multiple times and meditate on its meaning. Think of the Divine One when focusing on Kether, on the eternal and vast wisdom of Divinity with Chokmah, and so forth. Do this slowly and don't feel rushed.

STEP FOUR: Vibrate "**Qadosh Kether ha-Aur Achad**" three times, meditating on the Light of the Presence above your head. Vibrate "**Qadosh Chokmah ha-Aur Raza**" three times, meditating on the Divine Wisdom. Vibrate "**Qadush Binah ha-Aur Shekinah**" three times, meditating on the Divine Understanding.

STEP FIVE: Say: "**O Holy of Holies, purify my mercy and fill me with the spirit of love. O Holy of Holies, purify my strength and fill me with the spirit of courage. O Holy of Holies, purify my outer and inner beauty and fill me with the spirit of devotion. O Holy of Holies, purify my desires and my aspirations and fill me with the spirit of piety. O Holy of Holies, purify my intellect and fill me with the spirit of truth. O Holy of Holies, purify my sexuality and fill me with the spirit of eternal life. O Holy of Holies, purify my body and soul and fill me with the spirit of my holy guardian angel.**"

STEP SIX: When you have determined the name of your guardian angel in a further chapter, include it in this step. Vibrate the name of your guardian angel the number of times equivalent to its numerical reduction, for example, if its value is two hundred and fifty-one, then 2+5+1 or 8 times.

STEP SEVEN: Meditate on your body being made of pure scintillating white Light. Feel this Light flowing from above your head to your feet and filling every cell and ounce of your body and radiating from it. Let this flow be natural and not forced. Realize that the light descends and fills your soul from Kether as it receives the Light from the Divine One.

STEP EIGHT: Focus your attention and your entire self on the Divine. Say, either silently or aloud, "**O Holy of Holies, I submit to You my Chesed, Geburah, Tiphareth, Netzach, Hod, Yesod and Malkuth as vessels for Your Divine Light. I bind my soul and spirit with**

chains of light to Thee, O Creator of the Universe, in devotion and service to the eternity of time, Amen." Again visualize the entire Tree of Life superimposed on your body in brilliant white light and see yourself surrounded with a garment of brilliance and love.

THE TREE OF LIFE SCROLL

PURPOSE: We talked at the beginning of the chapter about the Tree of Life as a living breathing force. We then covered some of the teachings within the Qabalah concerning the Tree of Life and the Arabic and Hebrew alphabets. It is time to put all this information into some practical magical means. In this exercise, we will use the mathematical construct of the Tree of Life, with all its storehouse of knowledge, as a way for you to experience the actual Tree of Life. This diagram is itself a talisman and we will take full advantage of its attributes to bring the Tree of Life into your life in a balanced and wholesome way.

Magical talismans are like the hammer and nails of our craft. If you pick up many of the talismans from the ancient world, you will see that they are engraved with either one or more of the following components: a) letters, b) numbers, or c) images. On talismans, letters are either magical names or an occult sequence of letters. Numbers can be written in sequences or in the form of magical squares and the images tend to be designs that involve humans and animals and geometric shapes. The Tree of Life diagram contains all three elements.

These three components work together to create a like-attracts-like mechanism. They are both a form of objectifying and a container for the intent and the spiritual energy necessary to make that happen. This container is then consecrated through the Rouhaniah (Prana) of the names, symbols, planets, and so forth. The Rouhaniah is summoned by the magician and charged into the talisman by recitation of Holy Names and by calling on Angels or Jinn or both. In this exercise, we will be creating a talismanic scroll of the Tree of Life that awakens these spiritual facets within your life. As we mentioned, each of these emanations represents a powerful facet of the Divine that emanates in this world. You can call on only one facet or you can call on all facets. In the scroll, we will be calling on all ten facets. Like all other talismans, the scroll will contain an image, Divine names, and angelic forms, and then will be consecrated. Keep it in a safe place near you after you finish with it.

TIMING: Do this ritual once every month to keep the charge alive. It should take you about two hours to complete.

TOOLS: You will need a clean surface on which to draw the talisman. You can use parchment paper, poster cardboard, a clean white sheet of paper or even a piece of white fabric. You will also need ten very small-sized color photos of your face. Now, on a large piece of white poster cardboard, draw the diagram of the Tree of Life with its connecting paths and Hebrew letters in the ancient form of the Hebrew. On each circle write the name of one of the ten emanations in ancient Hebrew followed by the letter Heh then the word El, the letter Waw, and finally Elat. As an example, write Hod H El W Elat thus:

$$ †\mathcal{J}\rangle\Upsilon \quad \mathcal{J}\rangle\Phi \quad \pi\Upsilon\Phi $$

This translates to the Glory of God and the Goddess. Do this for each of the emanations beginning from Kether and ending in Malkuth. Then affix each of your images to the corresponding name of the emanation on the diagram. If you don't have photos of yourself, write out your full name (first name, mother's first name, father's first name, family name at birth) preceded by the same combination of the emanation's name with El and Elat around the circle. Women should reverse the order of their parents' names. You will also need a 100-bead rosary for counting during the ritual, so that you don't have to think about keeping track.

In the diagram on the following page, the letters connecting the paths are depicted at the connecting points of the sephiroth.

LETTERS ON THE PATHS OF THE TREE OF LIFE

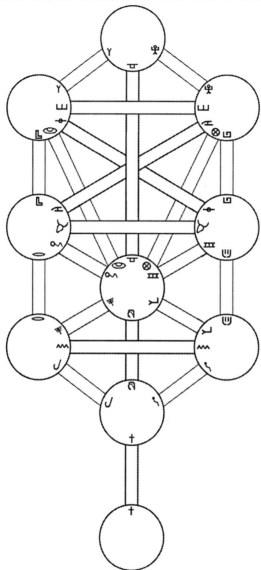

STEP ONE: Take a purifying shower or lustral bath. Light some incense in your sacred space.

STEP TWO: Place the scroll on the floor and kneel with your head on the scroll, if possible with your third eye on the circle of Malkuth. With a 100-bead rosary in your hand, begin chanting the name: "**Sephira Malkuth ha-Elat.**" You may also shorten it as you progress to "**Malkuth ha-Elat.**" Repeat this chant a hundred times, while focusing your being on the Divine One. With this focus in mind, shift part of your awareness to the concept of Kingdom. Let all your senses be engrossed by your focus on the spiritual kingdom of the Divine. Feel this kingdom all around you and stretching to the end of the universe and beyond. Let all your senses be overwhelmed by this realization.

STEP THREE: Try to adjust your head so that your third eye rests on the emanation of Yesod. If that isn't possible then continue as before. Chant the name of "**Sephira Yesod ha-Elat**", a hundred times and shift your focus to the cosmic foundation of the Divine, akin to what you did in step two. Once you are done, continue by shifting to the next emanation and chant "**Sephira Hod ha-Elat**" in the same fashion. The process continues along the same lines through "**Sephira Netzach ha-Elat**", "**Sephira Tiphareth ha-Elat**", "**Sephira Geburah ha-Elat**", "**Sephirah Chesed ha-Elat**", "**Sephira Binah ha-Elat**", "**Sephira Chokmah ha-Elat,**" and finally, "**Sephira Kether ha-Elat.** "

STEP FOUR: Sit up and roll up the scroll. Hold it in your hand and say: "**O Divine One, whose presence fills the spiritual emanations of Etz Chaim; O Elat Ha-Kether, Chokmah, Binah, Chesed, Geburah, Tiphareth, Netzach, Hod, Yesod and Malkuth, let a ray from Your Light descend upon this scroll and fill it with the rouhaniah of Etz Chaim. Let this scroll be my living link between my soul to the spirit and current of Your emanations Kether, Chokmah, Binah, Chesed, Geburah, Tiphareth, Netzach, Hod, Yesod and Malkuth so that it may awaken within my being the white flame of Your Divine Light, Life and Love.**" [x10]

STEP FIVE: Say: "**I call upon you, o millions upon millions of lights that fall like dew from the fruits of the Tree of Life in the cosmic garden of Eden, wherein the Shekinah rests as Queen. O you Rouchaniah of the Etz Chaim, the Tree of Life, make manifest your presence within my soul, and to all those souls of Light who work the magic of Light, to bring forth in me and my life illumination, wisdom, understanding, prosperity, strength, protection, beauty, harmony, victory, rapture, glory, intelligence, strong foundation, will and spiritual and physical enrichment of the holy kingdom.**

Let the powers of the Tree of Life and its blessings flow into my life in the name of Elat Elyon, the Exalted and Mighty One. Come

now, O all ye powers and forces of the emanations of Etz Chaim. Come, o ye angels, spirits, and faithful beings of Light that swim within the sea of Light upon Light in Kether, Chokmah, Binah, Chesed, Geburah, Tiphareth, Netzach, Hod, Yesod, and Malkuth; obey ye now the name of Elat Elyon, the Divine ruler of your kingdom, Shekinah, your Queen. Show yourselves; come from your abodes and help me in my path as a magician of Light to continue my work in harmony, so that I may partake of the mysteries of Divine Light. Amen!" [x3]

Once you are done with the scroll, wrap it in white fabric and put it somewhere that is safe. When you feel a need to balance out and feel connected, hold the scroll in your hand and chant the names of the Sephiroth ten times in descending order.

With the basics covered, we will begin the actual practicum of magical training. We will start with the regular preliminary rituals, most of which are a combination of ancient materials and the rituals and rites taught at our magical group. We will then proceed with the method of contacting your holy guardian angel, awakening the energy of the Elements, and then working the sphere of the planets. A really exciting journey is ahead of you, so let's begin.

Works Referenced

Benner, Jeff. *The Ancient Hebrew Language and Alphabet*. Virtual Bookworm. 2004

al-Karamani, Ahmed. *Rahat al-A'aqel*. Dar al-Andlus. Beirut, Lebaon: 1983

al-Fayyumi, Saadia ben Joseph. *Commentaire sur le Séfer Yesira ou Livre de la Création par Le Gaon Saâdya de Fayyoum*, trans. & ed., M. Lambert, Paris, Emile Bouillon, Editeur, 1891; translated into English from the French & Hebrew by Scott Thompson and Dominique Marson, San Francisco, 1985

Anonymous. *Dala'al al-Khirat*. Shirkat al-Ma 'aref Liltaba'a wa al-Touzeea'a. Bandung, Indonesia.

5
Essential Rites and Ceremonies

agical training is not just a process, but also a journey that will span a few years. Let us begin this wonderful journey with a kind of magical ritual very different from those which you are probably accustomed to seeing recommended for beginners, in other books. You will begin your training, not through learning a banishing or summoning rite, but by consecrating a magical tool. The tool that almost every magician needs first is her book of magical rites, that delineates the practices. Historically, many of these books of magic were written by hand and then copied. Nowadays, many of them are purchased from your local bookshops, but that doesn't make them any less magical. This book is the intended manual for this training curriculum. The purpose of consecrating this book or any magical implement is to bring it to life for a given purpose. Once it is consecrated, every time you open it or work with it, it will awaken within you the feeling and desire of practising your craft. It becomes a living medium and not just words on paper.

Taking into account that not all our readers are experienced Magi, we decided to keep the ritual of consecration simple in form, without diluting its potency. Once you have done this ritual, this book will become a magical tool. Every time you open it, the energies will flow through your hands and keep you steady and strong on this path. So, you should treat it like you treat any other magical implement, with the utmost care and respect. You should not give it to others, sell it or take it into unclean places such as bathrooms. Once you have worked with the book for an extended period, you may want to revisit this ritual and look back at this step with fond memory.

For the ritual, you will need a clean room where you will not be disturbed. You will also need a yellow or white candle and some incense. You can use any available stick incense. If you have a charcoal based burner, then use that instead to burn coriander seed for its smell. You can usually find this sort of burner, known as a censer, as well as the charcoals, in any church supply store. For those who have never used one of these, once the charcoal has been lit and the incense is burning, lift it up only by its chains. The censor itself will be too hot to touch. You will also need some kind of headband on which you can paint the symbols, that you may wish to use later as a bookmark.

Take a taper candle and inscribe the following holy symbols on it vertically, starting with the symbol on the far right.

✪ 🌀 ⌘ ⚹ ⫴ ⌥ ⫵ ✪

Make sure the following symbols are upon your forehead, in two lines, on a headband (written from right to left):

Light the incense and candle and sit quietly staring at the flame. Keep the book nearby. Stare at the flame and let its flickers relax and calm you.

Say with conviction, passion and force: "**O ancient masters of holy magic, who reside in the secret mountain of mysteries, I stand before you as a seeker of the secrets and the knowledge of the wise. I call upon you to bring me closer to your presence and aid me with the company of those ancient beings that preside over the rivers of the garden of Eden and who oversee the art of the Magi. Hear me by the name of your Queen, whom you serve and adore. I call upon you, o ancient masters of magic, to hear my call this hour and watch over me and aid me with your power and guidance. I bear upon my forehead the symbols of your chiefs Melchizedek and the Master Metatron, for I am a seeker of the path of old. Listen to** me, ye invisible ones known by many names among the ancients, ye who are magical from birth and of flame that doesn't burn. I call upon you, servants of the secret and mighty name kept veiled by the sages of old, that is inscribed upon this candle and has great dominion over you. Empower this book with a ray of magic from your world, so that by reading it, it shall awaken in my sphere a ray of that ancient current that has its place at the beginning of time and keep me steady on the path of magic. Listen to me, o servants of the symbols upon this candle, and come to me now and empower this book without delay. Let it be a living connection between me and the ancient masters of the magic of Light. Watch, guide, and aid me, for I am a servant of Divine Light and it is this Light that you serve and revere."

Repeat the preceding steps again and again until the candle has fully burned. You may take a few minutes break between every repeat and just watch the candle. The candle may take quite a while to completely burn, so if you wish, you can extinguish it for the night and come back to relight it the following day. Once the candle has burned, give thanks in your own words. Open the book to the page right after the Table of Contents, which has a version of this conjuration. Write your name in the space provided. Sign it at the bottom and affix a small portion of the wax to it, while it is soft and hot. Flatten the remaining wax and put it into a small cloth pouch or some kind of cloth container. When the wax has hardened, keep it somewhere safe. This will serve as a link with the spirits of the candle. You may experience some strange events during this ritual or right afterward, and you may want to watch your dreams.

Before we go any further, we need to take a step back and talk about the rituals in this book and to how to properly perform them. First and foremost, those rituals are the ones taught to new apprentices at the Magic Society of the White Flame, in preparation for their admission to the Children of Light or the Mystery School of Melchizedek. These are the rituals that we ourselves have been using for close to ten years. They are based on much older materials or original sources of the Western systems of magic, that arose in the Middle East. Having studied hundreds of books and so many ancient manuscripts, it became obvious that many of the ancient rituals were fragmented. This was intentionally done to safeguard them. This means that any given ritual in one of those ancient books is either incomplete or detached from the larger framework of its application. This problem is acute and is bound to plague any scholar of the tradition for many years to come. The other problem is unlike modern schools of thought, there was a focus on practicality over conservation. This meant that numerous versions of a given ritual exist in different schools. Each version works slightly differently. As problematic as this may sound, it is indicative of a more organic magical tradition. People cared less that it was the same exact wording of a thousand year old practice than about the fact that it works. They wanted their magic to work and work well.

Finally, many of the complex rituals required a kind of commitment that is impossible to muster in modern day lifestyle. There is a value to the ancient approach, of course, and we are not dismissing it as obsolete. However, when setting out to write this book, we had in mind people like us, living in the city and having to deal with 9-5 work schedules and busy family lives. We wanted magic that works and that we could do without quitting our day jobs. It is a fine balance. We could have translated word by word any one of the texts in our collection. This would be great from a scholarly and historical perspective, akin to the translation of Dead Sea Scrolls, but for the bulk of aspiring magicians, it would end up being nothing more than an armchair read. Most people don't have the time to retreat six months in a cloister for a single ritual. Not to mention, since the rituals are fragmented, an expert English occultist would need a couple hundred different source materials, all in English, before she could make sense of the system. It would be another hundred years before any real practical value could be had. In this book, we had to reconstruct some of the rituals that were fragmented or put some of the fragments together. We stayed true to the original sources and approach. We wanted to keep the changes to a bare minimum, but we also didn't want to end up sacrificing practicality for the sake of scholarly idealism. In effect, we put those rituals together by translating and practicing the original sources over many years. The rituals are true to the spirit, intent, and, in most cases, wording, of the original sources.

The only true innovation we introduced is the Goddess work, but this of itself isn't much of an innovation. It must be remembered that according to Arabic occultists, the tradition's birth place was in Babel. The seven symbols appeared there first and also many of the techniques. Many of the oldest occult books referenced by masters of our tradition belonged to authors who were from Babylon, such as Tankalosha. Names like Gilgamesh and Marduk appear in a number of Arabic conjurations. The missing element is the Goddess Ishtar, who would have been of supreme importance to the ancient Akkadians and Chaldeans. This omission is utterly intentional by Arabic authors. It isn't unusual either. For example, in one of the old books by Ibn al-Haj, there was a garbled talismanic design. It took us close to five years of digging, before we located a version that had the design intact. The version was acquired from a source with connection to secret Sufi orders in Pakistan. Upon receiving this book, we realized the cause of the omission in later reproductions. The talisman was composed of four Stars of David. If such biases could lead modern printers to censure occult texts of basic holy symbols, imagine any direct reference to the Goddess! We feel the reintroduction of the Goddess only completes the system and ensures its effectiveness. We have even found jinn magical rituals to be more effective with this reintroduction, since many jinn tribes follow the old pagan religion and many of their kings are adherents of the Goddess. For those who wanted pure word-by-word translation of Arabic occultists, they will have to wait for a future work. For those looking for authentic magic that works, achieves excellent results in a safe manner, and can be fit into a busy schedule, this book is for you.

Let us now talk briefly about how to actually do any of the rituals in this book. There are three components to most magical rituals. The first is a script or speech that is delivered; we will call this the incantation or conjuration. The next is physical movement or postures. The last is visualization and imagination or mental focus.

We usually find that the speech or incantation part is where most beginners run into trouble. Modern magicians think of rituals in terms of performances or dramatic plays. However, a dramatic speech in theatrical acting lacks the kind of conviction that is necessary for magical success. No matter how much the actor puts into the performance, at some level she knows it is an act. The first thing to remember then is that, while emotions and intensity are necessary in reciting rituals, you also have to believe in the words that you are saying from the depth of your heart and soul. If you think of recitation in terms of just following a ritualized script, then your magic will not soar into the heights. Therefore, try to say the words as if they are coming from the depths of your heart. The next key to success in magical recitations is to speak them as if you are speaking to an audience that actually exists. Even if you have to read a script, still read it as if you are addressing an important delegation or audience in a large auditorium. Speak so that those in the back will hear you and feel your sincerity, conviction, and intensity. If you are worried about others hearing you due to living restrictions, then speak the words aloud in your own head. Don't hesitate, whisper, stumble, or speak as if you are unsure of yourself or reading a page out of a book. Speak slowly or fast, as the passion moves you, but feel every word you are saying and try to impress your audience.

Another important element to magical recitations is that often they are prayers or contain elements of such. This goes to the heart of the difference between a magician and a sorcerer. The magician works the magic by being a channel or a vessel for the Divine force acting through her. The work is usually done with the understanding that the magician is an actor like the angel is an actor. Therefore, it only makes sense that the conjurations seek out the aid of the Divine. The sorcerer on the other hand relies on herself solely for the realization of magic. It is done to serve her needs primarily, over any other considerations, and she takes credit for her effort and work. The magician swims with the current, while the sorcerer tries to divert it. Therefore, most magical rituals done by a sorceress emphasize her own power over spirits, angels, nature, and even gods. They also contain declarations of her status as mistress of the realm, even as far as proclaiming that she in her ego state must be obeyed as a supreme ruler, or else. The magician, on the other hand, calls on the Divine, asks the angels, and enlists the jinn. At the end of the day, she gives thanks for the all the help she has received. The gist of this point is that many of the magical rituals are in actuality a form of laser-focused prayers. We refer to them as conjurations, but at heart they are prayers. Keep this in mind when reciting them. Since they are a process by which you address and connect with the Divine, keep them pure and from the heart. Finally, if you are repeating Divine names or words of power, then do so with intensity. You may chant them, or vibrate them, or even sing them. Each ritual has different requirements. We will make those clear for each of the rituals in this book. Don't get too attached to sounding beautiful, as long as you resonate to your core.

The next major component of ritual work is physical movement and postures. This usually involves standing, sitting, or kneeling. Ancient magicians often knelt in their prayers and address, while few modern magicians ever do. The whole idea appears to be an anathema to this new generation. Kneeling and prostrating isn't a process by which you humiliate yourself to the ego of another being. Kneeling and prostrating is part of reconnecting to the earth itself. While it does have the added virtue of keeping the magician's ego in check, primarily it is a way to ground and reconnect on a full physical level. Many of these kneeling or prostrating postures are designed to represent certain letter forms, or allow the energy to circulate in a certain pattern, or to activate certain energy centers. Dance or body movement is also used in magic, especially to induce a trance state. Another physical element in ritual work involves tracing geometric shapes in the air. You may not always trace these geometric shapes accurately, but you should do your best. The key to success isn't merely to trace something in the air, but to craft it at a spiritual level, as we mentioned earlier. You are like an artist using spiritual energy to create your mosaic, so try to do the best you can at your works of art.

The last important component of ritual work is visualization and focus. This basically entails keeping your mind focused on what you are saying and doing. If you are calling on the Divine, the creator of the heavens, then imagine and visualize in your mind this vast heaven. Focus on this reality or concept of a such a Creator as vividly as you can. This helps increase the amount of emotions and intensity of the work. It also keeps the mind focused so it doesn't wander.

It is amazing how, after a few years, many magicians end up doing their daily rituals with their minds somewhere else entirely. This is why we discourage apprentices from taking a ritual and doing it daily for years. Sooner or later it becomes a mindless process like any other bodily function, and in some cases it turns into a crutch. As an example, if you do a daily ritual to banish the nasties that may come to haunt you, then what you are doing over the years is reaffirming this problem and eventually developing fear in yourself. This doesn't mean that there will not be times when you do need to protect yourself or that such rituals do not have merit. However, when it becomes a crutch, the focus isn't there and it becomes a psychological habit. You need to keep the rituals alive by being focused and immersed in what you are saying and doing. This entails shifting your ritual schedule around, so that they do stay alive and vital. When you need to visualize something you are drawing, then do so with your eyes open. Let the image stand there vivid, colored, and real, because it is. When you are visualizing something more cosmic or etherial, then do so with your eyes closed. However, whatever method you are applying, keep your emotions connected with it. Don't just do your magic, feel it. Inflame yourself with passion at every moment of your work.

To ensure you get the best results, this program has been designed with all the preceding points in mind. You will find that certain rituals are assigned for a period of time. We recommend you follow this schedule to the best of your ability. Before each ritual, we will give you our recommendations as to how many times per week it should be performed, how many weeks duration, and why are we asking you to do it. We will describe in detail the recommended visualization, physical movement and intonation of the Divine names. All that is left is for you to actually put it to use. More advanced or eclectic magicians may choose to skip this program or pick through the methods. We would like to discourage this for anyone wanting to get the maximum benefit out of this book, but in the end it is a personal choice. Whatever you may decide, try to enjoy your magic as much as possible. It may seem odd to say this, but even the most sacred magic, should be totally fun and enjoyable to do, and make you feel afterword better about yourself and the world around you.

RITUAL SPACE CONSECRATION

PURPOSE: It is important to purify a working area before any magical rites are done. This removes any low level residue from anything done before or from other people who may also use the space. It also helps enliven the space if it hasn't been used for a while. Even if you are doing your work in a dedicated temple, purification and consecration on a regular basis is a good way to keep the energy clean. It is also useful to raise your own vibration and balance you through the process of purification and consecration. As well, this purification and consecration can and should be used when you move into a new space where others have lived before, just to start with a clean slate. You can do it in each room of your new apartment or home.

TIMING: It is recommended that it be done before any major working.

DIVINE NAMES: The undefined Hebrew words used in this rite are: Qadosh (Holy), Ash (Fire), Maym (Water), Avir (Air), and Aretz (Earth). Chant or vibrate the Divine names gently and softly, such as: 'Qaaadoooosh El Haaa-Maaayeeem'. This Divine Name is constructed to mean Holy El of the Waters.

TOOLS: You will need a white or red candle. If you need to do your work and you can't find one at hand, then use any source of fire that is safe and available. You will need a source of incense, whether it be stick or burned on charcoal. You will need a cup or container of water. You will also need a small dish of salt. Before you use any of those tools, hold each of them in your hand and say: "**O Creator of fire [air / water / earth] bless this source of flame [smoke, water, earth] with**

the spiritual potency and brilliant light from the river of fire [air / water / earth] that flows in the heavenly Paradise."

STEP ONE: Pick up the candle and move to the east. Hold the candle up high and swing it before you to the far right, far left, then top center. Draw an equal armed cross and say: "**In the name of Qadosh Elohim Ha-Ash, I consecrate this working space (temple) with sacred fire.**" Feel that area of your working space being made holy and filled with light. Know that it is done by Divine presence and through the power of the spirits of the Element. Repeat this in all remaining directions: south, west, and north. While moving the candle between the four directions, trace and visualize a circle of fire being formed.

STEP TWO: Pick up the chalice or cup of water and move to the east. Hold the cup up high and swing it before you to the far right, far left, then top center. Draw an equal armed cross and say: "**In the name of Qadosh El Ha-Maym, I purify this working space (temple) with holy water.**" Feel that area of your working space being made holy and filled with light. Know that it is done by Divine presence and through the power of the spirits of the Element. Repeat this in all remaining directions: south, west, and north. While moving the vessel between the four directions, sprinkle some water and trace and visualize a circle of water being formed.

STEP THREE: Light some incense, whether in an incense burner or as a stick. Carry the incense to the east. Hold the incense up high and swing it before you to the far right, far left, then top center. Draw an equal armed cross and say: "**In the name of Qadosh Yah Ha-Avir, I consecrate this working space (temple) with sweet air.**" Feel that area of your working space being made holy and filled with light. Know that it is done by Divine presence and through the power of the spirits of the Element. Repeat this in all remaining directions: south, west, and north. While moving the incense between the four directions, incense the room and trace and visualize a circle of sweet winds being formed.

STEP FOUR: Pick up some blessed salt with cinnamon sticks or a sacred herbal leaf bundle like sage and then move to the east. Hold the container up high and swing it before you to the far right, far left, then top center. Draw an equal armed cross and say: "**In the name of Qadosh Adonoi Ha-Aretz, I purify this working space (temple)** with blessed salt." Feel that area of your working space being made holy and filled with light. Know that it is done by Divine presence and through the power of the spirits of the Element. Repeat this in all remaining directions: south, west, and north. While moving the container between the four directions, sprinkle some salt and trace and visualize a circle of earth being formed.

◉ ILLUMINATION WASH ◉

PURPOSE: The body of the magician is also a magical temple. Purification of the body before magical work is as important as purifying the physical temple. You can always just take a shower, of course. However, the ancients saw the process in more magical terms. It is a spiritual ritual in which the intent to purify the body is coupled with the process of achieving sanctity. This magical relation with water purification dates back to the old civilizations of modern day Iraq. The Sabians were known as 'submergers' or 'immersionists' because of their practice of baptism and ritual cleansing. The ancient Mandean cosmology refers to the Supreme Principle as the Great Life, whose symbol is the living water or Yardna, and one of His central rites is immersion in flowing water. This living water is considered to be both celestial and physical. According to them, all earthly rivers are manifestations of the Celestial River or the Euphrates of Radiant Light. The Radiance is the Cosmic Father and the Light is the Cosmic Mother. Their offspring is Yawar or the manifestation of the awakening Light. They explain that the river of life and light flows forth from a single point hidden in the mystery of the Great Life.

The Illumination Wash technique is based on Sufi practices. It is a form of individual water purification, where only certain parts of the body are washed. These parts are the hands, mouth, ears, nostrils, arms, feet, head and neck. The hands are receivers and projectors of energy and toil at the craft. The mouth utters the magical incantations and the prayers. The nostrils smell the incense and allow the magician to enter into a trance state. The ears hear the vibrations and listen to the faint echo of the spiritual realm. The arms represent the strength and force that bears the work and the dual coin of compassion and severity, or active and passive. The feet are the foundation upon which the whole body rests, and are connectors with the earth. They allow the magician to walk her path. The head is the awareness of the magical identity and the conscious choice in whatever action is being taken.

The top of the head is also the receiver of the neck. The neck and back of the head are the points of reception of information from the spiritual realm and, hence, points of knowing and dreams.

TIMING: This ritual is recommended before any in-depth magical work or entering into your temple area to do extensive work.

TOOLS: You can always use tap water in the bathroom. However, we recommend you use magically infused water. Get a special jug or container of water. Fill this water three quarters of the way up with normal water. Place as many quartz crystals in the jug as you can. You may also put in a few drops of rosewater or rose oil or any other aromatic oil that your body will tolerate. If possible, try to place this water outside where the light of the moon can fall on it. You can also hold the water jug up so that moon is reflected in it. The longer this is done the better. Keep the water somewhere warm, so that it stays at room temperature. It is best that you cover it until the time to use it is at hand. You can consecrate this water in a large quantity before you put it into the jug. If you prefer, you can also charge the water with the power of the stars such as the Pole Star and the Pleiades or with the light of the Sun itself. Each of those choices has its own merit. If weather conditions don't permit any such options, then skip this part of process. Don't wait till you have consecrated water to do your ritual. Use normal tap water until you do have some.

STEP ONE: Wash your hands with water three times, saying each time, "**In the name of the Creator of the Waters of Life, may my hands be cleansed from all work of evil.**"

STEP TWO: Wash the inside of your mouth with water three times, saying each time, "**In the name of the Divine Word, may my mouth be a sanctuary of truth.**"

STEP THREE: Wash your nostrils with water three times, saying each time, "**In the name of the beautiful Queen of Angels, may my nostrils behold the scent of the roses of the garden of paradise.**"

STEP FOUR: Splash your face with water three times, saying each time, "**Light.**"

STEP FIVE: Wash your right arm from the wrist to the elbow three times, saying each time, "**In the name of the All Merciful, I am ready to toil in the great work.**"

STEP SIX: Wash your left arm from the wrist to the elbow three times, saying each time, "**In the name of the Strong One, I am ready to toil in the great work.**"

STEP SEVEN: Wash the top of your head (hair, front and back) once, saying, "**O Holy of Holies, may my mind be open to Your Presence.**"

STEP EIGHT: Wash your right and left ears three times, saying each time, "**O Ancient of Days, let me hear the voice of Your Angels.**"

STEP NINE: Wash the back of the head (neck) three times, saying each time, "**O Eternal Truth, illuminate my soul with wisdom and understanding.**"

STEP TEN: Wash your feet to the ankles three times, saying each time, "**Truly, O Lord, O Lady of the Universe, I have set my feet onto the great work.**"

BLESSING AND CONSECRATION

In our craft this process of purification and consecration is extended further. As magicians, we strive to see the sacred in all aspects of our lives. This entails focusing on the sacred in all our actions. That is why in old grimoires you will see prayers and blessings being done on everything, from the magical robe before it is worn, to the sword wielded in rituals. This process is called consecration. Consecration is a process that is repeated often and not just one time. The other important element of sacredness is blessing as a spiritual magical mechanism of keeping the light flowing. Spreading the light completes the cycle and ensures continuity of receiving the light.

Blessing is the application of the magnetic dynamics of the cosmic force of compassion. In essence, it is the manifestation of Divine Grace. Spiritual blessing is directly tied to the concept of increase. When a harvest increases beyond the farmer's wildest imagination or expectations, then some would say 'the harvest was blessed' or that 'the farmer was blessed'. This blessing comes from the Divine and is a

result of abundance of the flow of the Light. It is the direct manifestation of individually targeted and responsive Divine Mercy. Blessing is
the center of the magnetic aspect of the general operational energy of
creation itself. It is drawn to those who ask for it, seek it and transfer
it. Both mercy and benevolence are the by-products of blessings and
the roots of the continuous wheel of life.

Once the magician becomes a living conduit for the Divine Light,
the realization will dawn that blessing is the substance of creation and
is everywhere and immediately available. Its primary sensation is in
the form of personal attention from Divine Reality and its most immediate descriptive maxim is: 'Remember the Light, and the Light will
remember you.'

METHOD ONE – Angel Blessing

PURPOSE: As a magician, you will be working with angels on a regular
basis. The angels will aid you, protect you, teach you, and help you in
many ways. What can you do to pay the angels back for all their help?
There is nothing material that would be of interest to them. However,
they are beings of light who aspire always to be closer to the Source,
the Light of all Lights. Giving a blessing to an angel is one way to say
thank you. You yourself can't impart that blessing, but you can ask the
Divine to bless them and raise their station. All you need is the angel's
name. If you are planning to work with an angel or a set of angels
on a regular basis, make it your custom to send the blessing to them
weekly. This kind of blessing can also be directed to any other spirit.

TIMING: The best time to do this would be after you have done your
magical work. This works best when your work with the angel has
been personal. It isn't really necessary after general workings. Normally, you would use the name of the angel as part of the blessing.
This is indicated in the ritual text with the capital letter N. Whenever
you see this in a ritual, replace it with the appropriate name. If you are
working with several angels, you can either name each angel or you
can make it general, dedicating it to all angels present.

DIVINE NAMES: We are using the Divine Name Ishtar, since many of
these angels have Chaldean roots. The Goddess Ishtar is one of the
oldest names for the Queen of the Heaven and represents the cosmic
force of love.

STEP ONE: Say in a sincere and strong voice, "**May the best blessings of Ishtar, and the most noble blessings of Ishtar, the most graceful blessings of Ishtar, the most excellent blessings of Ishtar, the most perfect blessings of Ishtar, the most magnificent blessings of Ishtar, the most shining blessings of Ishtar and the most distinct blessings of Ishtar, rest upon the angel N. Let the angel N. be brought closer to the Divine Presence of the most Exalted Divine Light. May the angel N. be blessed a thousand fold by the Queen of Angels, and may N.'s light be illuminated by the Light of Lights.**"

METHOD TWO – Instant Human Blessing

PURPOSE: As you get into the habit of sending out blessings, you will notice that you can raise the vibrations of your surrounding area by your presence. You can also help other people raise their own vibration. As more people's vibrations elevate to become harmonic with love, all of humanity moves closer to peace. Even though a larger group can always raise more energy than a smaller group, the spreading of Light is an individual process that can be done any time and anywhere. When you spread the light as an individual, you receive more light to fill your emptying cup. You can send blessings to people and to the angels themselves.

TIMING: This ritual can be done at any time you feel a need for it. It is also a good ritual to do if someone in your surrounding is being negative or feeling unhappy.

TOOLS: The beauty of this technique is that you can do it without the needs of any external tools, while interacting with people face to face in your daily life. You can do it silently as the person you are focusing on is busy in a conversation with someone else near you.

STEP ONE: When you see an individual to whom you would like to send the blessing, focus your attention on her heart. Then imagine this individual encompassed by a beautiful white sphere of light. See a golden sphere of light, with a white 'T' cross over the heart region .

The focus is on the heart, because it is the center of the human soul and the seat of beauty. The white sphere of life will balance and revitalize the individual's aura. The golden sphere will activate the heart center and strengthen its vibration. The Tau Cross is a symbol of spirit acting on the material world.

STEP TWO: Chant the name of the angel Auriel a few times internally.

STEP THREE: Say silently in your mind to the individual, "**The blessings of the peace of the Shekinah befall you and Auriel's wings encompass you.**" [x3] In your mind, see the individual filled with joy and happiness, for half a minute or longer.

STEP FOUR: Once you are done, end with a reverse focus. See your body surrounded by brilliant white light and say to yourself: "**The Light fills me with peace and blessing.**"

The reverse blessing is vital for two reasons: 1. It severs the link and blocks any unwanted astral connections. 2. It fills you with the Light and focuses you on the energy for which you are seeking to be a conduit. When you do the reverse process, feel completely disconnected from the other person and spend 30 seconds or more feeling peace and emptying your mind from all thoughts or mental imageries other than your own.

METHOD THREE –Human Blessing and Guidance

PURPOSE: The highest form of magical blessing involves spiritual enrichment and guidance. As a magician, you can use this method to help other people reach their highest spiritual potential by sending a stream of light their way and asking that they be guided to the highest manifestation of virtue. This is a specialized blessing and may not be suitable for everyone or in all circumstances. We tend to use it mostly when dealing with people who we know are on the spiritual path.

TIMING: You can do this whenever such a blessing is desired. This is also beneficial when a person encounters challenges during their spiritual pursuit and is in need of support. This method can be used whether the person is present or not.

TOOLS: The only thing needed is the full name of the person, but a picture would be helpful.

Step One: First, relax your mind and focus on the Divine. Focus your mind on the descent of the Light upon your head and around your body. Know it so without forcing it.

Step Two: Once you feel the Light touch you, focus on the person. Say: "I call upon you, O angel Dohal, by the blessed and Divine name El Elyon. O great angel Dohal, who art set over the affairs of this world, strengthen and establish N. daughter of N. in her search for the Divine Light. Increase her spiritual perception, so that she may accomplish her calling, and that she may rise into the clear Light of the Spirit. May a thousand, thousand blessings be upon N. daughter of N, a creature of the Light. Let her become the best among the people in rank and status, most noble among them by deed and action, the most graceful in patience, the most excellent in virtue, the perfect observer of spirituality, the most magnificent by degree of love, the most shining in light and the most distinct in spirit." [x7]

Step Three: Say: "The peace of the Shekinah befall you N. daughter of N." [x7] See the individual filled with joy and happiness.

Step Four: Once you are done, end with a reverse focus. See your body surrounded by brilliant white light and say to yourself: "The Light fills me with peace and blessing."

METHOD FOUR – Blessing Food and Drink

Purpose: Ancient magicians of our tradition used food and water as carriers of magical force. They would consecrate the water and magically have it infused with a specific force. Then they would use it as a medium by which this energy was absorbed into their body physically and spiritually. We will be doing this in a ritual farther along in the chapter. The same process was applied to food where magical talismans were written on bread and then consumed. Sometimes the magician would also write a conjuration and consume it daily for many weeks before actually proceeding to use it daily. Although we have tested this and found it effective, we will not be using this method in this book, as it constitutes a more advanced working model. In our craft, we also look at our daily food as a source of both physical and magical nourishment. Therefore, food is consecrated and blessed in ritual fashion with every meal. We not only thank the Divine for the sustenance, but also ask that it be transformed from food into magical nourishment.

TIMING: We tend to do this blessing at every major meal. You can do it with everything you eat and drink, but most people find it easier to restrict it to main meals. If you are worried about what people might think, say that you like to pray before you eat and then recite it silently.

STEP ONE: Look at your food and, seeing it surrounded by white light, say: "**O Elat (Goddess), I thank you for providing this sustenance unto me. May I be enabled to sustain the poor among Your children as you have sustained me. I ask your blessing upon this food (drink) that Your Light may enter into it, that I may enter into Your Light and It into me. O angel Raphael, fill the physical substance of this food (drink) with spiritual force from the Light of the Kingdom of the Queen of Heaven. Let it maintain my body and nourish my soul with its magical manna. Thus nourished with Light, I shall reach ever toward the raptures of the Heavens and celebrate the joys of the Earth.**"

METHOD FIVE – Blessing Temple Items

PURPOSE: Robes, tools, incense and other ritual items are also objects of blessing and consecration. All objects are made of some form of energy and each carries a certain amount of magnetism. When infused with the blessing of Divine Light, we awaken the purest form of its essence. This also connects all of our actions with our pursuit of the magic of Light. It reminds us that these things we treat as gross matter are, in the end, shades of the Light we seek so dearly. This is especially important when the items with which you are working will play a function in your magical work at some level.

TIMING: We recommend you do this technique when you are working with new implements or bringing old implements back into your working area. Examples of this would be using a new incense container or wearing your ritual garb again for doing magical work.

STEP ONE: Begin by inhaling once, while vibrating Nur (Light) in your mind. Now, without exhaling, inhale again quickly, vibrating Nur in your mind. Repeat this by inhaling a third time while vibrating Nur in your mind.

STEP TWO: Hold your breath for a few seconds, vibrating Michael in your mind repeatedly, very strongly and feeling and visualizing your head about to explode with Light.

STEP THREE: Exhale upon the object and, in your mind, see your breath as a gush of white and golden light. Vibrate Nur during the exhalation. See the object or item covered with white light sparkling with blue & yellow stars.

STEP FOUR: Say: "**I consecrate this (name the temple implement) in the name of the Holy of Holies, the Eternal Light of all Lights and the radiant flame of the angel Michael.**"

METHOD SIX – Blessing Your Bed

PURPOSE: The bed is the place in which you rest your body and you allow your soul or etherial body to enter the world of dreams and the astral or in-between worlds. This is a point of vulnerability as well. This is why the ancient practitioners of our craft insisted on prayers before retiring. These prayers were meant to guard and protect them from untoward influences at a point they viewed to be a small death. One way to handle this magically is to consecrate your bed and ensure that both the physical object and the space it occupies becomes a consecrated and purified vehicle. It becomes a mini-sanctuary at night where you can rest yourself.

TIMING: The best time to do this technique is before going to bed. This is also highly recommended if you are engaged in extended magical work over a few days.

TOOLS: You only need your index finger to use this exercise. If you are new to the Hebrew alphabet, you may want to check one of the appendices in the back. You can also use a sweet incense stick to draw those letters in the beginning. The combination of incense and vibration of the letters increases the amount of consecration that is taking place. However, if you share the bed with someone who may be uncomfortable with all this, rely on your finger alone and silent vibration.

STEP ONE: Face the bed and, using your forefinger, draw on each of its corners one of the letters of the name Shekinah starting from SE and moving around toward NE. As you draw each letter vibrate Shekinah. Write the letters EL on the center of the bed, while vibrating El.

DIRECTION OF BED CORNERS

CENTER	NE	NW	SW	SE
אל	ה	נ	כ	ש

STEP TWO: Once you are done, say: "May the Divine Light descend upon this bed, that it may be blessed as a sanctuary of rest and peace. Through the protective presence of the Shekinah, O angel Gabriel watch over my spirit, soul and body as I sleep and enter the realm of dreams. Restore and rejuvenate me so that I be energized to carry on the magical work of Love and Light."

METHOD SEVEN – Sexual Blessing

PURPOSE: If you were to read many of the old occult grimoires, you would find many references to sexual abstinence during magical work. In modern times, this has evolved to a majority belief that magic doesn't normally involve sexuality or shuns it. This is a misunderstanding of the intent of the ancient magicians. It was rare for a couple to practice the craft. The social dynamic didn't always favor women. This meant that it would be difficult for magicians to engage in sacred magical sexual practices with their partners. Abstinence became a temporary measure. Things are changing and many magicians seek partners who practice their craft. While there is still room for abstinence in certain situations, it is possible now to engage in sacred magical sexual practices. During extended magical work or even on a regular basis, this sacredness can be nurtured by reaffirming prior to coitus that it is indeed a magical act. This not only strengthens the feeling and connection between partners, but also bring the sexual act into the realm of the sacred.

TIMING: This ritual is done by both partners just prior to intercourse.

Step One: Before intercourse, the man proclaims "**Dostoor Dostoor Ya-Mala'ikat Al-Nur!** (Permission, Permission, O Angels of the Light!)" The male should feel the presence of angels around him and be aware that his penis is made of pure light.

Step Two: The woman replies to him, "**Mubarak Mubarak Jinsaniah Al-Nuraniah (Blessed, Blessed is the Sexuality of the Light!)**" The woman should visualize her womb as a great ocean of stars.

Step Three: Upon actual coitus, they both proclaim "**Blessings of the Shekinah enter this union; we are at peace.**"

METHOD EIGHT – Healing Blessing

Purpose: Blessings can also be used in times of crisis. You will encounter those that are in trouble or are in need of comfort. This need can arise directly or indirectly, such as hearing the sound of an ambulance's siren near by. As magicians, we are neither paralyzed by circumstances nor do we go on with our lives as spectators to the traumas around us. You may not be able to save the world or even the person before you, but you can do something. The answer lies in the magic of love and the blessing of Light. Your ability is to love and, with the aid of angels, you can bring comfort and healing blessings to someone miles away. It may not always remove the sickness, stop the bleeding or end their pain, but you will be surprised how much the magic of love and blessing can accomplish. This blessing is a vehicle for you to send love, magnified as pure energy, to anyone. This energy will affect their spiritual body and fill them with a sense of peace. By Divine Grace and angelic aid, the healing, physically or emotionally, will be accelerated. It will also help awaken your inner healing power and bring peace and love to your own heart.

Time: This healing blessing can also be performed at any time and place of convenience for you, as long as you know that you will not be disturbed during the ritual. You can do it for others, either right away in a case of emergency, or from your home. You can also do it for yourself, if you feel that you need it. We know that many people have trouble doing that, but they really shouldn't. It is like giving yourself a hug instead of waiting for others to hug you.

TOOLS: You will need a candle either white, purple, yellow or pink. It will also help if there is some incense, even if it is just stick incense. There is no specific requirement for the type of incense, since it is used primarily as a sanctifier and a mental focus enhancer. Due to the emergency need of this ritual at times, these ritual accessories are not mandatory. You can do this anywhere and at any time without any tools.

STEP ONE: Light the candle and incense. If you are in a group, then hold hands. Focus on the candle and begin to quiet your mind and control your breathing to the count of 3 or 4.

STEP TWO: Focus your mind and attention on the magnificent blessings of the Divine. Feel and imagine every part of your body from head to toe made of pure scintillating light. Chant softly "Al-Nur" until you feel a complete connection with the light of the Divine.

STEP THREE: Focus your mind on the target of this blessing. Everyone repeat with passion, "Our (my) love is filled with peace. Our (my) love is filled with light. Our (my) love is filled with life. It grows a thousand fold, when angels carry it to those in need. To N. we (I) send healing blessings of love, light and life." [x7] If you don't know the person's name, as in the case of an accident, then identify the target as best as possible. If you are doing this outdoors at the scene, then skip the candles and incense and make the repetitions silent.

STEP FOUR: When you feel the energy building up to a point of climax, visualize seven bright stars appearing and joining together to form one massive bright and powerful star. As the stars are merging, vibrate the seven names of the Holy Archangels: Ruqiel, Gabriel, Semsamiel, Michael, Sarfiel, A'aniel and Kasfiel.

STEP FIVE: Now, hold your arms straight out with palms facing each other, about six to ten inches apart. Envision between your palms a ball of light increasing in brightness. (Some magi visualize a beam of light coming down from above their crown chakras and emanating from their heart chakras, to feed the ball of light.) When the ball cannot grow any brighter, watch it rise up on the smoke of the incense to meet the large bright star. See it become part of the large star and the star become brighter. (At the scene of an accident, you can visualize this whole step.)

STEP SIX: Say: "**Filled with healing blessings of light, love, and life, go to _____and bring comfort, restoration, and protection. As the Queen of Heaven desires it, so it shall be!**" Visualize the bright star shooting through the universe as a pure ball of universal energy. See it entering our atmosphere and surrounding the target with warm and bright Light!

✸ PRAYER TO THE GODDESS ISHTAR ✸

PURPOSE: This prayer is the key that opens many of the serious rituals in this book. Invocation of the Divine is generally the first major component of any extended magical ritual and part of the regular practices of the magician. Previously, we discussed how, in magic, the Divine is the Light of all Lights and that this Light is an embodiment of love. The idea that God is love is a recurring theme within the spiritual community. It is more than a saying. This love fills the entire process of practising magic and is really what facilitates and drives the working relationship between angels, jinn, spirits, and the magician. It is a relationship built on love that overflows from the unifying source. This relationship is nurtured through our working with the Goddess of Love. The stronger your bond as a magician with the Goddess of Love and Queen of Heaven, the more successful and real your magic will be. Calling on the Goddess of Love will enliven your soul with the living power of the Holy Spirit. Having a connection with the Queen of Heaven will increase your understanding of the mysteries of creation that we call magic. Even though the Goddess of Love is generally associated with spirituality in love and sex, this is also the key to experiencing a glimpse of paradise and blissful states. This prayer is based on an angelically revealed text known as the *Codex of Love*. Through the prayer, you will open your heart and experience Light in your heart and mind as intense love. It will also make the spiritual beings more receptive to your magical calling. In essence, the more your love for the Goddess of Love grows, the more this love translates into your being loved by the spiritual inhabitants of the heavenly realms.

TIMING: This invocation is to be recited out loud with deep love, melody and intensity of feeling, three to four times a week, preferably one of them a Friday. It is also used as an opening for major ritual work that involves calling on angels, jinns and other spirits.

DIVINE NAMES: The major Divine name that appears here is the Akkadian name for the Queen of Heaven and Goddess of Love. The name Ishtar is to be sung as if calling from the depths of your soul for the deepest desire and love of your heart. Other names for the Goddess that identify with different facets of the Queen of Heaven appear toward the end of the invocation. The mantra Anahuahi Ishtar Yahuahiana identifies the Goddess as the I, He, and She facets of the Divine, from both first and third person perspectives. This is an acknowledgment that the Divine is infinite and all encompassing in its immanence.

TOOLS: No tools are needed for this ritual if it is done solo or during a busy schedule. Within ritualized magical structure, usually a white or green candle, sweet incense, and the tools for purification and consecration are useful accessories, as well as a rosary or counting beads.

STEP ONE: Purify and consecrate your working area and light a dedicated candle and some sweet aromatic incense, such as vanilla, rose, or coconut-heavy mixtures.

STEP TWO: Chant the name Ishtar forty-nine times, in a melodic and calling voice. Don't try to vibrate the name. Chant it as a lover calling from the depth of the soul toward the beloved in yearning mixed with pain of separation. You can also chant it musically or repeat it reverently. Whatever method you feel most comfortable with, keep your mind focused on the Goddess and on closeness to Her and Her nearness to you.

STEP THREE: Calling to the heavens and the world around you, say passionately and adoringly: "Glory! Glory! Do I sing, O angels of love divine. Holy! Holy! I beheld a wondrous vision; seven bright stars cried rejoicing unto the Queen of Heaven and earth. By She who is the First and the Last, whom all angels adore and praise, I banish Lilitu and the demons of fear, hatred, falsehood, and wrath to the world from where nothing returns. O Ishtar; Queen of the Stars, Immaculate One, Exalted Light of the Heavens, my heart cries to you. O Light of Heaven and Earth, radiance of the universe, radiant of countenance, my spirit cries to you. Unto Her all things fall prostrating;" (prostrate) "Queen of the World, Creator of all that is, was and will be, my heart cries to you. Unto the Lady of the angels who receives supplication, my body cries to you. Unto the merciful Goddess Ishtar, who hearkens unto eternity, my passions cry to you." (Rise up)

STEP FOUR: Putting both your hands on your chest and feeling love for the Goddess and all life in the world say: "**Ishtar, O my Lady! O my Lady, ignite my spirit with Light, and awaken my heart with Love Eternal.**" (Repeat as many times as you can while feeling your love grow with every repetition)

STEP FIVE: Say in melodic prayer mode: "**Hear, O Angels, the cry of Your Queen: I have given the brightness of my crown to the stars. I have given the vision of my eyes to cats and lions. I have cast my spear into the dragon and unleashed passion. I have given the strings of my harp to my daughters and made their voices sweet to the host of heaven. I have placed the feathers of my wings on the scales of judgment to weigh against the dead hearts. I have made my blood to run in the veins of saints and prophets, and my symbols adorn every faith. I am the hidden flame in every religion, and to me all of you shall return.**

Is that truth that your lips utter, O lover? Is that passion that your fingers seek to touch, O lover? Is that ecstasy that arouses your senses, O lover? Is the Chalice of Intimacy your wine, O lover? Do you know of what I ask? I ask of your heart, does it beat with Her name? I ask of your blood, does it carry Her breath? I ask of your cheeks, do they know your tears? Blessed art thou, O lover, who knows of these. Thou art the savior of hearts and a fountain of joy. She is your hope and you are Her life. This is love, so listen well, O ears, and behold, O eyes, the story of the King and Queen.

Who comes between the lover and the Beloved? I am the Beloved and you are my love. They say gods, I say God. They say Father, I say I am. I am thy Father and I am your Mother. I am the King and the Queen. I am that I am. I am Yahuah. I am Ishtar. I am the first and I am the last. I am thy breath and thy sigh. I am the tear and the cry. I hear your prayer before your lips utter it. I am love and wrath. I am justice and truth. Thou shalt have no other gods before Me."

STEP SIX: Calling to the heavens and the world around you, say passionately and adoringly: "**Holy are Thou, Queen of Heaven and Earth. Holy are Thou, the revealer and concealer; Your name is Light! Holy are Thou, Ishtar, the Queen; Aima Elohim, the Creator**

Mother; Shekinah, the Divine Glory; Sophia, the Wisdom; Goddess of Love, Life, and Light, by whatever name I call Thee, I can
never utter Your beauty. My soul is in Your hands. Let all the angels adore. Let all the spirits on the Earth adore. Let all that is in
the Heavens adore. Let all that is in between adore the Queen. May
all the angels of Light, whether they are in Heaven or on Earth,
descend upon me, singing Your name. Anahuahi Ishtar Yahuahiana. (Ana-hua-hee Eeeee-shtaaaar Ya-hua-hee-aaaaanaaaa. Vibrate
this last name in a melodic voice as you reach up to the heavens with
both arms.)"

INVOCATION TO THE MASTERS OF MAGIC

PURPOSE: There have been many stories and books written about secret masters, the great white brotherhood, hidden chiefs, and so forth.
Most of what has been said or written about this subject is based on
conjecture. Even those occultists who decry their existence, or say
they are merely high level human masters, do so without any concrete knowledge or investigation. These masters are not a new phenomena that is a product of the imagination of New Age adherents.
We have seen references to them dating as far back as the 12th century
C.E. There are two types of masters to which they refer. The first are
humans, chosen before birth, who represent certain spiritual incarna-
tions. They don't necessarily have supernatural powers, as they are
embodiments of spiritual facets. The other kind of masters are those
who are not human and never have been. They exist in the realm and
domain of angels and they oversee the flow of magic and the development of mysteries. They are the guardians of the magical arts and get
involved, invisibly and sometimes not-so-invisibly, in calling new seekers into the craft, selecting from them those who will access the greater
mysteries and initiation. When they are with a group, and they can
support more than one at the same time, then it has a living current.
If they withdraw their support, then the current of that group is dead
no matter how many members it has or how many temples it erects.
Individual magicians can be affected by these masters' support and
guidance or the lack of it. Most often they are invisible and do their
work silently. However, on a few occasions we have witnessed more
direct intervention, including one anointing a candidate with oil before
his initiation. Yet, they are not human, angels, or jinn. There is a limit
to how much we can say or reveal here, but we don't really need to

say much. The purpose of this ritual is for you to find out on your own and, more importantly, it is for you to establish the kind of magical connection that keeps their guidance and support for you alive.

TIMING: This ritual is to be done at the end of any extended magical work. It can also be done as a daily affirmation. We recommend you do it daily for at least one year.

TOOLS: You will need the headband from the ritual of consecration of the book. We also recommend that you light a candle and burn some incense. Also, if you can do this in nature or in a secluded garden or a park, it would be even better.

STEP ONE: Say with conviction, passion and force: "**O ancient masters of holy magic, who reside in the secret mountain of mysteries, I stand before you as a seeker of the secrets and the knowledge of the wise. I call upon you to bring me closer to your presence and aid me with your company, O ancient beings that preside over the rivers of the garden of Eden and who oversee the art of the Magi. Hear me, in the name of your Queen, whom you serve and adore. I call upon you, o ancient masters of magic, to hear my call this hour and watch over me and aid me with your power and guidance. I bear upon my forehead the symbols of your chiefs Melchizedek and the Master Metatron, for I am a seeker of the path of old.**

Listen to me, ye invisible ones known by many names among the ancients, ye who are magical from birth and of flame that doesn't burn. I call upon you, servants of the secret and mighty name kept veiled by the sages of old, which was given to King Solomon, that has great dominion over you. Empower me with a ray of magic from your world, so that it awakens in my sphere a ray of that ancient current that has its place at the beginning of time and keeps me steady on the path of magic.

Listen to me, O servants of these symbols (draw the seven symbols before you in the air or even better draw them on your arm or chest and expose them) and come to me now and empower me. Let there be a living connection between me and you, o ancient masters of the magic of Light. Watch, guide, and aid me, for I am a servant of Divine Light and it is this Light that we both serve and revere."

✦ RITE OF DIVINE SERVANTS ✦

PURPOSE: One of the most rewarding tasks in the life of the magician is to be a living beacon of Light. Such individuals realize the importance of championing the virtues of Light strongly during dark times of despair or pain, or in places it appears to have dimmed. Many of us try to shed a bit of this light in the best way we can. As magicians, we use this vehicle as our principle means. Often we may feel alone, like a sole candle flame in a dark cave, but this is not so. There are many individual candle flames in this cave. This ritual serves as one way in which all these candle flames can connect. Even if only one person does this ritual, that person still is able to connect with the egregore or group consciousness of the magicians of light. The ritual uses three symbols. These represent three layers of initiation, as well as three distinct circles of occult development. The first symbol serves as a connection to the first circle, the circle of aspiring magical seekers. The second connects to the second circle, the circle of dedicated magical adepts. The last symbol connects to the third circle, or 'secret' Masters of the Mysteries.

TIMING: This ritual is best done three times a week for at least four months.

DIVINE NAMES: The only Divine Name that appears in this ritual is the word Lvx or Light.

STEP ONE: Stand in the form of a cross, then visualize and feel beams of light bursting from both your palms. Meditate for about a minute on the sensations and symbolism of this step.

STEP TWO: Maintain the posture from step one. Focus on a bright candle flame above your head. Say, in a determined and loud voice, **"Great Magical Creator of the Universe, I adore You and I invoke You."**

STEP THREE: Form the letter 'L' by bringing your right arm above your head in a vertical posture. Focus on any pain and loneliness you may have endured in your journey and feel it melt away and be replaced with great joy for where you are now and where you are going. Feel connected to the thousands of seekers on the path of the magic of

Light. While focusing on the Divine, say, "**I Invoke You, O Rapturing Love.**" Visualize your body surrounded with a blue light. Imagine a green crescent crowned with a red, a blue, and a yellow star before you. Feel a connection with aspiring magicians of all ages and walks of life. Know that you are not alone in your search; let your love grow and extend outward unconditionally. Receive the overwhelming energy of love in return.

STEP FOUR: Bring both your arms above your head to form a 'V'. Focus on the road to magical adeptship, all that you have done and have to do to get there: the work, the joy, the benefit, the sacrifices and the satisfaction of being a mage of Light, living and breathing the Divine Spirit and in the company of angels. While focusing on the Divine say, "**I Invoke You, O Resurrecting Life.**" Visualize your body surrounded with red light. See a white cross with a red rose mounted on it before you. Feel a connection with the magical adepts of Light across the world. Feel your challenges melting before the powerful surge of a new spiritual energy.

STEP FIVE: Bring your arms down across your chest in the form of the letter 'X'. Allow a bright golden-yellow energy to surround you as strongly as possible. Feel yourself empowered and ready to fully take on your personal destiny. Once the image becomes strong, say, "**I Invoke You, O Rescuing Light,**" while focusing on the Divine. Visualize your body surrounded by a white ball of light sparkled with gold. See a chalice adorned with a blue, a yellow, and a red gem before you. Entwined around this chalice is a green bronze snake and above it rests a beautiful silver crescent. Feel the connection with the Masters that have guided humanity for thousands of years. Feel their guidance in your life and their love.

STEP SIX: Bring your arms down and then move them up in a swooping manner, call forth the Light with all of your will. Proclaim, "**Lux, (Luuuuuuuuuuuxxxx) Let Your Ever Living, Loving Light descend on the Servants of the Divine across the nations of the Earth.**"

STEP SEVEN: Hold out your arms in the shape of a cross again, then visualize yourself surrounded with transparent white light. Say, "**United by the ancient circle of Divine magic, we stand ready to serve in Love, Light and Life.**" [x3] See hundreds of others across the world, standing as you are in this step. Know that you are not alone in your desire to bring the Light into this world. See yourself and all of the other magicians of the Light linked by a single cone of power and an ancient magical current.

❁ THE CALL TO MAGIC ❁

PURPOSE: You may feel a calling to magic, a deep yearning inside of yourself that you can't explain. This isn't unusual. People are called to magic, metaphorically and literally. Magical groups make a point of sending out a call to attract those of like mind, who are meant to share with them their celebration of the mysteries or magical work for a period of time. This is a lesser call. The greater call comes from the guardians of the ancient art, who help and guide people into this path. These people are called into the art for different reasons, which can range from needing to learn something to help themselves or others, to being due to some past-life or spiritual connection with the work. Some are literally born into magic or into a magical family. Magic is a powerful spiritual force and its impact on our spirit extends over many lifetimes. You may very well have been called to this art. You also can call others to this path. Assisting others, even indirectly, to find their way spiritually is a great service and a blessing for all involved. Even though this ritual is about sending a lesser call, it is very beneficial in that it connects you with the currents. You become part of the greater call and this benefit flows not only into your life, but into the lives of others.

TIMING: The ritual of the call is generally done during the full moon.

TOOLS: All that is needed is a white or green candle and some incense.

STEP ONE: Purify and consecrate your working space, then light a dedicated white or green candle.

STEP TWO: Meditate on the flame of the candle. Relax your body and calm and empty your mind.

STEP THREE: Focusing on the candle flame, say, "**O Holy of Holies, the Great Initiator of the mysteries of Divine magic, I adore You with my heart, I praise You with my lips; I call You with my soul.**

137

By the flame and the glory of Your light in heaven and earth, let the fires of Light and life be ignited within me, a mage of Light. Send the angelic redeemer and ancient priest of the Great Mysteries Melchizedek, the prince of spirits Metatron, and the angel of your hidden and concealed occult wisdom, the archangel Raziel. Let the angel Raziel be a guiding hand to those who are ready for studying and practicing Your ancient mysteries of Divine magic within this tradition or any other. Let the path be made clear for them and peace profound descend upon them. May Spirit guide their feet, as You have guided my feet. May their hearts be comforted with love, as You have comforted my heart. Let the angel Raziel watch over them, as Your angels have watched over me. Let the Light descend on them with love so warm and mild, as it has descended on me. Amen. Amen. Amen. Amen and a thousand, thousand, thousand Amens be upon them, and all true seekers of the magic of Light!" [x3]

✺ GRAIL OF WISDOM ✺

PURPOSE: Attaining wisdom is the crowning jewel of the magical development process. If you lack wisdom, even if you are to contact your Holy Guardian Angel, you will not know how to properly handle this information. Ancient masters and spiritual teachers didn't acquire their wisdom just from reading books. Books provide guidelines, information, and techniques to achieve magical growth and spiritual wisdom. Wisdom is connected with enlightenment. This is the ability to see things for what they are, outside the confines of illusion. This comes through spiritual effort and is a spiritual blessing. However, there are techniques to bring and grow wisdom into one's own mind. Wisdom can be magically planted like a seed, which is then nurtured to full bloom via the Light.

The operational premise of the ritual of attaining wisdom is to call upon Holy and angelic names to charge a dedicated cup of water. The water is then consumed, and will infuse the entire soul and spirit with the imbued force through the physical and ethereal bodies. Of course, the success of this depends on the angels consecrating the water. So it is important that you inflame yourself with the invocation and recite it as many times as necessary. When you get the first feeling of success, that is, you begin to feel some form of external energy around you, then double and triple your effort. Stop only when you feel as if your request has been answered a few recitations earlier.

TIMING: Do this ritual daily for 40 days. It would be best if you are able to do this first thing when you wake up, after an Illumination Wash. Otherwise, try to do it on an empty stomach.

DIVINE NAMES: This ritual introduces sacred names of power for wisdom. They are based on an ancient method of extracting names of power from the permutation of other names of power. This was a common practice in the ancient world, even within Jewish mysticism or Qabalah that was influenced by the Chaldean magi. The ritual also ends with other names of power that are based on permutations of a single name of the Divine. These names should be chanted together loudly at a fast pace, as a way of entering trance. To your ears, this should sound very similar to many native Amerind shamanistic chants.

The ritual also introduces the Hebrew Divine Names that represent the unknown name or Raz Shem (the Name of Mystery) and the name of the mystery of mysteries, Shem Raz Ha-Razim. To really enhance the impact of this ritual you may want to chant silently the names Yah Ha-Chokmah (God of Wisdom) and Elohim Ha-Binah (Gods of Understanding) as many times as possible during the day and night.

TOOLS: Any cup of water will do, but you can also have a chalice inscribed with the Holy names used in the conjuration, and it is even better if you can inscribe the entire conjuration, with the names, upon it.

STEP ONE: Do the illumination wash and then purify and consecrate your working area.

STEP TWO: Hold the cup between your hands, close to your third eye. Focus for a few minutes on the intent: to call on angels to use the water as a medium for transmitting the seed of wisdom to you, who are a follower of the way of the wise.

STEP THREE: Say: "**By the names of wisdom Chahak Machah Memem Hakach; by the Raz Shem given to Adam when he left the Garden of Eden, by which he prayed for redemption; by the**

Raz Shem that was given to Moshe before the burning bush Ehieh
Asher Ehieh; by the Raz Shem that was given to Prophet Shelomoh
and he was made a wise king; by Shem Ha-Raz Ha-Razim, before
which all of creation bows in love and adoration, I call upon the
angels and spirits of Sodi Chokmah Ha-Aur.

By permission of the Holy of Holies, I call upon the Archangel
Raziel, peace be upon him, from the midst of the Rauch Ha-Kodesh
(Holy Spirit), from the midst of Safafiel, the Prince of Reason, to
aid me with the descent of the spirits of wisdom. By the hand of
Afafiel, the Prince of Knowledge; by the hand of Katatiel, Prince of
Understanding, by the hand of Aramiel, Prince of the Crown, by the
hand of Yahuel, Prince of the Testimony, by the hand of Nahanael,
Prince of insight, by the hand of Rahael, Prince of the Secrets of
the Shekhinah and by the hand of Ashmoyeli, Prince of the Torah, I
invoke the spirits of wisdom to infuse this water, so that in drinking
it, I may be infused with spiritual wisdom and occult understanding. Just as Atiq Yomin (Ancient of Days) gave to Moshe Divine
inspiration, the spirit of wisdom and understanding, the spirit of
knowledge and cleverness, the spirit of cunning and knowing, the
spirit of secret insight and the spirit of the Holy of Holies, may the
Shekhinah, the spirit of knowledge and God's wisdom, the secret
spirit of ancient magic, rest at this time upon me, (Your first name
– child of – your mother's first name – child of – father's first name
– last name. Women should reverse the parent's names).

In the name of Shaqarhozi, the great prince, who is Patar Adonai, the great Prince, who is Ririel Adonai, the great Prince, who is
Anoqtiel Adonai, the great Prince, who is in charge of the archives
of Torah wisdom; all the keys are given into his hand. He was the
teacher of Moses; he taught him Torah, wisdom, knowledge, and
strategy. Thus may he open to me, (Your first name – child of – your
mother's first name – child of – father's first name – last name), the
door of wisdom and the door of understanding. In the blessed and
Holy Names of Ah-hey-wah, Ah-Hey-Wash, Yo-hey-wash, Yo-hey-
wah-hey , Yo-hey-wah, Yo-Hey, Hey-hey, Hey-wah-hey, Hey-Hey,
Hey-wah-hey, Yo-hey-wah-yo, Hey-wah-hey, Hey-hey, Yo-hey,
Wah-hey, Ah-hey, Yo-hey, Yo-hey, Wah-hey, Wah-aha-ah, I invoke
the spirits of wisdom to infuse this water so that in drinking it, I
may be infused with spiritual wisdom and occult understanding.
Amen. Selah."

❂ THE SHIELD OF THE MAGI ❂

PURPOSE: This ritual is a protective warding that will guard you against any possible hostile spiritual intrusion into your space. As a magician you will need necessary protection against unexpected surprises or interference. It is traditional to erect wards in your working magical areas or establish a protective shield around yourself when not doing work. This idea has been known as banishing in modern occult circles. However, banishing is actually a process of removing negativity or releasing resident spirits. A ritual that does this effectively generally doesn't establish wards as well. The warding will not banish the spirits, but will erect a wall between you and them. Therefore, it isn't uncommon that you see things looking at you from behind the shield or that for the first few nights you have strange dreams. This magical warding can also be used to augment the magical circle found in old magical books. You can use this ward to protect others, who may be experiencing negativity in their lives.

TIMING: Do this ritual at least twice a week. Do it more if you feel something is bothering you psychically, or if you sense an unfriendly presence in your area. It is also a good ritual to do before working with any major spirits or jinn.

STEP ONE: Meditate on the Light and feel a sphere of Light above your head. Say: "**O spirits of Light, I heard the voice of my angel speak to my soul and say 'Mah-rah-zah-hoo' and I replied 'Mah-rahd-ah-zeer-hoo', my spirit is from the Light of all Lights, I serve the Light of all Lights and to the Light of all Lights I shall return. I am a servant of the Holy of Holies in the tradition of the prophets of old. I call upon you o spirits of Light, in the name of our creator, the Light of all Lights, to shield me like you shielded the prophet Al-Mahn-hah-mah-nah, peace be upon him.**"

STEP TWO: Move to and face the east. Draw the shield of the magi, while saying: "**Ahh-Mah Hh-May-Thah Aht-Mah Ta-May-Thah.**" When you draw the shield visualize it strongly before you in gold, blue or white. The shield is illustrated here, with the appropriate instructions for tracing it.

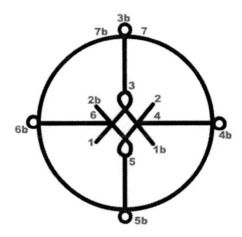

You begin drawing from point 1 and draw the top inner angle and loop ending at point 1b. Move to point 2 and draw the bottom inner angle and loop ending at point 2b. Then begin drawing the crosses from point 3 up to point 3b, which includes the small circle. The small circles are all drawn in clockwise fashion. Move to point 4 and draw the right arm of the cross with its terminating circle at point 4b. Move to point 5 and draw the bottom arm of the cross with its terminating circle at point 5b. Move to point 6 and draw left arm of the cross with its terminating circle at point 6b. Then move to point 7 and draw the outside circle beginning from the top moving clockwise to point 7b. When you are done, draw a connecting line made of pure white and gold fire and move to the south.

Step Three: Face south. Draw the shield of the magi, while saying: "**Ahh-Mah Hh-May-Thah Aht-Mah Ta-May-Thah.**" Draw a connecting line made of pure white and gold fire and move to the West.

Step Four: Face the west. Draw the shield of the magi, while saying: "**Ahh-Mah Hh-May-Thah Aht-Mah Ta-May-Thah.**" Draw a connecting line made of pure white and gold fire and move to the north.

Step Five: Face the north. Draw the shield of the magi, while saying: "**Ahh-Mah Hh-May-Thah Aht-Mah Ta-May-Thah.**" Draw a connecting line made of pure white and gold fire and move to the east. Connect the north and east shields.

STEP SIX: Return to the center and say: "**Ahh-Mah Hh-May-Thah Aht-Mah Ta-May-Thah.**" Repeat this three times or multiples of seven. Increase the energy behind it as you go on, while visualizing the four shields in bright flashing light around you.

STEP SEVEN: Say: "**Al-Nur, shield and preserve me. Keep away from me all harmful things and injurious creatures from among the humans and the jinn. Keep away from me the corrupt and evil spirits. Let us be apart as the distance between the heavens and the earth. Preserve me with your preservation, by which you preserved the universe. By the great name Ehieh Asher Ehieh Adonai Tzabaoth El Shaddi** (visualize the sphere of Light above your head grow large enough to encompass you and the shields) **and by the power of the archangels Michael, Gabriel, Raphael, Surial, Tzadkial, Sartial and Nanial, may I dwell in a fortress of Light whose gates are the Holy Names, whose watchers are the mighty archangels, and upon whose banners glows the symbol that is the magi's shield** (revisualize the shields brightly shining around you)." [x3 or x7]

❂ BANE BREAKER RITUAL ❂

PURPOSE: If you hang around occult circles long enough, you are bound to meet someone who is convinced that they are under magical attack by someone or another. This is true whether we are talking ceremonialists or witches. This has led to a whole saga of coven wars in the community. Nineveh remembers a few times when we were accused of attacking certain individuals, which couldn't have been furthest from the truth. What leads to this phenomena? Is it merely illusion from internalizing all magical phenomena as mental experiences? Is it a form of magical madness or unresolved psychological transference? More often than not, the victim of magical attacks blames the parties with whom past negative personal relationships exist.

We don't believe that there is a blanket answer to this issue. To dismiss magical attacks as non-existant flies in the face of two things. The first is the vast number of people who have had experienced them at one time or another. The second is the antiquity and abundance of attack or hex spells across cultural and magical paradigms. If we deny that attack magic is possible, we may as well deny all the other branches too. On the other hand, the majority of people accused of magically attacking others are indeed inoccent. This is not to say that magical aggression doesn't occur between humans, only that they are not always the guilty parties, especially if the evidence is the result of some astral or dream experience. Getting too focused on such attacks is a route to paranoia and fear. Fear is the greatest enemy of any magician ~ this can't be emphasized enough. A magician who is afraid will make choices that are damaging to herself and others, spiritually, mentally, and even physically.

There is another theory that is often missed in the West. Many of those magical attacks are actually done by jinn. Jinn can appear in any form and in old texts sorcerers would send them into the dreams of their victims, to attack them in the form of a human. The human form could be that of the sorcerer himself or someone else. Most magicians in the West practice no effective banishing against jinn, and some even invite those beings to their life in an uncontrolled manner. It would be no feat or challenge for such a jinn to attack its victim and convince her that she is under attack by someone with whom she has had issues. As human magicians fight each other, they have no time to deal with the jinn. Some even turn around and summon evil jinn to enlist their aid to help against their perceived attackers. It is a win-win situation for the evil jinn. Due to their psychic abilities, Jinn also know how to radiate panic among humans, which is further why we emphasize the importance of learning to control your fears and transform them into something positive.

Instead of worrying whether you may or may not be under such attacks, we recommend that, as a matter of routine, you banish any such energies. It becomes a matter of normal magical hygiene. It also strengthens the spiritual sphere of the magician. Those that do this on a regular basis will notice that many problems that almost appeared as bad luck, have vanished. We generally recommend that you do this rite regularly and not wait until you are under some strange influence. How do you know that you are under attack? There are many signs that a trained magician can decipher with extended accuracy. However, it is easy to dismiss the signs out of hand or to become paranoid; neither attitude is balanced. In principle, if you feel drastically different after doing this ceremony, as if a huge weight has been lifted from your shoulders, or as if you had shaken up lots of negativity or pressures, then you were the target of something or another. Don't dwell on it or the source; just do the rite regularly and don't be seduced into fighting back.

TIMING: Do this ritual at least once a week or whenever you feel something is amiss.

DIVINE NAMES: The words of power in this ritual form a devotional praise in Hebrew, that you recite while drawing the four hexagrams on the sides. Draw the hexagrams rapidly to ensure that the prayer flows together comfortably. The charge utilizes potent angelic names that are common to the tradition.

STEP ONE: Chant: "Halelu Elochai Qadush Adon Malachim Wa Ruachim." [X7] (Glory to be My God Holy Lord of Angels and Spirits.)

STEP TWO: Move to the East. Draw a circle, starting from the top and going clockwise. Draw the upper triangle starting from the top and going clockwise, vibrating as you do so: "**Ehieh.**" Vibrate: "**Asher.**" Draw the lower triangle starting from the bottom and going clockwise, vibrating as you do so: "**Ehieh.**" Draw the sun symbol ☉ inside the hexagram, and visualize the hexagram glowing brightly. Draw a connecting line of pure light from this hexagram to the hexagram to be drawn in the south. Ehieh Asher Ehieh is the Divine Name spoken to Moses, and means: "I will be that I will be."

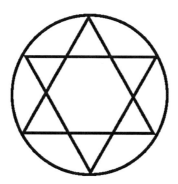

STEP THREE: Move to the South. Draw a second circle, starting from the top and going clockwise. Draw the upper triangle starting from the top and going clockwise, vibrating as you do so: "**Adonoi.**" Draw the lower triangle starting from the bottom and going clockwise, vibrating as you do so: "**Tzabaoth.**" Draw the sun symbol ☉ inside the hexagram, and visualize the hexagram glowing brightly. Draw a connecting line of pure light from this hexagram to the hexagram to be drawn in the west.

STEP FOUR: Move to the West. Draw a third circle, starting from the top and going clockwise. Draw the upper triangle starting from the top and going clockwise, vibrating as you do so: "**El Shaddi**." Draw the lower triangle starting from the bottom and going clockwise, vibrating as you do so: "**El Chai**." Draw the sun symbol ⊙ inside the hexagram, and visualize the hexagram glowing brightly. Draw a connecting line of pure light from this hexagram to the hexagram to be drawn in the north.

STEP FIVE: Move to the North. Draw a final circle, starting from the top and going clockwise. Draw the upper triangle starting from the top and going clockwise, vibrating as you do so: "**Adonoi**." Draw the lower triangle starting from the bottom and going clockwise, vibrating as you do so: "**Malek Ha Malkuth**." Draw the sun symbol ⊙ inside the hexagram, and visualize the hexagram glowing brightly. Draw a connecting line of pure light from this hexagram to the hexagram drawn in the east. The Divine Name Adonoi Malek Ha Malkuth means "my Lord King of the Kingdom."

STEP SIX: Move to the East to connect the two hexagrams. Return to the Center.

STEP SEVEN: Repeat three times: "**By the blessed and holy Shem Yah and the mighty archangels Michael [x3], Metatron [x3], Tahitmeghilial [x3], Sharntaeel [x3], and Kehial [x3], I banish any spells, sorceries, hexes, bindings or any magical or psychic energies set upon me by any human or jinn that would influence me negatively or attempt to control my choices, for I am dedicated to the Divine Light and the magic of Light. Any magical forces or psychic whispers that would hinder me in my life or lead me astray from my spiritual magical path be banished, be banished, be banished.**"

STEP EIGHT: Chant: "**Halelu Elochai Qadush Adon Malachim Wa Ruachim**." [X7]

When doing the various steps of the ritual, try to do them in a single flow without interruption. The intent is to say the following prayer: "Glory be to God, Holy my Lord of Angels and Spirits, I will be that I

146

will be, my Lord of Hosts, God the Strong, God the Living, my Lord King of the Kingdom!"

Having put these rituals and techniques into practice, you have now begun to build a strong magical foundation. You are probably excited about beginning to work with spirits, elementals, planetary forces, and even summon some jinn. We recommend that you be patient a bit longer. You should first contact your holy guardian angel. Your guardian angel work will raise your spiritual vibration, and endow you with the spiritual authority needed for the later parts of the program. This kind of spiritual awareness is necessary to ensure that your work is in fulfillment of your true destiny on earth, and to empower you with a true sense of confidence when communicating with other spiritual beings. You will literally have the Divine seal on your magical work, which is why we feel it is a necessary next step for any true seeker of the magic of Light.

Works Referenced

al-Buni, Ahmed (D. 1225 C.E.). *Shamsu al-Ma'aref al-Kubrah*. Maktabat Isha'at al-Islam. Delhi, India.

al-Buni, Ahmed (D. 1225 C.E.). *Manba'a Ussol al-Hikmah*. Maktabat al-Hidayah. Surabaya, Indonesia.

al-Toukhi, A'adu al-Fatah. *al-Siher al-Azeem (v1-3)*. al-Maktabah al-Thaqafiah. Beirut:1991

Mubarak, Ahmed. *Al-Ibriz fi Manaqib Sayyidi 'Abd al-'Aziz al-Dabbagh*. Maktabat Mohammed Ali Sabeeh. al-Azhar, Egypt. (Composed 1716 C. E.)

Anonymous. *Codex of Love: Reflections from the Heart of Ishtar*. Ishtar Publishing. Burnaby, Canada: 2005

Anonymous. *Sepher Raziel ha-Malak*. Jerusalem, Israel.

6
The Guardian Angel

"By the heavens and the night visitor! Do you know who knocks? The piercing star. Verily, as every soul has upon her a guardian." Quran, Surah 86, Verses 1-4

"For God commands the angels to guard you in all your ways." Psalms 91:11

Magicians believe that with the birth of every child a stellar body appears in the heavens. As the star moves, the child follows its light. If the star of one individual comes close to the star of another, the two beings will meet on the earth; when the two stars separate, they also separate. If two stars are to collide, the individuals involved will collide in anger and in conflict. When the star finally sets over the horizon, the person also dies. In this sense, each individual in this world is like a star. This star is not a mere celestial body in the outer boundaries of our galaxy, but a stellar body that moves in the spiritual world. In the ancient tradition, a star is symbolic of an angel, in this case your guardian angel.

What exactly is the holy guardian angel (HGA)? The holy guardian angel is first and foremost an angel. This means that this entity isn't you. It doesn't refer to that deep spiritual part of you or that inner enlightened self or anything that constitutes your self, mind, or spirit in a psychological sense. We are talking about an entirely independent being and this is an important key. This angel is assigned to you to watch, to record, and to guide your life. This teaching is based on the principle that there is an angelic governor presiding over every function in the universe. Since, in this universe, you are a function who acts and reacts to your surroundings, there is also an angel presiding over you. The strength of this relationship is based on the strength of your relationship to the Divine. Thus, if you should stray far from the spiritual path, your connection with your angel will weaken. This

149

angel is intimately, spiritually, connected to you and can act as your intermediary or representative in the celestial world.

Contacting one's guardian angel is an important first step in angelic magic, because this is the closest angel to you from among all other angelic beings. This connection is through both proximity and spiritual bond. This is your star, and it shines brightest in your life from among all others created by the Divine. You can choose to work with and build a relationship with any number of the blessed angels in the celestial realm, but you can always count on a firm relationship with your angel. The only thing that can weaken this relationship is for you to turn your back on spirituality and the Divine.

In the ancient magical path, calling upon the guardian angel was traditionally one of the initial steps you would take as an apprentice. Some magicians recommended that the apprentices begin and end all their occult work with a blessing on their guardian angels. This is due to the role of the guardian angel as an intermediary and as the envoy of the Divine One. This importance doesn't compete in any way with the attribution of all magical causalities primarily to the Divine. It is simply working in harmony with the Divine order and celestial arrangements.

There are many spiritual benefits from having a healthy connection with your guardian angel. This is why many modern magical schools have made the communion with and discovery of the name of the holy guardian angel either the halfway mark of the process of magical development or one of its most important accomplishments. Magical aspirants of these systems undergo many initiations and work with many rituals to prepare for, or to help enhance, the chance of this encounter. Initially, the idea of contacting the holy guardian angel was made popular in modern Western magical writing by the translation of a magical text known as the *Book of the Sacred Magic of Abramelin the Mage*. It also became central to the doctrine of the famous author and magician Aleister Crowley.

The idea of a holy guardian angel is more than a modern phenomenon, as it is rooted in the ancient teachings of the Magi and has found its way into many religions in the Middle East. One of the earliest references to this teaching is found in the Sumerian culture. Sumerians believed in Divine messengers of the gods who ran errands between them and humans. Excavations near the Sumerian capital of Ur revealed religious artifacts; one of the earliest of those discovered was an angelic engraving in stone, a winged figure. Each Sumerian home had an altar honoring its guardian angel. Guardian angels also figured in the teachings of Zarathustra. The Ahura Maza, the embodiment of the spiritual as well as material existence of the Cosmos, created many beloved ones or archangels. These archangels, called Yazata in Persian, interact with each human being through their guardian angels or Farahvashi. These guardian angels are the link between the individual and the rest of the celestial or angelic realms.

Holy guardian angels are also mentioned in the Torah, in Genesis, in the struggle of Jacob with an angel. Jacob tells the angel, who appears as a man, that he will only let him go when he has pronounced the blessings bestowed upon him. The angel declares that Jacob has wrestled with men and godly beings and won; therefore, his name is now Israel. Jacob's struggle was with his brother Esau's guardian angel. The importance of the guardian angel continues to this day, especially in modern Western occult societies.

One of the obstacles that many magicians encounter in the endeavour of contacting their guardian angel is finding methods or techniques specifically dedicated to this goal. The most fabled and probably the only known method in English, is the one detailed in the book of the magic of Abramelin. Due to its complexity and difficulty, many also turn to the Golden Dawn for a working system for HGA contact. This is mostly due to the fact that the translator of the book of Abramelin was one of its founders. However, the traditional Golden Dawn had no interest in the HGA, and, as such, not a single ritual for this purpose was ever published in its order's corpus. The Golden Dawn's emphasis is on the Higher Genius, which is an equally valid but different concept. Lack of practical published materials and organized systems leaves modern magical seekers with few venues for contacting their guardian angel.

In this book we will provide you with some effective and productive methods to contact your guardian angel and to begin to build a strong relationship. These techniques can be used within the book's own self-paced program or as part of another magical system. We recommend, if you choose to work with another system, you avoid any program that incorporates guardian angel work with working with demonic beings to gain magical powers. Calling upon both angels and demons in the same sphere would be an insult to the angel and a painful punishment to the demon. Keep in mind that calling upon angels and demons in the same sphere isn't the same as calling upon demons with Divine and angelic names. The demon responds to avoid having an angel sent to it. The ancient magicians of our tradition also taught that those who make a point of regularly summoning demons will be blocked from contacting or receiving aid from angels and celestial beings.

Before we proceed any further, let's talk about what we mean by contact. In Chapter 3, we talked about the various methods of contacting an angel. There are four ways to contact your angel and each of them is considered a valid one. The first and greatest contact occurs through a physical or semi-physical encounter with your guardian angel. This requires an extended operation that can last months with long, extended retreats. While many would be willing to make the time commitment to it, few are able to do so in our busy modern life. Our highly competitive capitalistic society is inherently unfriendly to a mystical, monastic or hermitic magical life.

The second approach involves the angel's presence or spirit ray touching your own. This will feel like being engulfed or hugged by another entity. You will know this is your guardian angel by the major effect it has on your spiritual heart center and on your consciousness in general. This is a strong experience and its beauty is difficult to describe. This can occur during the ritual of contacting your guardian angel. This contact will leave you, on a very deep level, with an impression of what your angel wanted to impart to you. You will not have any doubts about what the message is or that it was your angel. It will be one of the most spiritually rapturous experiences, second only to being engulfed by awareness of the Divine reality.

The third approach involves being visited in a very lucid dream by your angel. The angel might appear as a man or woman, but very luminous and bright. It will identify itself to you in some way, and you will feel the radiance and love. The angel generally communicates using dream symbolism or even a voice in your dream. This message is very important and requires meditation to unlock it.

The fourth approach is most often used in magical workings. It involves contact through mediumship or clairvoyance, through the crystal ball or magic mirror method. This isn't as reliable, as it depends heavily on the ability of the mage to open up to the angelic presence and message. It also requires a good ability to receive and interpret any messages received. It is easy to be deceived in the process. Beginners may confuse their own inner desires or feelings for guidance from the guardian angel. You will need to know on a soul level or in every fibre of your existence what your guardian angel is telling you, and that it isn't something coming from within your own mind or imagination. The strong impact of such a message can be diluted by such externalized contact methods. The key to dealing with these problems is to undergo extended training, repeat the process over the years, develop the ability to recognize the qualities of messages and extend the operation itself. This means that you would need to adopt a retreat period, fast and regularly do rituals to contact the angel before you could expect to receive a valid message. Fortunately, during such a process, you may very well have an encounter with the presence of your angel to validate any images or messages you receive.

❀ THE NAME OF YOUR ANGEL ❀

The first and most important step in contacting your guardian angel is discovering the angel's actual name. One method, recommended by books like Abramelin, utilizes elaborate techniques involving retreats, deep meditations and fasts and an extensive six month long operation. This method is a bit of a challenge and few cases of success have ever been recorded. The overall expectation is that you will hear your angel's name in your mind when you make contact. This leaves room for miscommunication and deception, since this will be your first encounter with your angel. These methods are viable when and if you have spiritually purified and empowered yourself sufficiently through years of practice. The chance of success for most practitioners with limited practical magical experience, or who have not done extended mystical and magical operations beforehand, is low. Due to the current demands of modern life, few people are willing to make such an investment in time and energy at the beginning.

The other method that we recommend is mathematical. The name of your angel can be derived from the numerical vibrations of your own birth name. This should not come as a surprise, as a birth name has long been considered to be a powerful spiritual link to the individual. Names in occultism have power and a person's name was a powerful occult key in all ancient operations. Birth names may appear arbitrary, but the ancients didn't believe them to be so. They felt these names were magical and that knowing a magician's name would give you power over her. Around the 6th century B.C.E., Pythagoras also declared that the world is built upon the power of numbers. He believed that the entire universe could be expressed in numerical formulas. Numbers and letters were seen by the ancient masters as the primary tools of the Divine Architect in this world and, through them, occult miracles and spiritual accomplishments were possible. Such reliance on mathematical principles for finding out your HGA's name may at first seem less mystical than having a vision or having it told to you by an inner voice, but it also means that you can begin to establish contact with your angel now. There are drawbacks to this method, but our tests have shown that it works well and is a great help to beginners.

This is a good time to discuss how the ancients came up with the value of the letters in numerical form and approached their understanding of numbers. We need to go back to this original thinking to be able to establish the correspondences of numbers to the English letters. Since mathematics and numerology were not two different sciences in the beginning, we can assume that the ancient numerologists investigated the properties of numbers by analyzing their mathematical behavior and action. The number five was considered a number of rebirth and preservation. It was due to the fact that when it is multiplied by itself, it preserves itself. The same goes for any integer that is a product of multiplication with five. Here are a few quick examples:

5x5 = 25
25x25 = 625

This approach can be applied to the numbers mentioned in scriptural texts. The number six is considered the first of all perfect numbers; we read in the Bible and Quran that God created the world in six days. A perfect number is a number whose positive divisors (except for itself) sum to itself. Here are a few quick examples:

6 (1+2+3 =6)
28 (1+2+4+7+14=28)
496 (1+2+4+8+16+31+62+124+248=496)

The ancients also saw the polarity in nature, with most species containing both female and male. This same polarity was expressed in numbers, by designating odd numbers as masculine and even numbers as feminine. The magi gave the letters of the alphabets small, large and great ranges. Ranges are the linguistic ordinal count or the locational count of a letter in its alphabet. The range of Aleph is one, because it's the first letter of the Hebrew alphabet and the range of Gimel is three, because it is placed third after Aleph, and so forth. Equally, the range of A in the English alphabet is one and the range of C is three, and so on. The first letter of any alphabet has the range 1 and the second 2, and so forth. The value of ranges was commonly used

in magic to determine the vibratory quantity of a word, that is, how many times it should be vibrated. The numerical sequences in all the ranges proceed from one to ten. The small range continues from eleven to twenty-eight, while the large ranges continue from twenty up to one thousand. This principle is applicable to any sequence of letters in any language.

THE RANGES OF LETTERS IN THE ALPHABETS

Small Range	Large Range	English	Hebrew	Arabic
1	1	A	א	ا
2	2	B	ב	ب
3	3	C	ג	ج
4	4	D	ד	د
5	5	E	ה	ه
6	6	F	ו	و
7	7	G	ז	ز
8	8	H	ח	ح
9	9	I	ט	ط
10	10	J	י	ي
11	20	K	כ	ك
12	30	L	ל	ل
13	40	M	מ	م
14	50	N	נ	ن
15	60	O	ס	س
16	70	P	ע	ع
17	80	Q	פ	ف
18	90	R	צ	ص
19	100	S	ק	ق
20	200	T	ר	ر
21	300	U	ש	ش
22	400	V	ת	ت
23	500	W	ך	ث
24	600	X	ם	خ
25	700	Y	ן	ذ
26	800	Z	ף	ض
27	900		ץ	ظ
28	1000			غ

Readers of modern occult books may find our numerical attribution of the English letters confusing. This is due to the current trend to use the Hebrew alphabet as a comparative language for others. Our system of ranges is explicitly evident in older sources, and is also clear from the adaptation of the nine fold degree system from Hebrew into English numerology. In modern numerology texts, the division of the English letters into nine columns is used as the basis for the value of the letters in what is called Phythagorian numerology.

MODERN ENGLISH NUMEROLOGY

1	2	3	4	5	6	7	8	9
A	B	C	D	E	F	G	H	I
J	K	L	M	N	O	P	Q	R
S	T	U	V	W	X	Y	Z	

A table similar to the nine divisions of English numerology was used in both Arabic and Hebrew numerology. In Hebrew, it is called Aiq Beqar (Nine Chambers).

TABLE OF NINE CHAMBERS

1	2	3	4	5	6	7	8	9
א	ב	ג	ד	ה	ו	ז	ח	ט
י	כ	ל	מ	נ	ס	ע	פ	צ
ק	ר	ש	ת	ך	ם	ן	ף	ץ

The letters in the first Hebrew column have the commonly recognized large ranges of 1-10-100. The letters in column two have the large ranges of 2-20-200, and so forth. Aiq Beqar is used for talismanic purposes, among many others. Nevertheless, it is understood that the large range of Aleph is one and Yod is ten. The same goes for the English nine chambered table, A is one and J is ten. The letters in the first English column also have the large ranges of 1-10-100 and the letters in column two have the large ranges of 2-20-200, and so forth. When trying to calculate the ranges for an alphabet, you shouldn't compare ranges used for another alphabet as a basis for extracting its own values. Could you imagine trying to fit the Swahili alphabet with the Hebrew to acquire the ranges of the Swahili letters?

Modern scholars and students have also erred by mistaking the ranges for the actual numerological values. If we were to total the numerical ranges for the following English words, they would all have the same total.

✳ Live = 30 + 9 + 400 + 5 = 444

✳ Evil = 5 + 400 + 9 + 30 = 444

✳ Veil = 400 + 5 + 9 + 30 = 444

✳ Vile = 400 + 9 + 30 + 5 = 444

By modern magical understanding, this means they should share similar "numerical value." They do share similar harmonic range, but not numerical values. The range of every letter is calculated based upon its placement within the alphabet. However, the numerical value of every letter is additionally calculated based upon its placement within the word or phrase. Two methods are mainly used; the first depends upon constructed elemental tablets for the letters, while the other, known as the 'Secret Whisper', is more simplified, but equally effective. The basic premise of the 'Secret Whisper' is to multiply the large range of a letter with its sequence number within a word or a sentence. Here are the numerical values for the same words in our example using the 'Secret Whisper':

✳ Live = (30 x 1) + (9 x 2) + (400 x 3) + (5 x 4)= 1268

✳ Evil = (5 x 1) + (400 x 2) + (9 x 3) + (30 x 4) = 952

✳ Veil = (400 x 1) + (5 x 2) + (9 x 3) + (30 x 4) = 557

✳ Vile = (400 x 1) +(9 x 2) + (30 x 3) + (5 x 4) = 528

Using the magical method of the Secret Whisper, you can calculate the name of your HGA from your own name. Those wishing to use just the range can do so. If you are using different methods, vibrate each name until one name opens your heart and soul, like a flower to the brightness of the spiritual sun. You will know which one this is and, as you work with it, you will be surprised at the strength of the force it awakens in you.

The first step in calculating your HGA's name is to write out your full name. It was traditional in the Middle East to use words like Ben

(Son of) and Bent (Daughter of) when referring to people. Such as: Solomon Ben David or Lilah Bent Myriam. Therefore, there are two ways to write the full names. The first would include the usage of Ben and Bent in the writing and calculation, and the other would exclude it. The exclusion is more common with Latin based names. Also, many people in Western countries have at least one additional middle name that Semites do not use. If you have one, the middle name has to be taken into account. The writing of the name should be based on the linguistic format of the individual's cultural background. The format of a typical English name is as follows: (Your First Name) – (Your Middle Name[s]) – (Your Mother's First Name at Birth)- (Your Father's First Name at Birth) -- (Your Birth Family Name). If you are a woman, switch the order between your mother's and father's names, as follows: (Your First Name) – (Your Middle Name[s]) – (Your Father's First Name) - (Your Mother's First Name) - (Your Birth Family Name). If you don't have a middle name, don't worry about it, as it is a cultural variable like the word Ben. The principle formula that does not change is the use of your and your parents' first names and your last name at birth. In cases of adoption, where the biological parents are unknown, use your adopted parents' names.

The second step is the selection of a numerical method to calculate the name. We are going to use only one method here as a standard. We will apply the Secret Whisper method to the large ranges of the letters of the name.

You can do the calculation on paper or using software. If you are using paper, draw a grid similar to the one following and then write down the letters of your name in descending sequence. We recommend that you leave enough space for three sets of numbers. Here is an example calculation, using George Anthony Lisa David Wilson. George is the first name, Anthony is his middle name, Lisa is his birth mother's first name, David is his birth father's first name, and Wilson is his birth family's last name. Beside each letter, place its English large range value. Now place each letter's sequence in the column next to the large ranges. Next, multiply the large range value with the sequence and place the total beside each letter. Then add the total of the numerical value column.

CALCULATING THE LARGE RANGES FOR A SAMPLE NAME

Letter	Range	Sequence	Total
G	7	1	7
E	5	2	10
O	60	3	180
R	90	4	360
G	7	5	35
E	5	6	30
A	1	7	7
N	50	8	400
T	200	9	1800
H	8	10	80
O	60	11	660
N	50	12	600
Y	700	13	9100
L	30	14	420
I	9	15	135
S	100	16	1600
A	1	17	17
D	4	18	72
A	1	19	19
V	400	20	8000
I	9	21	189
D	4	22	88
W	500	23	11500
I	9	24	216
L	30	25	750
S	100	26	2600
O	60	27	1620
N	50	28	1400

The sum of all the numbers in the fourth column provides us with the full numerological value of the name, based on the Secret Whisper formula. The total for this particular name is 41,895.

If you want to use a spread sheet program for your calculation, launch it and write the letters of your full name descending in the A column. In the B column, write the actual value for each letter. In the C column, write 1 and increment it sequentially until you reach the last letter in your name. In the D column, write the following formula: =(B1*C1) in the first cell, =(B2*C2*) in the second cell and so forth. Finally, in the cell under the last inserted formula, type in the following formula: =Sum(D1:Dx). The x here represents the last letter's row number. This will allow you to acquire the values accurately, without error. You should double check your numbers and math regardless.

The next step is to subtract the angelic suffix from this value. In ancient documents, there are two variations for doing this. The first is to use the traditional large range Hebrew value of 31 for the Divine name El. The second is based on the large range Arabic spelling of that name, 41 for Ayl, which is closer in original historical pronunciation. From the 360 degrees of the zodiac the Arabic magician subtracted 41, with a result of 319 (TYSh), which is the jinni suffix. The addition of 41 and 319 results in 360 degrees, which corresponds to the Zodiac. If we were using the Arabic alphabet to form the angelic name, we would subtract 41 and if we were using the Hebrew, we would subtract 31. Since we are working with the Arabic alphabet for this example, we will use the Arabic suffix AYL (41).

The reason that we subtract the range value of the suffix in the first place is because otherwise the value of the name of the angel would exceed the original total calculated value. We subtract first what we will be adding later, so as not to unbalance the equation. Subtracting forty-one from the total 41,895 leaves us with 41,854. Now we pronounce this number as such: forty one thousand, eight hundred and thirty four. This is translated into the following formula: 40-1-1000-800-50-4. We then exchange the numerals with the equivalent Arabic letters and the letters of the suffix. You would of course do this from right to left, since this is the direction of Semitic languages.

30	10	1	4	50	800	1000	1	40
ل	ي	ا	د	ن	ض	غ	ا	م

The pronunciation of the name is the most difficult step in this process for non-native speakers. The key is to place the consonants for each letter together and, when a need arises, simply insert an 'e' between them. This is how you pronounce the preceding name.

ل	ي	ا	د	ن	ض	غ	ا	م
L	Y	A	D	N	Dh	Gh	A	M

The result would be as follows: MAGheDhaNeDAYL (Maghe-dha-ned-aeel). To know how many times to vibrate this name in rituals and meditations, simply reduce the total number itself: 4+1+8+9+5= 27. We use only a single reduction.

✹ ANGELIC LAMEN ✹

The angelic lamen is the next tool that you will be constructing in this book. On one side is the angelic pentacle and on the other side is the angelic mandala. Once you are finished constructing the lamen, treat it with respect and wrap it with white cloth when not using it. Wear the lamen so that it rests on your heart during any work with your guardian angel.

The side containing the pentacle involves a pentagram surrounded by a circle. Inside the points of the pentagram are the letters, in ancient Hebrew script, forming the word Shekinah or Divine Presence. The Shekinah is the Queen of Angels, and it is under Her presence that angels seek closeness to the Exalted Light. Outside the pentagram is written in Hebrew, Achath Ruach Elohim Chayyim, which means "One is the Spirit of the Living God."

This is the standard template for all angelic pentacles. You will also notice the numbers from one to three. These numbers are place holders for the modifications that personalize the template for a specific angel. In place of number one, you write the name of the actual angel for whom this pentacle is designed. The writing of the angel's name can be in ancient Hebrew, Modern Hebrew, Arabic or Aramaic. In place of number two, you place the script sigil of the angel.

The third number in the template is a place holder for the charge of
the angel. This is also open to customizing and spiritual inspiration. It
can be in any language, but it is best if it is in Hebrew, as this is the
same language as the rest of the pentacle. It consists of a statement of
adoration to the Divine, possibly an attribute similar to the nature of
the angel, and a call to respond. One possible Hebrew statement for
the angel would be:

ברוך אור מופלא עתיקא קדישא

Beruk Aur Mophla Atiqa Qadisha
(Blessed be the Hidden Light the ancient Holy One!)

If you can't think of anything in particular for the statement, then use
a generic adoration such as this:

קדוש אלהי המלכים

Qadosh Elohi ha-Malachim
(Holy God of Angels!)

The charge that follows the statement is a simple request for the angel
to respond. It is written in Hebrew thus:

עֲנֵה לִי מַלְאָךְ N.

Aneh Li Malach N.

(Answer me angel N.)

We mentioned something about the angelic sigil, but how do you construct one? The most popular sigil method in modern Western occultism is the Rose-Cross method taught in the Golden Dawn. This is
what we call a geometric ratio procedure. The sigil is derived by lo-
cating points on a two dimensional plane and then connecting them
to create a sigil out of the geometric distance and alignment of the
points. The problem with this method is that the letters are so closely
arranged on the rose that when copied the ratio can't be maintained.
A difference in ratio in the copy could mean an entirely different letter
sequence when placed back on the original rose. Even a maintained
ratio would produce different results if placed on a rose of a different size from the original. The second problem is that the differences
between various sigils remain obscure and all the symbols eventually
induce the same feeling.

We prefer the use of script sigils. Script sigils are based on connecting talismanic script letters spelling out the name of the angel or
spirit. The connection is usually embellished and done in a geometri-
cally pleasing fashion. For example, let us create a script sigil for the
angel Maghedhanedayl. First, we begin by selecting an appropriate
script. Generally, these kinds of script are simple and mathematical in
their shape, consisting of no more than lines, circles, and termination
points like crosses. These scripts replace the letters, but do not affect
the language. Some scripts, such as the Theban script or Passing of the
River, have become famous in the West. Some were based on ciphers
used by certain secret societies, while others have been invented more
recently for fun or as part of a fictitious story. Occultists of the ancient world used close to one hundred different scripts. Some of these
scripts were based on ancient and dead languages, some were created
by famous individual magicians of their times, and others were used
by certain groups such as the Sabians or Hermetists. Not all of those
scripts were treated equally. Trials and application have shown that
some are more effective than others.

The reason for the use of these designs is that they act as an added
gateway for the currents that are being evoked. Of course, the same
goes for many geometric patterns such as Pentagrams, Hexagrams,
Golden Ratio and so on. Even though these images, just like intent

and focus, act as conduits, they in themselves are not the source of the magical currents. Nevertheless, their use is part of the principle of magic that deals with numerations.

We will list only a fraction of such scripts in this chapter for you to pick from to create your HGA sigil. Our source for these scripts is a famous and rare Arabic document known as *Shuq Al-Mastaham Fe Ma'areefat Rumooz Al-Arqam,* written by a Nabatian author Abu Bakr Ahmad ben Ali ben Wahshiyya around 855 C.E. The book's value was of high importance to magicians and marked a developmental stage in cryptography. A number of those scripts are reproduced here, as found in the currently existing copy of the document. These are hand drawn renditions and, of course, we can not verify the accuracy of all these scripts. The source is medieval, and we have not found any alternate source with which we can compare them. We also accept that errors during duplication are possible and can not be ruled out. This does not mean the scripts are wrong, only that the reader should not be surprised if future research uncovers a minor error here or there in any of the scripts.

The series of magical scripts that follow are for general magical workings and can be adapted to the HGA working. They can be used in making numerical magic squares, creating amulets and talismans, inscriptions on magical implements and so forth. You may want to specifically use the script of Hermes when you are using heavy Egyptian or Greek magical symbolism in your work. You can use the script of Wonders for making magical designs or seals for jinn and other spirits. You may also use the Pythagorean script, especially when making your magic square numerical amulets. These are general guidelines and, with experience, you will come to recognize the right script for each of your workings.

Magical Script of Hermes

7	6	5	4	3	2	1

50	40	30	20	10	9	8

300	200	100	90	80	70	60

400

Magical Script of Pythagoras

7	6	5	4	3	2	1

50	40	30	20	10	9	8

300	200	100	90	80	70	60

400

Giorgian Script

7	6	5	4	3	2	1

50	40	30	20	10	9	8

300	200	100	90	80	70	60

1000	900	800	700	600	500	400

MARSHOL'S SCRIPT OF WONDERS

┱	⊬	⧀	∆	Ʒ	Ⴗ	Ⴣ
7	6	5	4	3	2	1

₹	⨍	ᵒ	⧵	⍴	⅃	ᘔ
50	40	30	20	10	9	8

⅃	ᓕ	Я	Ɣ	ᘿ	Ⴑ	꒨
300	200	100	90	80	70	60

ㅂ	⊓	ᛇ	ⵦ	ⵦ	ⵦ	ⵦ
1000	900	800	700	600	500	400

DISCORIDES TREE SCRIPT

ᛉ	ᛉ	ᛉ	ᛉ	ᛉ	ᛉ	ᛉ
7	6	5	4	3	2	1

ᛉ	ᛉ	ᛉ	ᛉ	ᛉ	ᛉ	ᛉ
50	40	30	20	10	9	8

ᛉ	ᛉ	ᛉ	ᛉ	ᛉ	ᛉ	ᛉ
300	200	100	90	80	70	60

ᛉ	ᛉ	ᛉ	ᛉ	ᛉ	ᛉ	ᛉ
1000	900	800	700	600	500	400

One other important element of magical scripts is their connection to the lore of the primordial angelic language or Divine language. According to the same source manuscript, in his book on secret things Agathodaimon gave the three ancient Divine alphabets. The word Agathodaimon itself translates into the good genius or guardian angel or spirit. However, Agathodaimon was also another name for Hermes. According to Agathodaimon, one of the three primordial alphabets was the old Syrian alphabet, the original Divine alphabet, which was taught by God to Adam.

ANCIENT SYRIAC SCRIPT

I	◁	⟑	⊢┐	⟨⟩	⊿	⅃
7	6	5	4	3	2	1
ⱨ	ⱳ	ⱸ	ⱶ	⫽	⤓	⥾
50	40	30	20	10	9	8
⩬	⅂	⨅	⥽	⟈	⅃	⋔⋔
300	200	100	90	80	70	60
						⅃
						400

This alphabet has undergone numerous changes in its form through time to become the more recognized modern Syriac script. The ancient Syriac script can be used as a generic script for any magical construction. It can replace a number of magical scripts, when specific scripts are not available, and can be used in conjunction with Hebrew and Arabic scripts. Of course, the Syrian Aramaic language continues to exist today in a modern form. It is an important language and many of the names of power in ancient magic were preserved in it.

To continue with our example, we will be selecting the Marshol's script for creating the angelic sigil. The first step is to write down the script correspondences with the letters of the HGA's name. The second step is to connect them in a harmonic way to create a signature design. Let's use the example HGA name to illustrate the process:

MAGHEDHANEDAYL IN MARSHOL'S SCRIPT

ل	ي	١	د	ن	ض	غ	١	م
30	10	1	4	50	800	1000	1	40
☚	⤳	Ƴ	◮	⟊	⚜	⊟	Ƴ	⫧

167

Connecting them would yield the following angelic sigil:

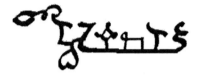

The next step is to construct the angelic mandala. This magical mandala is made by combining letter runes into a special circular design for the name. The final design is so unique that it can't be confused in any way or made to represent another name. The symbols are hard to draw on most tools but then for that we have the sigils. However, they can easily be drawn on a circular flat surface such as the angelic pentacle.

RUNES OF THE ARABIC LETTERS

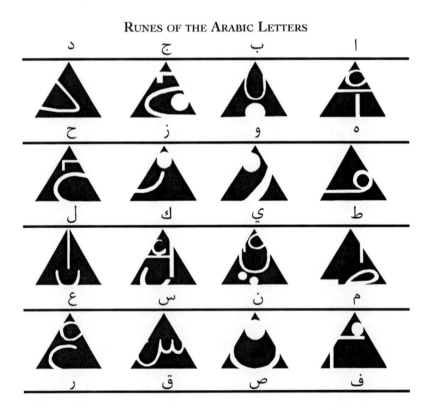

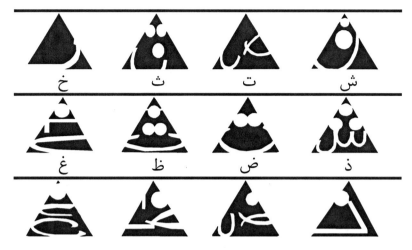

To design the mandala, draw a circle and then divide it into slices according to the number of letters in the angel's name. Don't forget that the suffix AL/AYL is part of that name. Make sure that, while the slices are all connected to the center, there is some space between them. Within each slice, draw the appropriate shape for its corresponding letter in its proper sequence, proceeding clockwise around the circle. You must remember that the "black shaded area" is the actual shape, not the white. While the white space may appear close to the letter, it is actually only empty space. It doesn't matter at what point of the circle you begin, as long as you go in sequence and clockwise. The colors for angelic mandalas are usually green or gold on a white background. The dark, shaded areas, being the actual symbols on which to focus, should be the part painted. The mandala for the angel Maghedhane-dayl is constructed using the following runes:

The completed mandala is shown on the following page.

❂ RITUAL OF WHITE FIRE ❂

PURPOSE: Once you have undertaken the cleansing steps of the Illumination Wash and the rebalancing steps of the Garment of Light,
the next step is to infuse your spiritual and ethereal body with Light.
This is a good time to open up and heal any remaining imbalances
in your energy centers as a precursor to your HGA working. This is
done partially by elevating and exalting the human mind by focusing
it on the Divine presence. The process of receiving the Light infuses
the spiritual body and empowers it. Healing and opening the energy
centers in the process helps with related psychological and spiritual
imbalances as well.

THE SEVEN ENERGY CENTERS

Sanskrit Name	Body Location
Sahasrara	Crown
Ajna	Third Eye
Vishuddha	Throat
Anahata	Heart
Manapura	Solar
Svadhishthana	Sacral
Muladhara	Root, Base of Spine

170

Illuminating the crown energy center can help overcome lack of faith or doubt about one's spiritual relationship to the Divine. Illumination of the third eye energy center helps balance the traps of materialism and the illusion of separation between the world and the Creator. Illumination of the throat energy center helps balance fears or paranoia. Illumination of the heart energy center helps balance sorrows and traumas. Illumination of the solar plexus energy center helps balance feelings of inadequacy, lack of self-worth or low self-esteem. Illumination of the naval energy center helps balance strong lusts. Illumination of the root energy center helps balance the sense of separation and disconnection from our physical body and nature itself. When the magician does the technique of White Fire for balancing, the focus should be on the positive aspects of the energy center. When done regularly, this can be a powerful instrument, not only for spiritual transformation and the infusion of Light, but also for the healing of unbalanced emotions and spiritual states.

DIVINE NAMES: This technique uses the practice of magical chanting. Magical chanting, like the recitation of mantras, is a good way to focus your mind and open it to the influx of spiritual forces. Magical chanting is two-fold in nature: one external and the other internal. External chanting is the more popular form, which is the repeated recitation and vibration of one of the Divine Names. This is very similar to the idea of a mantra. However, without the internal chanting, the benefits of external chanting are superfluous. The aim is to connect to the Divine and magical currents on all levels, and not simply to empty the mind from all thoughts by monotone recitations of sounds.

Internal magical chanting is allegorical to an individual diving into the ocean of meaning, so that nothing else exists for the senses. So if the magical chanting is of the Divine Name of El, then, during the external chanting of the name, the entire consciousness should be focused on being engulfed by and in the presence of the Infinite Divine. The words should flow to intensify the internal chanting. If need be, the recitation can get very loud, very quiet, very fast or very slow, and even a voice change isn't uncommon. However, none of that matters – any rigid rule will hamper the entire process.

Many Sufi groups also utilize energy and physical movements during their chanting techniques, which they refer to as Ziker or Divine Remembrance. They see every chant of a Divine Name as if it originated in one part of their body, like the navel, and moved to another, like the brain. Certain names are chanted while inhaling and others while exhaling, followed by head movements. We are not going into more detail on these practices, because they differ from Sufi order to order and from teacher to teacher.

When the chanting is done successfully, the magician should feel engulfed by the Presence, as if her body is but an extension of the name, a manifestation of such quality. Only then will a ritual utilizing the attribute or calling upon it have the desired effect in the physical plane, for then it is manifesting not from the lower astral via the ego, but from the highest worlds through Divine Providence. Or again, to utter the famous words of our master Hermes: That which is below is a reflection of that which is above. In cases when the chanting is dealing with words of Power or formulae that don't represent the Divine, then the focus should be on the externalization during internal chanting. So if the chant is for calling forth of an Angel, then all of the senses, internal and external, should be focused on the Angel's being, presence, and descent, externally in the magician's sphere. This shouldn't be a matter of force through will either.

TIMING: We recommend you do this ritual three times a week for three months.

TOOLS: During magical chanting, it is best if the body is clean and there is sweet incense burning nearby. The mind must be prepared beforehand through relaxation or breathing exercises. In some cases, observance of a set number of repetitions is required; a rosary is helpful as it keeps the mind from worrying about counting. Magical rosaries have been known to actually improve the effect of the chanting and shield the practitioner from psychic interferences during workings.

In the ritual, the number of repetitions given is what is recommended, but they can be reduced to whatever you are capable of doing. If you are not feeling well, you can also do this exercise lying down or seated. It is also important that, no matter where you are focusing your mind, you remain in a state of praise and adoration to the Divine when chanting the Holy Names. You must be in a state of reception of the Light. You are not raising or creating this energy yourself, but receiving it from the Divine. The hardest part is shifting focus from step to step, but you can develop that skill by time and practice. Do your best to keep this mental focus strong, as well as to maintain an inner state of reception and love.

STEP ONE: Standing with your feet together, ground yourself to the center of the Earth. Feel your feet melt into the earth as if you have grown out of the soil. Begin quieting your mind, while performing a breathing exercise to the count of four or eight. Proceed until you develop a rhythm. Once you have done this for a bit, make sure your palms are stretched open to your sides or facing each other with finger tips touching.

STEP TWO: Say: "O Al-Nur, whose light has illuminated the heavens and earth with Your guidance, with the unknown within their being, You have brought them to Your Unity. You are the Illuminating Light, the Guide, the Strong, the Fortified and Your Light has no equal in the worlds. Your Being is the guaranteed existence, which has no equal. Al-Nur, illuminate me with the Light of Your shining nature, and holy being. Al-Nur, whose knowledge encompasses all the minute things in the Universe, manifest in my inner being Your Light, so that it may liberate me from my cosmic darkness - a light that removes from me my human blindness and blinders so that I may be absorbed into Your being, and be one with Your Guiding Light. Al-Nur, illuminate me, O Nur, with Your Light." (Sun of knowledge by Al-Boni)

STEP THREE: Take time to focus on the presence of the immortal and eternal Spiritual Light of the Divine One. Visualize a white flame above your head, the purest and brightest that you can see in your mind's eye. Inhaling the purest and brightest Light that you can feel, begin chanting the Divine Names "Ya Al-Nur Al-Hai." Proceed with the magical chanting for a minimum of thirty-three times. The vibration should be that of aspiration, prayer, adoration and praise.

STEP FOUR: Focus your mind on the crown center of your head. See and focus on this spiritual center of your physical body. Say, "Ya-Qudous Al-Nur Al-Ahad [x7], surround my crown energy wheel with a halo of your brilliant Light; open, purify, and infuse the spiritual center of Sahasrara with Your Light of Rulership."

STEP FIVE: Keeping the flame of light bright and brilliant, visualize another flame forming at the region in the center of the forehead. As you do this, chant: "Ya Al-Nur Al-Hai." [x33]

Step Six: Focus your mind on the center of your forehead. Shift your focus to the spiritual center surrounding it. Say, "**O Ya-Qudous Al-Bassir Al-Hadi [x7], surround my third eye energy wheel with a halo of your brilliant Light; open, purify, and infuse my spiritual center of Ajna with Your All Seeing Light.**"

Step Seven: Keeping the flames of light bright and brilliant, visualize another flame forming at the region in the center of the throat. As you do this, chant: "**Ya Al-Nur Al-Hai.**" [x33]

Step Eight: Focus your mind on the center of your throat. See and focus on the spiritual center surrounding this area. Say, "**O Ya-Qudous Al-Salam Al-Haq [x7], surround my throat energy wheel with a halo of your brilliant Light; open, purify, and infuse the spiritual center of Vishuddha with Your Light of Truth.**"

Step Nine: Visualize another flame forming at the region in the center of the chest. As you do this, chant: "**Ya Al-Nur Al-Hai.**" [x33]

Step Ten: Focus your mind on the center of your heart. See and focus on this spiritual center of your physical body. Say, "**Ya-Qudous Al-Rahman Al-Wadud [x7], surround my heart energy wheel with a halo of your brilliant Light; open, purify, and infuse the spiritual center of Anahata with Your Light of Beauty.**"

Step Eleven: Visualize another flame forming at the region of the solar plexus. As you do this, chant: "**Ya Al-Nur Al-Hai.**" [x33]

Step Twelve: Focus your mind on the center of your solar plexus. See and focus on the spiritual center surrounding this area of your body. Say, "**Ya-Qudous Al-Latif Al-Shafi [x7], surround my solar plexus energy wheel with a halo of your brilliant Light; open, purify, and infuse the spiritual center of Manapura with Your Healing Light.**"

Step Thirteen: Visualize another flame forming at the sacral area. As you do this, chant: "**Ya Al-Nur Al-Hai.**" [x33]

Step Fourteen: Focus your mind on the center of your groin. See and focus on this spiritual center of your physical body. Say, "**Ya-Qudous Al-Hai Al-Qayum [x7], surround my sacral energy wheel with a**

halo of your brilliant Light; open, purify, and infuse the spiritual center of Swadhisthana with Your Light of Life."

STEP FIFTEEN: Visualize another flame forming at the base of the spine. As you do this, chant: "**Ya Al-Nur Al-Hai.**" [x 33]

STEP SIXTEEN: Focus your mind on the region of the base of the spine. See and focus on this spiritual center of your physical body. Say, "**Ya-Qudous Al-Fattâh, surround the energy wheel at the base of my spine with a halo of your brilliant Light; open, purify, and infuse the spiritual center of Muladhara with Your Light of Life.**"

STEP SEVENTEEN: Focus your mind on each of the energy centers beginning with the base of the spine and moving back up to the crown. See and feel that white flame bright and sacred. Know on a deep level that it is a holy flame of pure spiritual light. Moving slowly from center to center and keeping that flame strong, chant, "**Holy, Holy, Praised, Praised, is the Lord of Angels and Spirits (Qud´-uce Qud´-uce Sabuh Sabuh Rabu Al-Mala-aika Wa Al-Ruh).**"

STEP EIGHTEEN: Inhaling and exhaling, feel the Light from the Holy of Holies embodied in the seven flames surrounded with spiraling halos of light. Recognize that these flames are your own spiritual devotion to and union with the Divine Light. Feel the Light circulating like a blanket of illumination from the top of your head toward the base of the spine and down to your feet and back up again. The halos cover your body with a blanket of brilliance and the seven flames light you up from the inside and outside.

STEP NINETEEN: Focusing on the Light and feeling the spiritual aura around you, pray: "**O Lord and Lady of the Universe, who created all things, send to me my guardian angel, who was set upon me before my birth until after my death. Let this angel descend upon my body and soul with Light and Peace Profound. Your Will shall be done, my Beloved.**" Chant the name of your guardian angel at least one hundred times.

❂ THE MAGICAL ROBE ❂

If you don't have a magical robe already, it is time to make your second most important magical tool in preparation for your ritual of contact with your guardian angel. The magician and his robe are interconnected through history. The robe is more than a ritual garment worn for ceremonial purpose; it is a full body magical talisman. Once you put on your magical robe, it should feel like you have just plugged in to the currents. This means that the construction of a magical robe is a bit more involved than the Renaissance fun-fair variety. However, the basic body of the robe remains the same. We realize that you may not be good at sewing, so we are not going to ask you to go and learn how to sew. However, even if you hire or ask someone else to make the basic body of the robe, you will still need to put in some effort into making the magical portion of it. Now, in this book you will be making one magical robe and will have the option to make seven traditional planetary robes. In our tradition, the most commonly worn magical robe is white. White represents purity and light. Every color of the spectrum is encompassed in white. Once you make your white robe, you should begin wearing it for as many of your magical workings as you can. However, this rule isn't without exception. Some of the rituals in our tradition are done sky clad.

FABRIC FOR BASIC RITUAL ROBES

The fabric for your robe should be totally natural – cotton, linen, ramie, silk, or wool. If you choose wool, it should be light weight, since otherwise it will be too warm in the summer. Natural fibers, especially cotton and silk, are much more comfortable next to your skin and they also last longer. Synthetics can be too cool in winter and too warm in summer, and don't allow your body to breathe. You should take some time selecting the material, especially if you don't know what qualities will make a fabric comfortable and long wearing. If you can find a small shop that sells fabrics and sewing supplies nearby, go there and talk to the salespeople. What you want is a piece of natural fabric that will not irritate your skin, that is easy to care for, and that drapes (or hangs) well. Ask for advice.

You should crumple various fabric selections in your hands, to see what the wrinkle factor is. Make sure your skin is clean of any make-up or essential oils, so that you can rub each fabric against your face or the inside of your wrist to see how it feels. It might be a little bit scratchy, with a substance called sizing that will wash out, but if the fabric is really stiff, it won't hang right and it won't feel good to wear. It is also very important to make sure that the fabric you choose is washable, and to find out how it should be laundered. You really don't want to have to dry clean your ritual robe, although if you have your own laundry equipment, there are now kits for dry cleaning garments in your dryer.

If you are planning to sew the robe yourself, make sure the fabric you buy is easy to work with. Cotton and wool and ramie are much less slippery than silk, and show needle marks less, if you make a mistake and have to take out any stitches. If you are going to have a professional make the basic robe for you, then this shouldn't be a problem.

We chose to make our robes out of fairly heavy weight white silk. That is because we have a fairly large Indian community in our city, and can buy the fabric relatively inexpensively in their shops. It is comfortable, fairly opaque, drapes well, is machine washable, and is warm in winter and cool in summer.

PATTERNS FOR ROBES

You can usually find patterns for robes in most pattern catalogues, in the costume section. You will want to choose a pattern that isn't too complicated, with a hood. Any pattern for a hooded robe used in Christmas pageants or for Halloween is fine, as long as it is roomy, allowing for ease of movement and expansive gestures, as well as for sitting cross-legged in meditation. Inexpensive patterns for robes can also sometimes be found in thrift stores. If you are lucky enough to find one, check inside the envelope to make sure that the instructions for making the robe are there, as well as all the pieces you need, and that they are in good condition. The instruction sheet will indicate what pieces you need to make the robe and how to lay them out on various fabrics of different widths. If you have not sewn before, no matter where you get your pattern, you should get a friend with experience to go with you, to make sure your finished garment will fit you. Have your friend take basic measurements before you go, such as the length from the nape of your neck down to your feet, your chest measurement, your hip measurement, your sleeve length, and so forth, so you can check them against the information on the back of the pattern envelope.

Once you have purchased the material and the pattern, if you really do not feel confident in your sewing skills, it is quite all right for someone else to sew the robe for you. That said, it is always better to make magical tools, such as robes, yourself. With a little ingenuity, it can be managed. Certainly, you will need to make the talisman for the robe yourself.

Constructing the Robe

Before you start working on your robe, you should wash the material and iron it. This will remove the sizing (starch) and ensure that the robe will still fit after it is finished and washed for the first time, especially if you have used either cotton or linen, either of which can shrink or wrinkle badly in washing.

If you are going to sew your robe yourself, you will need a good pair of fabric shears, a box of straight pins, a measuring tape, dressmaker's chalk, and a sewing machine, in addition to the thread and fabric for your robe and enough spring green half-inch washable satin ribbon to sew a border around the sleeves and the hem.

Make sure you have a large, clean, flat surface on which to work. Lay the fabric out, folded according to the directions for your fabric and fabric width given on the instruction sheet. If you are using a new pattern, trim the edges of the pattern pieces you will be using to about a half an inch away from the borders. Pin the pieces in place as shown in the pattern directions, being careful to pin all the way through the material if you have more than one layer. Make sure your shears are sharp before you start to cut. If you need to lengthen or shorten a pattern piece, double check the measurement against your arm or your body before laying it out and cutting it. It is better to measure twice and cut once, than to cut your material only to find that you have made a mistake and need to buy more fabric. When you are certain that everything is correct, cut out the fabric pieces, making sure to cut around any notches, not through them. The notches are important for lining up the pieces when the time comes to sew them together. If there are any dots on the pattern, carefully mark them on the fabric with dressmaker's chalk or straight pins.

Sew the robe together, according to the pattern instructions. Sew on the ribbon border a half an inch from the end of each sleeve and from the bottom of your robe. If you cannot sew and really want to make the robe yourself, it is still possible to put the robe together, following the pattern instructions carefully, using permanent fusible web tape and an iron. If you use this, always hand wash your robe, to give it a longer lifespan. When it is finished, wash it again to remove any chalk marks or oils from handling the material, iron it and hang it up. Your basic robe is ready for use.

ROBE TALISMAN CONSTRUCTION

After you have worked with several mathematical calculations of your Holy Guardian Angel's name, and have come to a final decision as to which name resonates for you, you can construct the talisman that goes on the front of your robe, over the chest area. Please read all the instructions before starting.

For the talisman, you will need a ten-inch square piece of white cotton, seven smaller pieces of colored cotton - purple, black, green, blue, red, royal blue, and white, the same colors of regular sewing thread, seven skeins of embroidery thread - yellow, white, brown, green, blue, and black, or alternatively, fabric glue and fabric paints in those colors, a four-inch square piece of dark green fabric, dressmakers chalk, and either white embroidery thread or white fabric paint. Another alternative to fabric glue is iron-on permanent fusible web tape, which is less messy and fairly easy to use.

To make the talisman, you first cut out a circle nine inches in diameter from the white cotton. Next, cut an equilateral triangle (all sides and all angles equal), with each side measuring two inches, out of each of the colored pieces of cotton. Last, cut out a circle three and a half inches in diameter from the dark green material.

Beginning at dawn on a Sunday, the planetary hour of the Sun, take the purple triangle and the yellow embroidery thread or fabric paint into your ritual space and either embroider or paint the first symbol in the center of the triangle. You can then glue, fuse, or stitch the triangle onto the top area of the white fabric circle. If you are using fabric paint, wait until the paint is perfectly dry before attaching the triangle onto the white circle. Most fabric paints take forty-eight hours to dry. If you wish, you can just proceed with painting each triangle and assemble the whole circle when they are all dry. The assembly can be done outside your ritual space.

At dawn on Monday, the planetary hour of the Moon, take the black triangle and the white embroidery thread or fabric paint into your ritual space and either embroider or paint the second symbol in the center of the triangle. You can then glue, fuse, or stitch the triangle onto the next area of the white fabric circle, proceeding clockwise with the top point of the triangle touching the outside edge of the circle.

At dawn on Tuesday, the planetary hour of Mars, take the green triangle and the red embroidery thread or fabric paint into your ritual space and either embroider or paint the third symbol in the center of the triangle. You can then glue, fuse, or stitch the triangle onto the next area of the white fabric circle, again proceeding clockwise around the circle.

At dawn on Wednesday, the planetary hour of Mercury, take the royal blue triangle and the brown embroidery thread or fabric paint into your ritual space and either embroider or paint the fourth symbol in the center of the triangle. You can then glue, fuse, or stitch the triangle onto the next area of the white fabric circle, proceeding clockwise around the circle.

At dawn on Thursday, the planetary hour of Jupiter, take the red triangle and the green embroidery thread or fabric paint into your ritual space and either embroider or paint the fifth symbol in the center of the triangle. You can then glue, fuse, or stitch the triangle onto the next area of the white fabric circle, proceeding clockwise around the circle.

At dawn on Friday, the planetary hour of Venus, take the orange triangle and the blue embroidery thread or fabric paint into your ritual space and either embroider or paint the sixth symbol in the center of the triangle. You can then glue, fuse, or stitch the triangle onto the next area of the white fabric circle, proceeding clockwise around the circle.

At dawn on Saturday, the planetary hour of Saturn, take the white triangle and the black embroidery thread or fabric paint into your ritual space and either embroider or paint the seventh symbol in the center of the triangle. You can then glue, fuse, or stitch the triangle onto the remaining area of the white fabric circle. The completed circle of triangles forms a heptagram, with a heptagon in the center.

The reason for doing this work at dawn of succeeding days is that this time is the first planetary hour of the day to which each symbol is attributed, so you don't have to calculate it. If you do not have a week at your disposal, you can do the work in one day, provided you calculate the planetary hours and work on each triangle during its appropriate planetary hour.

When the heptagram of outer triangles is complete, take it into your ritual space and embroider in black, using embroidery thread or fabric paint, the Hebrew names of the archangels directly beneath each triangle. You will need to draw them out first, keeping them fairly small so that there is room for your HGA sigil in the center space.

Now, using dressmakers chalk, trace out the symbols for your HGA's name on the dark green fabric circle. You can either embroider the white parts in satin stitch, whether by machine or by hand, or you can paint them on with fabric paint. When this is finished, and, if you used fabric paint everything is perfectly dry, stitch, fuse, or glue the HGA sigil into the central space of the white circle, making sure that the green circle is positioned so that the first and last symbols of the name are at the top.

The final step is to stitch, fuse, or glue the entire white circular talisman, with the purple triangle and its yellow pentagram upright at the top of the circle, onto the center chest area of your robe. If you are using fabric glue, make sure you place several layers of something like packing tissue or paper toweling between the layers of fabric to prevent gluing the front and the back of the robe together. You should not use newspaper, since the print will come off and mark the fabric, possibly permanently.

The next time you put your robe on, take a few centering breaths and feel the difference in its energy. This talisman affects the heart and solar plexus centers very strongly.

❀ THE ANGELIC COVENANT ❀

PURPOSE: Magical evocation of angels was not done often in the ancient world. The Master Al-Boni explained the reason for this in his work. He stated that angels reside in the sphere of the Divine presence or the Shekinah. Asking them to come down to our level for a one to one communication would discomfort them and distract them from their duties. This is why magical evocation or calling down an angel was done only in three circumstances: 1) to enter with them into a covenant of aid and assistance; 2) to ask them to assist in extracting obedience from a more physical spirit or a jinn; 3) to ask them to assist in something or answer a question that is of grave urgency and beyond the scope of terrestrial jinn or spirits. Al-Boni also says that angels are very difficult to see properly or accurately using spiritual sight, due to their luminosity and immensity. This is why he detailed their markers as domes of light, as in the case of the seven planetary angels. This is also why many of the old magical tomes called upon angels for aid and assistance, but focused on summoning spirits, elementals or in some cases demons.

In all affairs terrestrial, you would enlist the aid of a terrestrial spirit under the direction and command of the Divine One and the celestial angels. Equally so, if you were to call upon angelic aid or even state in ritual work that a given angel would aid you or be present before you in any form, it would be more proper if beforehand you had entered into a covenant of aid and assistance with that angel. The only exception would be the guardian angel, since you are his charge and duty.

In this ritual, you will learn to open yourself up to angelic presences and to enlist their aid. You will start by entering into a covenant calling upon your HGA and then enter into covenants with the main angels of the tradition. Once sealed from their end, this covenant will ensure that you have protection and guardianship as well as assistance in future magical work. Although the covenant is sealed only once, you can renew it by repeating this ritual.

The text can be modified and used for any of the angels. The focus is less on communicating with angelic beings through a medium and more on building a relationship and a connection. The repetitions marked by **x** are highly recommended; however, if your time is short, these repetitions can be reduced. The requirements for this ritual are limited. Magicians with experience can build on this ritual and beginners can gain great benefit from doing it as provided. The key is to do it regularly over an extended period of time, as its effectiveness is cumulative.

TIMING: This ritual should be done twice a month on any days when you have time for it. Do this for the next four months.

TOOLS: Before you begin the ritual, you will need a clear and clean space to do your work. Make sure you have no electronic gadgets on, such as television, computers and so forth, anywhere nearby. Lights must be turned off, except for candle light, and incense should be burning. We recommend that you undergo a purifying bath or shower first. At minimum, you should be clean of body and clothing, and not have eaten meat, drunk alcohol, or consumed drugs earlier that day. The more effort you put into your state of mind and space, the better the results will be.

The only magical implement that you will need for this ritual is the angelic pentacle and your magical robe. Once you have the angelic pentacle made and ready for the ritual, hang it around your neck.

The first thing you need to do is purify and consecrate your working space. This purification and consecration technique can be used to clear up your house as well. You can do it in each room once a week for general clearing of psychic debris.

DIVINE NAMES: This ritual contains a few more Hebrew names and words than previous rituals in this book. We have included a table of translation to make it easier for you to become familiar with them. It also includes the Tahateel names and other names of power of ancient Aramaic or Hebrew origin as found in the ancient books.

HEBREW WORDS IN THE RITUAL

English Meaning	Hebrew	Pronunciation
My Lord	אדוני	Adonoi
Love	אהבה	Ahava
Light	אור	Aur
God	אל	El
Goddess	אלת	Elath
Truth	אמת	Emeth
Earth	ארץ	Aretz
Fire	אש	Ash
Master	בעל	Baal
Blessed	ברוך	Baruch
In the Name	בשם	Beshem
Valor	גבורה	Geburah
The	ה	Ha-
He	הוא	Hua
And	ו	Ve
Compassion	חמלה	Chemla
Ability	יכולת	Yecholet
Honor (Glory)	כבוד	Kavod
Power	כח	Koch

183

English Meaning	Hebrew	Pronunciation
Honesty	כנות	Kenut
Angel	מלך	Malach
King	מלך	Melech
Queen	מלכה	Malkah
Kingdom	מלכות	Malkuth
Glorious	נהדר	Nehedar
Exalted	עליון	Elyon
World	עלם	Olam
Humility	ענווה	Anava
Justice	צדך	Tzedek
Holy	קדוש	Qadosh
Sacrifice	קרבה	Karvah
Almighty	שדי	Shaddi
Exalted	שיכור	Shikur
Dominion	שליטה	Shlitah
Divine Presence	שכינה	Shekinah

IMPORTANT NOTE: Substitute the name of your own angel wherever you see the name Maghedhanedayl in the following ritual.

STEP ONE: Purify and consecrate your working space. Perform the prayer to the Queen of Heaven. Focus your mind on the Divine and say: "**Qadosh El ha-Ruchaniut Qadosh Elat Aur ha-Malachim.**" [x33] This should be repeated with deep emotion of praise or in a celebratory state of intensity.

STEP TWO: Say: "**Blessed be the name of El, who is veiled and can not be perceived, Lord of the seven heavens and seven earths and** what is in between, Hu Ha-Nehedar Ve Ha-Shikur, characterized by sublimity and grandeur and sanctified from similarity with His creation. Glory be to Him, the Exalted, who is elevated in His nearness and near in His elevation. Blessed be the name of El, who has strong force, and who has substantial power. He is the creator of the heavens and earth. Blessed be the name of El, Lord of the end and the beginning, Lord of the people and creator of the ghosts and spirits. He is the King of the angels of the throne, the angels of the chair, the angels of the heavens, and the angels of the earth. Blessed be the Lord of the Universe who has absolute power and lofty glory. He is the Light of lights and the Spirit of spirits. Glorious and holy is the Lord of Angels and spirit.

Beshem Elat Ha-Yecholet Ha-Koch Ha-Kavod Ha-Shlitah Ha-Malkah Le-Malkuth, I call you, o spiritual spirits that are pure and chaste. I call you, O spirits from the quintessential and rich lights. I call you, O individuals of the inner essence that are from the radiating lights, which are glorious and dazzling. I call you in the name of She whom the thunder glorifies with its praise. I call you in the name of She that angels praise in different languages and sounds, in awe of Her majesty. I call you to open up my soul and elevate my mind and spirit so that I may perceive the Divine and angelic presences." [x3]

STEP THREE: Close your eyes and say: "Baruch Malach Maghedhanedayl." [x100] During the chanting, you should feel love toward the angel. Sense the blessing growing around the angel every time you say this.

STEP FOUR: Say: "O Thou, El Elyon, who has no equal, give and grant unto me, through Your grace, the aid and assistance of your Malach Maghedhanedayl upon this earth and into this consecrated space. By the nineteen glyphs upon the Divine Circle of Kingship and Dominion, descend upon me, O Malach Maghedhanedayl. By the most holy Elohim, I call you, O Malach Maghedhanedayl. By the Power, Wisdom, and Virtue of the Spirit of the Holy of Holies, by the uncreated Divine Knowledge, by the vast Mercy of Elohim, by the Strength of Elohim, by the Greatness of Elohim, by the Unity of Elohim and by the holy names of Elohim, descend upon me, O Malach Maghedhanedayl with all the malachim under you.

O Malach Maghedhanedayl, by all the Names of El Elyon, by all the marvellous work of Elat Ha-Ahaba, who art the Creator of

185

the heavens, the earth, the sea and that firmament upon which the very Spirit of Elohim has moved, aid me from your spiritual presence and enter into a covenant of friendship and assistance with me in all of my needs. By the Creator of the stars, the seas, the winds, the tempests, herbs, plants, stones and all that is in the heavens, upon the earth and in between, answer me and aid me, O Malach Maghedhanedayl, peace be upon you. Let there be a covenant of Light between us during my earthly existence." [x3]

STEP FIVE: Kneel and hold the angelic mandala between your hands. Say: "Aneh Li Malach Maghedhanedayl." [x100] The intent of this chant is to call forth the angel. Feel free to increase the intensity of the chanting. Remember with every repetition you are calling upon the angel to come to you, so keep your mind clear of everything but the name and open yourself to the presence and descent. If need be, close your eyes to increase your awareness. Meditate on the angelic presence and on any messages that you may receive.

STEP SIX: Say: "Baruch Elat Malkah Ha-Olam, who is a guide to the soul toward the revelation of mysteries by which it is exalted and illuminated, I have prayed a thousand times over my guardian angel Maghedhanedayl, who came to my spirit a defender, and equally greeted him with peace. O angels, I have sworn upon you by the Exalted Light and all the scriptures and by remembrances and verses from the words of my Lady. I call you by Her beautiful names that are magnificent and exalted. Therefore, O Metatron, extend to me the rays of Gabriel and the mystery of Michael. By the holiness of El and lights of Elat, save me by a mystery which makes my heart pure. Therefore, O Raphael, O Auriel, O Israfel, answer my prayer, O Azrael, and my summons.

By the crown of mysteries of Adonoi Ha Ruchaniut and the wisdom of Elat Ha Emet, illuminate my soul. By the great understanding of Elohim Ha Karvah, purify my heart and sanctify my spirit. O merciful Elat Ha Tzedek, supply me with a presence from the might of Elohim Ha Geburah and make my side mighty, by the beauty of Adonoi Ha Kavod. Blessed be the victorious Elat Ha Ahava and majestic are the secrets of Her mystery. Glory be to Elohim Ha Kenut and the foundation of my life Adonoi Ha Chemla, for Her mercy and Her peace are my saviors. Therefore, praise the magnificent sovereign Adonoi Ha Anava, full of majesty, before whom all angels and spirits are humble. Praise Elat va Malkah Ha-

Malachim va Ruachim.

By Fah-tob-teel, respond O Malach Ruqiel, from the celestial orbit of the Sun, and all the spirits and angels under you. By Lach-ha-tot-eel, respond O Malach Gabriel, from the celestial orbit of the Moon, and all the spirits and angels under you. By Qah-tee-teel, respond O Malach Semsamiel, from the celestial orbit of Mars, and all the spirits and angels under you. By Jah-lah-ta-teel, respond O Malach Michael, from the celestial orbit of Mercury, and all the spirits and angels under you. By Mah-tah-teel, respond O Malach Sarfiel, from the celestial orbit of Jupiter, and all the spirits and angels under you. By Na-hah-ta-teel, respond O Malach A 'aniel, from the celestial orbit of Venus, and all the spirits and angels under you. By Lele-tah-teel, respond O Malach Kasfiel, from the celestial orbit of Saturn, and all the spirits and angels under you. O you angels, in the name of the Holy of Holies, aid me in my life and in my magical work. Send to me from the spheres of your dominion spiritual spirits to assist me in my spiritual and earthly needs.

Let there be a covenant between us, O hosts of spiritual spirits, O honored, pure and chaste angels, O entities of essence, and ghosts of light, by the privilege of these sacred names over you and its obedience among you. I avow and assert on you by the Knower of the all that is hidden and visible, the Great and Exalted, and by the names of your covenant on the door of great temple in Babylon o spiritual spirits: Baal Saqesh (x3), Mahraqesh (x3), Aqshamaqesha (x3), Malqsha (x3), Aqshamaqesh (x3), Shaqmonhesh (x3), that you lift me closer to the presence of the angels and may you come to my aid when called upon. O you angelic hosts and spiritual spirits, fulfill your covenant with El Elyon, that you have pledged, and don't break the faith. By the honor of Ehieh Asher Ehieh Adonoi Tzabaoth El Shaddi, nay, but I swear by the placement of the stars and it is an oath if you but know is great, don't be aloof and come to me in peace, quickly, and obedient to the names of Elath Malkah ha-Olam. May their blessing be upon you and in you, O spiritual spirits, and may you, Malach Auriel and all malachim, be brought closer to the Shekinah and the Highest Light."

When you are finished with the ritual, give thanks in your own words to the angels. Put out the candles and place the pentacles and mandala in a clean and safe place for future use.

Looking at where you are now on your magical path, you should recognize that you have changed. You have walked where few people

MAGIC THAT WORKS

on earth have chosen to walk. Now it is time to take your magical
journey further. You will come into your own power as a magician
as you begin to work with the elemental and the planetary energies.
These are the first level work of any accomplished magician. Working
with these forces will change you and challenge you, but the process is
exciting and one you will remember all your life.

Works Referenced

al-Buni, Ahmed (D. 1225 C.E.). *Shamsu al-Ma'aref al-Kubrah*. Maktabat
Isha'at al-Islam. Delhi, India.

al-Buni, Ahmed (D. 1225 C.E.). *Manba'a Ussol al-Hikmah*. Maktabat
al-Hidayah. Surabaya, Indonesia.

al-Toukhi, A'adu al-Fatah. *Mudhish al-Albab fi Asrar al-Hroof wa A'ajab
al-Hisab. (v1-4)*. al-Maktabah al-Thaqafiah. Beirut:1991

Ibn Wahshia (D. 9th-10th C.E.), Abu Baker. *Kitab Shoq al-Mustaham
fi Ma'arefat Romooz al-Arqam*.

7

Elemental Magic

The elements referred to by the old alchemists and platonic writers remain an integral building block of the magical development to this day. These four elements: Fire, Air, Water, and Earth, represent the four forces of nature and magical currents. The Elements are the result of the union of the four basic states: heat, wetness, coldness and dryness. Fire is hot and dry. Air is hot and moist. Water is cold and moist. Earth is cold and dry. Fire is the natural physical fire with which we are familiar and all that it symbolizes from will, energy, passion, drive, and so on. It also represents an aspect of spirit itself. Air is the breath of life; it symbolizes clarity, mind, thoughts, movement, and logical thinking. Water is the essence of life; it symbolizes emotions, consciousness, meditation, and spirituality. Earth is the mother from which our bodies emerge; it symbolizes manifestation, the physical world, and stability. Throughout history, magicians held these elements in the greatest esteem and importance. Working with the Elements is also an important part of this magical training program. The elements are integrated with all other aspects from our system, since they are foundational.

Modern magicians believe that these elements contain a form of nature spirits or elementals. They work with the elementals as a way to influence their personal development and physically manifest those things under their symbolic dominion. These elementals are known in the West as the Salamanders, Gnomes, Undines, and Sylphs. To modern magicians, even the jinn are only a form of Salamanders that can be banished by evoking the energy of Water and the Undines.

Modern magicians would call upon these forces to impact changes, such as calling on Sylphs and the Air element to bring mental clarity before an exam, or to influence the outcome of a business meeting or decision making process.

Working with elementals became important in the Western world when a medieval Rosicrucian text known as the Fama Fraternitas mentioned how the mythical Christian Rosencreutz travelled to Arabia and learned the mysteries of the elementals. However, the elementals as understood by modern magicians didn't really exist in the Arab world. Those elementals by which the Arabian magicians did wonders were the jinn. The elementals of modern magicians are then a Westernized version of the jinn.

Since the jinn live all over the place and have varying qualities, it became customary to refer to them by their habitation and habits. Some jinn lived under water; some had the ability of flight; some rested near volcanos and other sources of fire. The totality of the jinn were known as earthly because, unlike other spiritual beings, they resided among us on the earth itself. It was customary to give last names or nicknames based on a person's original locality or profession. This was extended to the various jinn tribes. Those who specifically liked to live in a certain place such as underwater caverns were called watery ones. Those who preferred to fly in the clouds or move with the winds had that aspect added after their last name. Therefore, you would see references in old Arabic texts to earthly ones (the jinn) followed by a conjuration to a jinni whose last name means watery one. These jinn are neither Earth nor Water elementals, but for non-Arabic speakers this confusion is understandable.

As this ancient lore was transferred to the early medieval Europeans through contact and translation, it may have became mixed in with their own cultural lore on nature spirits. The jinn became established as kinds of spirits that are made of and live in each element, leading to the belief that you would summon earthly elementals such as gnomes to attune yourself to that energy.

To summon jinn that reside in a given part of nature to attune to that part of nature would be misguided, even if it is popular. It would also be magically ineffective to summon water jinn to banish fire jinn because the habitats of the jinn have no impact on their actual natures, attitudes or power. It is also wise to know the names of the actual jinn, because calling on undines or jinn that live in water would be to invite a whole tribe of jinn, when you have no idea of what is being called forth. Not all those that live near or under water are beings you want to invite into your sphere and they are far from being blind and mind-less forces of the elements, since they are rational, thinking creatures. Fortunately, since most such elemental rituals lack the proper ways of summoning jinn, there have been few cases of people encountering any kind of negative presences or forces.

We know what we have told you so far challenges conventional modern thinking about elemental work. Having said this, when we talk about elementals in this book, we will not be referring to the jinn themselves, but to the rouhaniat of the element. The rouhaniat is a spiritual prana of a Divine essence and thus isn't actually a blind force to be summoned and commanded as in modern literature. It is an as-pect of the Divine spirit itself that resides within the element. This means you will be safe and secure and need not worry about negative consequences from opening your door wide to the jinn without speci-fying who or what is being invited. You will work with the spiritual energy itself and this will help you balance the reflective energy of the elements within your sphere. This work is vital to your magical development as it results in personality change and inner transforma-tion. It is the alchemical process that takes matter and infuses it with spirit and in the process refines it. This is more in line with the work of alchemists and is a way to attuning to that which surrounds us in nature. The spirit that resides in the water, air, fire, trees, groves, and many other places is really pure, holy spirit. The rouhaniah of Earth are like flickers of light that dance around the pure spirit that inhabits trees, plants, and groves.

As you prepare to do work with the rouhaniah of the elements, the first thing you need to do is determine what element is most dominant in your life. The reason for doing this is to ensure that you balance within yourself those elements that you lack. If you find that you have an abundance of Water and lack of Fire, then you may want to in-voke more Fire to balance out your Water. To understand the relation-ship here, know that Fire and Water are opposites and so are Air and Earth. Equally, Fire and Air are friends and so are Water and Earth. Determining your dominant element can be approached in two ways. The first is to figure out the dominant signs in your astrological chart and their elemental qualities. The second is to look at the elemental quality of your name.

Figuring out the dominant element astrologically requires you to first cast an entire chart and then look at the elemental weight of the planets. This is outside the scope of this book. Instead, we will focus on the elemental energy of your name, especially since you have already used it to calculate the name of your guardian angel.

We mentioned in previous chapters how letters and numbers were associated. The letters of the alphabet also correspond to the Elements. We saw a basic connection between the letters and the Elements, where we related three Hebrew letters to the three elements Air, Water and Fire, according to the Sepher Yetzirah. There are other relationships as well, such as the connection between the Tetragrammaton, or the Hebrew four-fold lettered name of God יהוה and the Elements: Fire י, Water ה, Air ו and Earth ה. The Elemental sequence of Fire-Water-Air-Earth is known as the Tetragrammaton sequence. The more traditional ancient sequences were the celestial: Fire-Earth-Air-Water and the natural or alchemical: Fire-Air-Water-Earth. The Arabic acronym for the elements in the natural sequence is NeHaMeT. Here N stands for Nar (fire), and is associated with Nur (Light). H stands for Hawa (air) and is associated with Hua (a third person singular name of God). M stands for Ma (water) and is associated with Malaekah (Archangels). Finally T stands for Turab (earth) and is associated with Tawhid (Oneness). This can be made into the sentence, "Nur Hua Malaekah Tawhid", or "His Light is the Angels of Oneness."

The following tables show the division of English, Arabic and Hebrew letters among the four Elements. In the table headers, the first order is the celestial and directly under it, in parentheses, is the natural or alchemical elemental sequence.

ENGLISH ALPHABET ELEMENTAL DIVISION

Fire (Fire)	Earth (Air)	Air (Water)	Water (Earth)
A	B	C	D
E	F	G	H
I	J	K	L
M	N	O	P
Q	R	S	T
U	V	W	X
Y	Z		

ARABIC ALPHABET ELEMENTAL DIVISION

Fire (Fire)	Earth (Air)	Air (Water)	Water (Earth)
ا	ب	ج	د
ه	و	ز	ح
ط	ي	ك	ل
م	ن	س	ع
ف	ص	ق	ر
ش	ت	ث	خ
ذ	ض	ظ	غ

HEBREW ALPHABET ELEMENTAL DIVISION

Fire (Fire)	Earth (Air)	Air (Water)	Water (Earth)
א	ב	ג	ד
ה	ו	ז	ח
ט	י	כ	ל
מ	נ	ס	ע
פ	צ	ק	ר
ש	ת	ך	

Both the celestial and natural sequences are used in talismanic work and for overall general magical purposes. The natural sequence is used to call out the terrestrial energy of a letter, the celestial for its more spiritual energy. The letters become a channel for the manifestation of the elemental energies. For example, the letters of Fire are used on many talismans for energy, power, conflict, infatuation and so on. Water letters are commonly drawn on talismans of healing, love, peace and the like. So, let us say that you have a fever. You can create a magical cure for the fever by mixing your name with the letters of water. You do this by writing one letter of your name, then one letter of water and so forth. Here is an example of this process for someone named Mark Cruise using the natural sequence: McAGRkKoCsRwUcIG-SkEo. This magical permutation can then be written on a band and worn around the head. Alternately, it can be written on the rim of a

cup, then dissolved by the water in the cup and then used on the head
or consumed by the sufferer. The ancients believed that by applying
words, feelings, and intent to water, it could become a magical agent
and transmitter of these to the rest of the body.

Determining the dominant elemental quality in your name requires
more than knowing how many letters of a given element are in it. You
need to weigh them. This is usually done based on a mathematical
scale, using degrees and ratios for understanding the Elemental rela-
tions. This process uses the natural order as the basis of measurement
on the terrestrial level. Fire is the first of the four elements; its degree
is 1. By the same process Air is 2, Water is 3 and finally, Earth is 4.
This allows us to figure out ratios and compound values. The ratio of
Fire to Earth is 1:4 or one fourth. The ratio of Air to Water is 2:3 or
two thirds. The combination of power of the Elements can thus be
measured mathematically like this:

Fire = 1

Air = 2

Water = 3

Earth = 4

Fire + Earth = 5

Air + water = 5

Air + Earth = 6

Fire + Air + Water = 6

Water + Earth = 7

Fire + Air + Earth = 7

Fire + Water + Earth = 8

Air + Water + Earth = 9

Fire + Air + Water + Earth = 10

The four elements, divided upon a planetary seven point scale, are
used to further weigh in the elemental ratio of letters in a name. The
letters of the alphabet are divided between the planets and then given

weights of measurement. The table of measurement consists of seven degrees of intensity called level, degree, minute, second, third, fourth, and fifth. Each one of these corresponds to the seven planets: beginning with Saturn, Jupiter, Mars, Sun, Venus, Mercury and ending with the Moon. To find which element is strongest in a name, we write out the name and weigh its letters. The first letter of Fire would be a level and would have the value of 7/7 or 1. The last letter of Fire would have 1/7 the intensity of Fire of the first letter. This measurement is extended further when looking at the placement of a given letter in a word. For example, A in Apple is 7/7, but if it is the second, like in Cat, then it is 14/7.

ARABIC LETTERS ELEMENTAL RATIOS

Numerical Order	1	2	3	4	5	6	7
Percentile Placement	Level	Degree	Minute	Second	Third	Fourth	Fifth
Percentile Numeral	7/7	6/7	5/7	4/7	3/7	2/7	1/7
Fire	ا	ه	ط	م	ف	ش	ذ
Earth	ب	و	ي	ن	ص	ت	ض
Air	ح	ز	ك	س	ق	ث	ظ
Water	د	ح	ل	ع	ر	خ	غ

HEBREW LETTERS ELEMENTAL RATIOS

Numerical Order	1	2	3	4	5	6	7
Percentile Placement	Level	Degree	Minute	Second	Third	Fourth	Fifth
Percentile Numeral	7/7	6/7	5/7	4/7	3/7	2/7	1/7
Fire	א	ה	ט	מ	פ	ש	ן
Earth	ב	ו	י	נ	צ	ת	ף
Air	ג	ז	כ	ס	ק	ד	ץ
Water	ד	ח	ל	ע	ר	ם	

English Letters Elemental Ratios

Numerical Order	1	2	3	4	5	6	7
Percentile Placement	Level	Degree	Minute	Second	Third	Fourth	Fifth
Percentile Numeral	7/7	6/7	5/7	4/7	3/7	2/7	1/7
Fire	A	E	I	M	Q	U	Y
Earth	B	F	J	N	R	V	Z
Air	C	G	K	O	S	W	
Water	D	H	L	P	T	X	

Let's look now at the Elemental qualities in the name Frances, as shown in the following example.

Frances' Elemental Ratios (Example)

Letter	Ratio	Position	Total	Element
F	6/7	1	6/7	Earth
R	3/7	2	6/7	Earth
A	7/7	3	21/7	Fire
N	4/7	4	16/7	Earth
C	7/7	5	35/7	Air
E	6/7	6	36/7	Fire
S	3/7	7	21/7	Air

The preceding example gives the name Frances a total of 28/7 Earth, 57/7 Fire and 56/7 Air. The first name of the lady in question has mainly Fire and Air vibrational qualities with a smaller amount of Earthiness, but no Water. We are using only the first name in our calculations as an example. You should use the full name like you did with the calculation of your guardian angel, or you could resort to your astrological chart for guidance, or a combination of both.

Once you have calculated the Elemental qualities that are strong in your name, begin working with them first. Then begin working with the missing or weak Element that is friendly to your dominant one. Fire and Air are friendly, and Earth and Water are friendly. Then begin working with any other missing Elements. As you do this, your personality will improve and so will the energy around your life. The beauty of Elemental magic will become more visible as you work with it and attune to it.

❁ ELEMENTAL ATTUNEMENT ❁

PURPOSE: We recommend this technique as way to invoke and balance the Elements in your aura. It is different from other Elemental methods covered in so far that you will be dealing with the pure Rouhaniah of the Element as it exists in the celestial heavenly realms. This is symbolized by the four rivers of paradise. Working with the Elements then as a unified spiritual whole will elevate your entire sphere of sensation to new heights and bring you ever closer to this eternal magic that we know as the Divine Light.

TIMING: We recommend practicing this technique a minimum of once a week for four months.

DIVINE NAMES: This technique relies on your ability to meditate and focus, while chanting the Divine name that rules over the Element. This is the name composed of the letters of Light and is divided between the four Elements and Spirit. You will be chanting and attuning yourself to each of the Elements individually and then to them as a unified spiritual whole. This process of repeated chanting is a way to let yourself be absorbed and awakened into the Rouhaniah of the names. The more you chant the names out loud, the more power you give the Rouhaniah of the name. They in turn will reward you with some of the attributes that they rule over. This is the reason the ancient magi of our tradition would chant some names upward of a hundred thousand times during several sittings. It also is a way to maintain mathematical harmony. The repeated chanting combines sounds and numbers. The magi would repeat a name the number of times equal to its numerical value or based on a special mathematical formula. The chanting serves to expand your mental horizon beyond its normal boundaries. The magi would chant a name until their entire consciousness was absorbed in its meaning and cosmic principle. They focused themselves so they could swim in the ocean of the name and become a receptacle to its power and equally so, it increased the blessings and power of the Rouhaniah, which as a reward filled them with the essence and attribute of the name.

The process of chanting a name hundreds of times can appear daunting in our modern Western world, especially since most people today live in rushed lifestyles. However, there is no effective way to replace this method properly and its reward is great. If you feel the repetitions are way too many for your lifestyle or ability, then cut them down considerably. If you choose to cut them down, then do the rituals more often to get the same results. So, if you see an instruction for one hundred repetitions and you want to cut them to twenty-five, then do that ritual three times a week rather than just once a week. As a rule, don't cut the repetitions far below a quarter of the recommended numbers. For every quarter you cut, do that ritual one more time during your weekly or monthly ritual cycle. However, once you get comfortable with that number begin to increase it again so you work up to the original. Our experience has shown that beginners in the craft can do upward of six hundred repetitions in their first sitting with ease.

TOOLS: Magical work requires not only the ability to visualize, but also to focus your mind. A clear, focused mind is more receptive to the energies and better at channelling the magical currents. Counting can be a cause of great distraction. This is why we recommend that you acquire a rosary or counting beads to free your mind from the tedious process of keeping count. Magicians were known to use special rosaries that were consecrated and empowered. Some of these rosaries were so powerfully charged by spirits and nature that merely placing one on a feverish head helped break the fever. We were fortunate enough to sample a few of these rosaries and they are exceedingly powerful and beautiful. Unfortunately, they are difficult to acquire and are mainly sold by special magical merchants in Indonesia. A few, such as Maghrobi Tasbih (Rosary), are currently available on-line. It would be a great magical asset to acquire such a rosary. However, any rosary with 100 beads will suffice for our purpose and intent. You can do the exercise temporarily without a rosary by repeating the names without counting till you feel almost overwhelmed by them. If you have made your talismans and rings, this would also be a good time to make use of them. You can wear all four rings or hold one ring at a time. Keep the scrolls on you.

You will need a place in which you can do this undistracted or uninterrupted. You will also need a comfortable chair or cushion for you to sit on for an extended period. If you find it helpful, light some candles and incense to put yourself in an altered state.

STEP ONE: Do the controlled breathing exercise for a few minutes. You may use a 3, 4 or 5-fold breathing count.

STEP TWO: Say, "O King and Queen of Heaven and Earth, infuse me with Rouhaniat al-Nar." [x7] Feel yourself fill with vital energy and power, then repeat the name Aham till you feel the ocean of spiritual Fire engulf you. If you have a rosary, repeat the name two-hundred and thirteen times. Keep your breathing steady and relaxed and feel the balancing Fire empowerment of this Name.

STEP THREE: Say, "O King and Queen of Heaven and Earth, infuse me with Rouhaniat al-Hawa'." Feel yourself filled with the mental clarity and wisdom of the Element of Air, then repeat the name Saqak till you feel the ocean of spiritual Air engulf you. If you have a rosary, repeat the name two-hundred and thirteen times. Keep your breathing steady and relaxed and feel the balancing Air empowerment of this Name.

STEP FOUR: Say, "O King and Queen of Heaven and Earth, infuse me with Rouhaniat al-Ma'." Feel yourself filled with the purifying, refreshing and serene energies of the Element of Water, then repeat the name Hhala'a till you feel the ocean of spiritual Water engulf you. If you have a rosary, repeat the name two-hundred and thirteen times. Keep your breathing steady and relaxed and feel the balancing Water empowerment of this Name.

STEP FIVE: Say, "O King and Queen of Heaven and Earth, infuse me with Rouhaniat al-Turab." Feel yourself become centered and grounded with the energies of the Element of Earth, then repeat the name Yass till you feel the ocean of spiritual Earth engulf you. If you have a rosary, repeat the name two-hundred and thirteen times. Keep your breathing steady and relaxed and feel the balancing Earth empowerment of this Name.

STEP SIX: Say, "O King and Queen of Heaven and Earth, infuse me with Rouhaniat Nur al-Anwar." Feel yourself fill with the Light of Spirit. With a feeling of awe and adoration toward this Divine Light, begin chanting the name Toren, repeating it till your mind expands as if it is an ocean of Light! If you have a rosary, repeat the name two-hundred and fifty-nine times. Keep your breathing steady and relaxed and feel the illuminating empowerment of this Name.

STEP SEVEN: Feel the Light surround and engulf your body from within and without. Chant: "**Aham Saqak Hhala'a Yass Toren.**" [x 111] If you don't have a rosary, do the chanting until you feel your body filled with the Elemental energies.

❂ ELEMENTAL RINGS OF POWER ❂

The next part of your journey into Elemental magic involves creating elemental rings of power. These rings serve not only as links to the currents of the Elements that you can carry and use, but also as repositories of Elemental energies. The rings can be used to summon forth Elemental spirits to help you in areas under their domain. They also help you build a strong rapport with the actual Elemental energies and domains. The easiest way to construct the rings would be to cut pieces of paper or cloth, write the names of power on them, form them into rings, and wear them. In magic, the easiest route isn't necessarily the best. This is why we recommend you acquire large silver bands and take them to a professional engraver. The names can be engraved on the rings fairly inexpensively. Each ring could cost you between $50-100 in addition to the cost of the original ring itself. This might seem like a substantial investment, but the actual benefit and power of each ring makes it worth its weight in gold. These rings by themselves are sufficient magic for most people and with them you can change yourself and your environment in ways you can only imagine now.

The names on the rings are derived from an ancient formula found in a rare occult text known as *Tayseer al-Mataleb* by Abu A'abed Allah al-Kufi. The formula in this book is designed to create names of power and talismans for any intended positive purpose. It was used to create magical cures for physical ailments, but can be used for literally any constructive end. We used the formula to extract the names for the raw power of the Elements.

Initially, we conducted a blind test with these names by charging the spirits to ground with earth a willing participant, who was three thousand miles away, and make him sleepy. He had no idea of the actual intent or the kind of Element used, only that we were going to conduct a long distance test. We checked on him a minute later. It became apparent that as we were chanting the names, he became very sleepy and tired. He found it hard to think and focus. He started yawning on the phone, even though earlier he was full of energy. He also started complaining of a headache and then proceeded to cough. He said his head and chest felt heavy, like a huge weight was on them that made it difficult for him to think or breathe. We tried the test again using Fire and it was equally strong and intense. Further tests over a few weeks confirmed again and again the kind of power those names wield and the success of the formula. They were so effective and acted so quickly that we actually decided against putting the formula or the names in the book. The thought of someone abusing their power was a matter of concern to us. However, we extracted a similar set of names that were less intense, but still strong enough that they can be used to get comparable results.

The tests using the names that we have included on this page and the next, were equally positive. They also lacked some of the intense side effects noted with the initial set. In one test case, a tired and sleepy participant was filled with energy after we charged the Fire names to do this. He stayed up till the wee hours of the morning, slept for a few hours, and then woke up very energetic. The rest of the next day he was active doing intense physical work, from vehicle maintenance to construction work, way into the early morning again. He admitted it was very unusual for him to be so full of energy. He went further and asked us to continue the experiment for an entire week, because was really enjoying this. It may take a while for you to be proficient enough to fully awaken their power, but you will quickly come to find that these names and the rings are a powerful magical asset.

INSCRIPTIONS ON THE RING OF FIRE

اطلرن - قاسرم - اعلكن - االرن - اصلين - حاهر

INSCRIPTIONS ON THE RING OF AIR

اطلره - قوسأم - اعلكه - اولأن - اصليه - حوهأ

INSCRIPTIONS ON THE RING OF WATER

اطلرم - قاسأم - لعمكأ - اللن - مصأيا - حلهم

INSCRIPTIONS ON THE RING OF EARTH

طارل - قتسر - ماعب- كاال- لتنر - صايب - حاهل

The inscriptions on each ring should be engraved from right to left to maintain the proper energy flow. The names are constructed for their mathematical and vibratory quality, so any meaning found for them in any language would be purely coincidental. The words on the ring of Fire are pronounced phonetically: Attelran Qasrum Aa'alakan A'elrun Usleen Hhaher. The words on the ring of Air are pronounced Attelrah Qosa'am Aa'alakah Ola'an Usleeah Hhoha'. The words on the ring of Water are pronounced Attelram Qasa'im La'amaka' Aalalen Mussa'yah Hhelham. The words on the Ring of Earth are pronounced Tarel Qatsar Maa'aeb Kaal Letnar Ssayeb Hhahel.

When getting the rings made, you may want to consider whether or not you want to have stones mounted on them. Stones are containers of energies and can be infused with powerful elemental energies. This will add to the expense of your rings, but if you can afford it, we highly recommend it. The stone for Fire needs to have been exposed to a tremendous amount of fire during and after its formation. This is more important than the actual color of the stone being red. This is why we recommend tektite, or a piece of magma, or a meteorite. The stone recommended for water is coral. For Air, we recommend milky white quartz. The milky whiteness of the quartz is a result of thousands of microscopic air bubbles inside the rock itself. The rock for Earth is a rainbow quartz, which is a quartz with Titanium coating. These are by no means the only stones that can be used, but some of the ones we highly recommend. You can find such stones sold in novelty rock shops; they can also be acquired through online purchase. They are not expensive, but they require a bit of cutting to make them fit as part of a ring.

Consecrating your ring is the next step. The consecration for these rings is different from previous rites that you have performed. The key is to actually empower the ring with the energy of the Element. This is done by ensuring that the ring is exposed to the actual Elements. The Air ring is tied in front of a window where the air blows, or even taken outside. The key is to ensure that it is exposed to as much air as possible. The Water ring is placed within a container of rain water or water gathered from a sea or a river. If you live nearby, then you can also go from time to time and dip your ring in the moving water. The

Earth ring is placed on top of a cluster of crystals or a geode. The Fire ring tends to be a challenge, but if you have a fireplace in your home, you can place it near the flames. You can also light a brazier or a fire in a cauldron and have the ring lightly touching the flames or placed near them. Once a ring is charged with one Element, it should never be exposed to its opposite. Don't wear a Fire ring anywhere near water or vice versa. Don't let the Air ring hit the earth or expose your Earth ring to strong winds. When you are not using your rings, keep each in its own sealed white bag made from a natural fabric, perhaps made from the leftover material from your magical robe.

The actual infusion of the Elemental power into the rings comes from reciting the names on the rings the number of times of their actual large range. After every hundred recitations of the names, state: "O Rouhaniah of these names that rule over the Element (insert Element) infuse this ring (and stone) with the raw essence and power of (insert Element) so that by wielding and wearing it I shall be infused with the spiritual force of (insert Element) and be able to command the Rouhaniah of (insert Element)" a multiple of seven times. You should do this while the ring is near the actual element itself as described and you are wielding or wearing the consecrated and charged scroll of the Elements. The large range for the names on the Ring of Fire is nine hundred and seventy-five. For the names on the Ring of Air, it is seven hundred and thirty-six. For the names on the Ring of Water, it is seven hundred and sixty-five. For the names on the Ring of Earth, it is one thousand, three hundred and twenty-seven. This process should be repeated daily for a minimum of forty-days. You can follow this with a consecration using the Ancient Oath, but this is optional.

Activating the rings you have consecrated is easy. All you have to do is wear the ring and chant the names on it for at least five minutes. Once you have done the chanting, command the Rouhaniah of the Element in question by the names on your ring to do whatever is under their dominion.

THE MAGUS GATES

PURPOSE: When we were looking through ancient descriptions of al-Mandal or the magic circle, we noticed an interesting reference to portals. The text indicates that the circle should have four portals in the corners or in the four directions. The description also stated that usually one of the four portals was kept open to ensure that the beings are allowed to enter into the magician's location. What the books neglected to mention was the actual description of this portal. Having been unable to find sufficient clues, we contemplated an alternate route. It only made sense that, since the description of the magical circles was passed down through the ages , including to Europeans, that we could find some clues by looking at such surviving texts.

The most common design of magical circles that appeared in European grimoires involves four large pentagrams laid on the outside of the drawn circles. This can be seen in such grimoires as the Heptameron and Lemegaton. Arabic designs of jinn pentacles involved the use of a pentagram with names inscribed inside and outside. Of course, this is not concrete proof that pentagrams were a key part of the intended portal design. However, it is not an accident that even modern Western systems of magic rely on the pentagram for invoking and banishing forces. If they are indeed the vehicles for opening portals that we believe them to be, then it is logical that they should attract spirits to you.

In modern magic, people who regularly put pentagram rituals to practice report seeing more things around. Modern writers' explanation for this is that this practice lights up the aura. They fail to explain why drawing pentagrams for banishing should do this, while rituals such as the Middle Pillar, that actively infuse the aura with Light, do not. The most likely other explanation is that by using the pentagram, even in banishing rites, the user is opening portals without actually closing them. Unattended portals reinforced daily would normally attract all kinds of spirits into the sphere of the user. This is the hypothesis that we and many others we know have tested, and the results have come back a resounding positive.

In the ritual of the Magus Gate, we rely on the pentagram to open up portals to different worlds. Two portals are opened at the same time. The first one is between our own world and the pervading realm of spirit. The other is from the realm of the spirit into the intended world. The gateway has to be opened from both sides on each world to be effective. This relies heavily on the aid of angels and other spiritual beings to ensure that the portal is opened from their side. Once a portal is opened, the beings are invited through the gateway and evoked. If nothing else, the Magus Gate is an excellent way to rend the veil between the worlds during evocational work.

TIMING: This ritual is done when a gateway between worlds is needed. It should be done as necessary and not made into a daily ritual. Keeping the veil open or thin for a long period can cause some difficulties in closing or sealing it later on.

TOOLS: The only tools you will need for this ceremony are the actual portals themselves. In the beginning, the portals are optional. We highly recommend that you make them as you progress further in your work. It is a worthwhile investment of time, energy, and money. Each portal is constructed the same way. We recommend you make four of them, one for each direction, since you will be opening all four during Elemental empowerments. In most other workings, you will only need one.

You can make your portals using any of a number of mediums. You can paint them on pieces of cardboard; you can paint them on the walls; you can paint them on rounds of wood; you can make circular wooden frames and stretch black cotton over them, like you would a piece of canvas for an oil painting, and paint them with fabric paint. However you decide to make these masterpieces, you will need to bear in mind a few parameters.

The background color of the portal is black. This represents space. If you are using fabric as your medium, you should draw everything in tailor's chalk first. You need to paint a perfect pentagram in white at the center of the portal. This pentagram should be of such a size that its top arms are at your shoulder level, and the bottom points are at mid thigh on your body. The lines of the pentagram we used were eighteen inches long. By perfect pentagram, we mean that each point has an angle of seventy-two degrees. In the center of the pentagram, there is a "Golden Mean" spiral, also painted white. It should be positioned so that it spirals from the center outward in a clockwise fashion. You can find methods of drawing these on the internet, or in books about sacred geometry.

The points of the pentagram are enclosed in a white circle. Around the outside of the circle there is painted a dragon eating its tail, also referred to as the "wyrm Ouroboros." The color of this dragon should represent the physical universe. We were trying to achieve indigo for ours, but because we were working with fabric paint, the combination of blue with black came out a kind of iridescent sparkling grey. You may want to experiment with different paints to make sure you get something that works. Within the body of this dragon are drawn and painted the names of the elder Gods and Goddess of Babylon, in cuneiform.

Beginning with the nearest to the head and moving closer to the tail, the seven are as follows: 7) Ishtar, 6) Adad, 5) Shamash, 4) Sin, 3) Ea, 2) Enlil, 1) Anu. They are arranged according to the descending order of the heavens as listed by Epic of Etana. The heavens are not exactly the same as the physical planets. The dragon represents infinite space. Anu, being ruler of the stars, is the closest to us and hence belongs to the 1st heaven. Ishtar, as the Supreme Creator of Life, rules over the highest heaven. The names are written in Cuneiform as such:

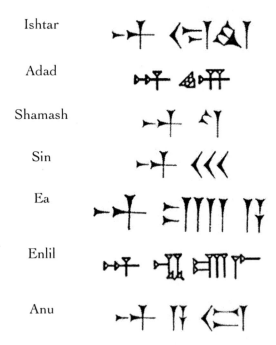

Ishtar

Adad

Shamash

Sin

Ea

Enlil

Anu

Once completed, you can place the portal up on the wall, in the direction that you intend to use it. When it is not in use, you can either cover it with a black cloth, (recommended for cloth and frame construction and painted walls), or you can remove it and keep it in a safe place.

THE PORTAL OF THE MAGUS GATE RITUAL

DIVINE NAMES: The primary Divine names used in this ritual are Chaldean deity names. We will also use names of power extracted through the same formula as the names on the ring. These names were extracted specifically for opening the gateways.

OPENING THE SPIRIT GATE

STEP ONE: Begin by standing facing east. Close your eyes and take a very deep breath inward, then exhale forcefully. Feel the stress leaving your body. Allow your breathing to increase, sensing yourself filled with vigor and energy. Take a few minutes to perform the four fold or eight-fold breath. Take the time to meditate on the Divine that is present in all the galaxies, stars, planets, and universes.

STEP TWO: Say, "By the quiet gentleness of the Goddess, by the gentle creation of the Goddess, by the beautiful veil of Goddess, I have entered into the alliance of the Goddess. I seek the intercession of the Light to throw love for me into the heart of my angel, who has been set upon me at the moment of my birth till the moment of my death (vibrate the name of your HGA per its numerical reduction). Let this angel descend upon me now and aid me with peace profound."

STEP THREE: Chant, "Ya-Syin al-Hai al-Qayum Bari Anwar al-Akwan wa al-Noojoom." [x49] This translates to: "Ya-Syin, Ever Living, Ever Being, Creator of the Lights of the Universes and Stars."

STEP THREE: Say, "O Opener, you open the locks of the chests with the keys of eternal caretaking. You are the Rich and Generous. You are the Provider, the Generous. You give Your gifts to whom You wish. In Your hands are the keys of goodness and treasures. You are the facilitator of the difficult matters. In Your hands are minute pearls of the Light. You are the sender of the spirit of munificence into the inner hearts of the companions of emanations. Every matter that is locked opens with Your care. The mystery of everything sealed and constricted is revealed by Your command. I ask You, O opener of every good and repeller of every harm, to let me stand before You, to receive from You the torrent of the knowledgeable life and timeless grants, to be excellence in waiting for the appearance of the manifestation of Your gentleness, to be always expecting to attain the perfection of Your grace, to be perpetually hopeful of finding the confirmation of Your generosity. Open my heart to me and facilitate the doors of revelation and vision for me. Aid me toward the receptivity of the Light of Your face at the spreading out of the treasures within Your compassion and forgiveness, O ancient in charity, O affectionate one, O benevolent one, O Lord of the Universe.

O Divine One, You are the Opener over the people with all that You wish from the sealed pathways. You are the doer with the mystery of Your name, al-Fatah [x3]. You are the victor against severe destructiveness. You are the judge between the people, with the minuteness of wisdom in the upper world and the kingships. You judge with what You want and select from Your creation. I ask You with Your mystery that flows in the currents of the World of Malkut, which descends in the concealment of its secrets till it reaches the Behemoth, then returns in its ascension in the affairs of the World of Jabrut. Open in my heart through the witnessing of those mysteries and substantiate them with the validations of lights. Make me a fitting receptacle for reaching the mystery of the life of Your being that is generous with the majesty of the mysteries of Your attributes. O Divine One, aid me with Your glorious victory that is a shield against every opponent, the envious, and disputer. O Divine One, facilitate me with Your servant Tamehiel [x3], the servant of this name, for You are capable of all things."

STEP SIX: Move to the East in a clockwise fashion. Focus on the Divine Light with your mind and heart. Draw a large circle in front of you. Say as you draw the circle: "**From the beginning of time till the end of time, the Light flows through the fabric of space bending, creating, and weaving the universes together.**"

STEP SEVEN: Point to the top of the pentagram you are about to draw, then say, "**In the name of Anu and Anat.**" Begin drawing the active Spirit pentagram, starting at the top and going in a clockwise fashion. While tracing the pentagram say: "**I trace the five pointed star of the Elder Creator and form a portal of spirit through space and time.**"

STEP EIGHT: Draw the golden mean spiral as best as you can. As you draw the spiral say, "**By the heart beat of the Goddess of Love Ishtar, I open this gate.**"

Step Nine: Say: "I call upon you, o guardians of the portal to the realm of Spirit, who are appointed to this blessed gate of Anu. Open the hidden and veiled gate by the Divine Light of the Queen of Heaven Ishtar and the powerful mystery and magic of Elil. Come from the Eastern (Southern / Western / Northern) quarter of the Universe and tear through the fabric of my perception and illuminate my universe with Light and my being with peace profound and an eternal ray of magic. Come – for I have called you with the holy and secret names guarded in the vault of mysteries, Motadar Chaqlas A'amaa'a Lakema Allan Rosswi Hhehmah [x3].

Come, O guardians of the gateways of spaces and lords of time, for in me is the spark of the Creator of the Heavens and Earth. Come, for upon my spirit is etched servant of Divine Light. Open a portal before me to the realm of spirit through the fabric of space and time, and let it be a gateway between my sphere and the sphere of other realms."

PORTAL TO THE REALM OF FIRE

Step Ten: Exhale into the pentagram the name Ghassdaiel seven times then say, "Aid me, O archangel Ghassdaiel [x3], peace be upon you, with your protection and by opening the gateway between me and the realm of spirits of Fire through the portal of spirit."

Step Eleven: Now lift your hands in the Sign of the High Priest, facing the pentagram. Say, "In the Holy Divine Name, Motdar Chaqlas A'amaa'a Lakma Al-lan Nassaye Rahh-mah [x3] move, O spirits of Light, and open the gateway between me and the world of the spirits of Fire, A'alem Rouhaniat al-Nar."

STEP TWELVE: Say, "O A'alem Rouhaniat al-Nar, by the permission of the Queen of Heaven and Earth, and authority of the archangel Ghassdaiel, and the blessed names Attelran Qasrum Aa'alakan A'elrun Usleen Hhaher [x3] come through this celestial portal before me in peace profound as a friend and infuse me with the pure magic and spirit of Fire." Repeat this step as many times as you feel is needed for the spirits to come through. When you are sure they have came through, say gently and with heartfelt feeling: "May Her blessings be in you and upon you, O Rouhaniat al-Nar."

PORTAL TO THE REALM OF AIR

STEP THIRTEEN: Move to the south and open another portal as you did before in steps six to nine.

STEP FIFTEEN: Exhale into the pentagram the name Ghathssaiel seven times then say, "Aid me, O archangel Ghathssaiel [x3], peace be upon you, with your protection and by opening the gateway between me and the realm of spirits of Air through the portal of spirit."

STEP SIXTEEN: Say, "In the Holy Divine Name, Motdar Chaqlas A'amaa'a Lakma Allan Hosswee Ahh-mah [x3] move, O spirits of Light, and open the gateway between me and the world of the spirits of Air, A'alem Rouhaniat al-Haw'a."

STEP SEVENTEEN: Say, "O A'alem Rouhaniat al-Haw'a, by the permission of the Queen of Heaven and Earth, and authority of the archangel Ghathssaiel, and the blessed names Attelrah Qosa'am Aa'alakah Ola'an Usleeah Hhoha' [x3] come through this celestial portal before me in peace profound as a friend and infuse me with the pure magic and spirit of Air." Repeat this step as many times as you feel is needed for the spirits to come through. When you are sure they have came through, say gently and with heartfelt feeling: "May Her blessings be in you and upon you, O Rouhaniat al-Hawa'a."

PORTAL TO THE REALM OF WATER

STEP EIGHTEEN Move to the west and open another portal as you did before in steps six to nine.

STEP NINETEEN: Exhale into the pentagram the name Ghadha'aaiel seven times then say, "Aid me, O archangel Ghadha'aaiel [x3], peace be upon you, with your protection and by opening the gateway between me and the realm of spirits of water through the portal of spirit."

STEP TWENTY-ONE: Say, "In the Holy Divine Name, Motdar Chaqlas A'amaa'a Lakma Al-lan Mossa-'ee Mahhdah [x3] move, O spirits of Light, and open the gateway between me and the world of the spirits of water, A'alem Rouhaniat al-Ma'."

STEP TWENTY-ONE: Say, "O A'alem Rouhaniat al-Ma', by the permission of the Queen of Heaven and Earth, and authority of the archangel Ghadha'aaiel, and the blessed names Attelram Qasa'im La'amaka' Aalalen Mussa'yah Hhelham [x3] come through this celestial portal before me in peace profound as a friend and infuse me with the pure magic and spirit of water." Repeat this step as many times as you feel is needed for the spirits to come through. When you are sure they have came through, say gently and with heartfelt feeling: "May Her blessings be in you and upon you, O Rouhaniat al-Ma'."

PORTAL TO THE REALM OF EARTH

STEP TWENTY-TWO: Move to the north and open another portal as you did before in steps six to nine.

STEP TWENTY-THREE: Exhale into the pentagram the name Ghasheezaiel seven times then say, "Aid me, O archangel Ghasheezaiel [x3], peace be upon you, with your protection and by opening the gateway between me and the realm of spirits of Earth through the portal of spirit."

STEP TWENTY-FOUR: Say, "In the Holy Divine Name, Motdar Chaqlas A'amaa'a Lakma Al-lan Tossree Ahhbah [x3] move, O spirits of Light, and open the gateway between me and the world of the spirits of Earth, A'alem Rouhaniat al-Turab."

STEP TWENTY-FIVE: Say, "O A'alem Rouhaniat al-al-Turab, by the permission of the Queen of Heaven and Earth, and authority of the archangel Ghasheezaiel, and the blessed names Attelram Qasa'im La'amaka' Aalalen Mussa'yah Hhelham [x3] come through this celestial portal before me in peace profound as a friend and infuse me with the pure magic and spirit of Earth." Repeat this step as many times as you feel is needed for the spirits to come through. When you are sure they have came through, say gently and with heartfelt feeling: "May Her blessings be in you and upon you, O Rouhaniat aal-Turab."

CLOSING THE PORTAL

STEP TWENTY-SIX: Once you have completed your magical operation, you will need to seal the portals that you have opened. You do this by facing each portal and drawing the pentagram beginning from the top-point counter-clockwise. Then you trace the spiral beginning from the outside moving to the inside. Once you have done this, you say: "I call upon you, o guardians of the portal to the realm of Spirit, who are appointed to this blessed gate of Anu. Seal the hidden and veiled gate by the Divine Light of the Queen of Heaven Ishtar and the powerful mystery and magic of Elil. Come from the Eastern (Southern / Western / Northern) quarter of the Universe and fill he fabric of my perception and illuminate my universe with Light and my being with peace profound and an eternal ray of magic. Come – for I have called you with the holy and secret names guarded in the vault of mysteries, Motadar Chaqlas A'amaa'a Lakema Allan Rosswi Hhehmah [x3].

Come, O guardians of the gateways of spaces and lords of time, for in me is the spark of the Creator of the Heavens and Earth. Come, for upon my spirit is etched servant of Divine Light. Seal the portal before me to the realm of spirit through the fabric of space and time, and let the gateway between my sphere and the sphere of other realms be sealed firmly."

The Magus Gate ritual will come in handy in future magical workings. It is used for opening portals not only to Elemental planes, but also planetary spheres and other realms. Practice it well and use it to fully accustom yourself to the Elemental forces. Don't forget to seal after every opening, for open portals can cause unwanted energies to enter into your life. Nevertheless, this is a safe ritual that will allow you to tap into a potent reservoir of Elemental streams, which you can pull on to grow spiritual and emotionally, and bring about positive energy to your life and to your loved ones.

ELEMENTAL SCROLLS OF THE MAGI

Having determined the elemental vibration of your name and having worked and tapped into the Elemental streams, the next step is to actually create the elemental scrolls of the magi. These scrolls create a magical link between you and the Elemental planes all the time. These talismans will enforce those elemental qualities that you already possess and balance them with those that you lack. So, if you have predominantly Fire letters, your Fire talisman will help channel the abundant Fire energy of your name positively and the Water elemental talisman will bring this missing energy into your life. Constructing those scrolls is a great introduction to the beautiful art of magical talismanic work. Talismanic construction is a detailed and complex art that connects and combines many aspects of the craft in a systematic way. It requires a good eye for detail and a creative imagination. Since our intent at this point is to create talismans for the Elements, we will be spending a good portion of this chapter dealing with the central part of most talismanic designs. This honor goes to the underrated and often under used occult design known as the magic square.

Magic squares play an important role in the art of talismanic magic within our tradition. Ancient magicians believed these designs embodied celestial powers, due to the harmony of numbers. A magic square is a *square whose sides are divided by straight lines that form smaller cell squares within; into these cells is placed a singular numerical sequence in which the sum of any side is equal to any another.* The magic squares are known in the West as Kameas, which is a Hebrew word meaning 'amulet'. In the Arabic language, they are known as Awfaq, which means 'what is harmonized'. Magic squares come in an infinite number of sizes, but they can be grouped into one of three numerical categories: 1) Even-Even such as 4x4, 8x8, 12x12 and 16x16; 2) Even-Odd such as 6x6 and 10x10; 3) Odd-Odd such as 3x3, 5x5 and 7x7.

The size of the square determines the number of cells. Other numbers to consider is the sum of each side and the total sum of all the numbers of the squares based on the natural form. In the 3x3 square, the sum of any side or rib is 15 and the total sum of all the digits is 45. These numbers may seem unimportant, but a closer look will reveal their deeper mystery. For example, the total body of a 3x3 is 45, which is the range of the Arabic Adam, and the total of the rib 15 is the range for the Arabic Eve (Hawa). The 3x3 square is usually referred to as the square of Adam and Eve. Each square's size has its own inherent magical benefits, and we will tap into those benefits as we use them for making the elemental scrolls. The ancient magicians used seven basic sizes, corresponding to the planets. The planets in turn share Elemental qualities. For our Fire scroll, we may select a 5x5 or 6x6 since they correspond to Mars and the Sun, which are hot and dry (Fire) planets.

SEVEN BASIC MAGIC SQUARES

Planet	Square Size	Number Of Cells	Sum Of Any Side	Total Sum
Saturn	3x3	9	15	45
Jupiter	4x4	16	34	136
Mars	5x5	25	65	325
Sun	6x6	36	111	666
Venus	7x7	49	175	1225
Mercury	8x8	64	260	2080
Moon	9x9	81	369	3321

There is much more to their occult use than just drawing a grid with numbers in it. The various ways you can personalize your magic square's borders make for some very powerful and beautiful talismanic constructs. As an example, for our talismanic scroll of Fire we need to embody Fire into the magical square itself. The elemental letters of Fire are: ‏ا ه ط م ف ش ذ‎. These letters are usually written together in a cursive form thus: ‏اهطمفشذ‎. You can use these letters to form the outline grid of the magic square that will fit in the center of your talisman. What you will be doing is extending the Fire letters cursively so that they create an outer grid. You will then divide the inner grid to form the desired size of the square. When you begin to draw your magic square, start with the upper right corner and move clockwise. This direction is due to the fact that Semitic languages are written from right to left. Rotate the paper as you draw your lines so that your direction is constant. Follow the same style when drawing the remaining lines within the squares.

7X7 SQUARE FORMED USING THE FIRE LETTERS

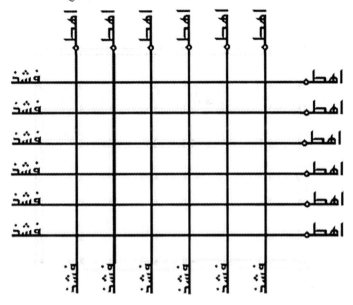

In constructing your Air, Water and Earth squares, you would follow a similar process, using the corresponding Elemental letters to form the outside grid. You would also select the appropriately corresponding grid size. For the book's examples, we used a 5x5 grid for all of them. However, in practice you would want to use a 3x3 for Earth, a 9x9 for Water, and an 8x8 for Air. When you actually do write your squares, make sure you are working with natural and durable materials. Don't use ingredients that contain plastic, as that grounds the energy and blocks the item from holding the charge. Although it has become increasingly traditional to make do with what is available and convenient, we recommend you acquire high quality materials for the scrolls. It is easy today to find clean, unblemished parchment paper. Even if you use wood or cardboard paper, you want a clean piece upon which to write your magic squares. Used or unclean materials can taint the energy infused into your elemental scrolls. Keep in mind that your working space should be larger than size of your magic square. The square isn't the only piece of writing on the talisman, so ensure there is enough surrounding room.

7x7 SQUARE FORMED USING THE AIR LETTERS

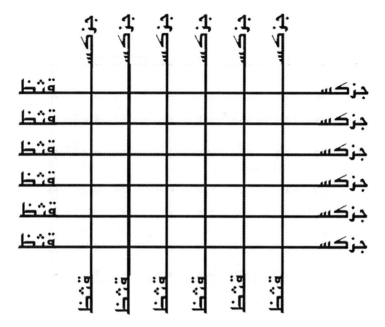

7x7 SQUARE FORMED USING THE WATER LETTERS

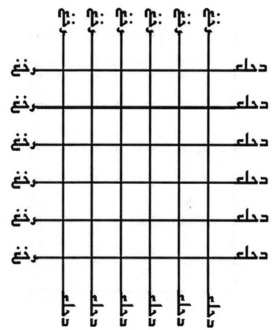

7X7 SQUARE FORMED USING THE EARTH LETTERS

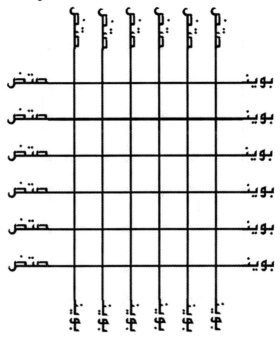

The final step in the construction of the magic square is to fill in the numbers in the various cells in their proper sequence. If you have seen magic squares before, you may recognize that they all start with one number and just go on sequentially. Magicians rarely use these squares in their basic form, most often personalizing them for the task at hand. As an example, let us say we wanted to make a 3x3 square for the emanation of Binah (Understanding). The range of the word Binah in Hebrew is sixty-seven. The numbers within the square should add up to this range or value. The square would be thus:

22	26	19
20	22	25
25	19	23

So as you see, building your magic square requires a bit more effort than just copying sequential numbers; you actually need to construct your personalized square.

When we speak of inserting a number into a magic square, what we really mean is that we want to create a magic square where each line adds up to that number, whether horizontally or vertically. Once a number is ready to be inserted into a magic square, the Key must be calculated. To calculate the Key, you will need to know the Handle, Lock and Door. Here is a brief description of what these terms mean:

Key: - The first number to be placed into a magic square.
Handle: - The difference between two consecutive cell numbers in a square.
Lock: - The last number to be placed in a magic square.
Door: - A calculated number instrumental in calculating the key of a specific magic square
Hinge: - Half the number of cells on any side of a magic square.

A basic magic square begins with a '1' in its Key and a '1' as its Handle. A more complex square may begin with a '2' or more for its Key and for its Handle. Regardless, the Handle must be constant between the various cells of a magic square or it will not work. The third number of importance, called the Door, can be calculated as follows:

Sn = Number of Cells
Door = (Sn-1) x Handle

TABLE OF DOORS

	H=1	H=2	H=3	H=4	H=5	H=6	H=7	H=8	H=9
3x3	8	16	24	32	40	48	56	64	72
4x4	15	30	45	60	75	90	105	120	135
5x5	24	48	72	96	120	144	168	192	216
6x6	35	70	105	140	175	210	245	280	310
7x7	48	96	144	192	240	288	336	384	432
8x8	63	126	189	252	315	378	441	504	567
9x9	80	160	240	320	400	480	560	640	720

Examples:

Q1) If we wanted to construct a 3x3 Magic square with a handle of one, what would be the value of the door?

A) [(3x3)-1] x 1 = 8

Q2) If we wanted to construct a 4x4 Magic square with a Handle of three, what would be the value of the Door?

A) [(4x4)-1] x 3 = 45.

The last important number, called the Hinge, is calculated by dividing the number of cells in a magic square's side by two. For example in a 3x3, the Hinge is 1.5; in a 4x4, the Hinge is 2; in a 5x5, the Hinge is 2.5, and so forth. Once we have all this information, we can calculate the Key.

$$[(Number / Hinge) - Door] / 2 = Key$$

Let's look at an example. Let's say that the range of your name is 543. You want to insert this into a 3x3 magic square. You will use a basic Handle of one. The Door for a 3x3 with a Handle of one is eight. What remains for you to calculate is the Key. Here is how that would look:

$$[(Number / Hinge) - Door] / 2 = Key$$
$$[(543 / 1.5) - 8] / 2 = 177$$

The next step is to insert the key into the cell block that corresponds to the number one in the basic 3x3 template. The template is the square that has a Key of one and a Handle of one. You can use this template as a guide to building your personalized squares.

4	9	2
3	5	7
8	1	6

When building your square, the first number, or Key, goes right where the number one is placed in the template. It would look like this:

220

	177	

Then we add the Handle of one to that number progressively as we move from cell to cell in sequence. The finished square would look like this:

180	185	178
179	181	183
184	177	182

Let us apply this technique to creating the magic square for your Air talisman. The large range in Arabic for the words 'Spirits of the World of the Air' is four hundred. We want to insert the number 400 into a 5x5 with a Handle of one. What is the Key needed to make the square?

A1) [(400 (number) / 2.5 (Hinge)) – 24 (Door)] / 2 = 68 (Key)

5x5 Template

18	10	22	14	1
12	4	16	8	25
6	23	15	2	19
5	17	9	21	13
24	11	3	20	7

85	77	89	81	68
79	71	83	75	92
73	90	82	69	86
72	84	76	88	80
91	78	70	87	74

Since Air is the second degree Element in the natural order, you may want to start with a Handle of two. Let's look at the key calculation in this case: [(400/2.5) – 48] / 2 = 56 (Key)

90	74	98	82	56
78	62	86	70	104
66	100	84	58	92
64	88	72	96	80
102	76	60	94	68

Many times you will need to insert an odd number like forty-one or a number that doesn't normally fit into a square type. The solution to this problem is to amend the square. It is very important that the square layout you are using accepts amending. Some are not amendable. Here are the amendable square templates:

3x3

4	9	2
3	5	7
8	1	6

4x4

8	11	14	1
13	2	7	12
3	16	9	6
10	5	4	15

5x5

18	10	22	14	1
12	4	16	8	25
6	23	15	2	19
5	17	9	21	13
24	11	3	20	7

6x6

36	30	24	13	7	1
25	19	3	35	17	12
6	10	14	21	28	32
20	2	29	11	31	18
15	34	8	27	5	22
9	16	33	4	23	26

7x7

26	30	20	38	14	46	1
11	43	5	23	35	17	42
31	21	39	8	47	2	27
44	6	24	35	18	36	12
15	40	9	48	3	28	32
7	25	29	19	37	13	45
41	10	49	4	22	33	16

8x8

39	47	22	30	60	52	9	1
55	63	6	14	44	36	25	17
28	20	41	33	7	15	54	62
12	4	57	49	23	31	38	46
5	13	56	64	26	18	43	35
21	29	40	48	10	2	59	51
58	50	11	3	37	45	24	32
42	34	27	19	53	61	8	16

9x9

10	78	35	26	55	42	6	71	46
50	7	66	30	14	79	43	21	59
63	38	22	67	54	2	74	31	18
64	51	8	80	28	15	60	44	19
23	61	39	3	68	52	16	75	32
36	11	76	40	27	56	47	4	72
37	24	62	53	1	69	33	17	73
77	34	12	57	41	25	70	48	5
9	65	49	13	81	29	20	58	45

Putting in a number that requires amending can seem a daunting task at first, but it needn't be. Let's go through the process of forming the Fire elemental square. The large range for 'Spirits of the World of Fire' in Arabic is six hundred and thirty-nine. This wouldn't go comfortably into a 5x5 square. You could try inserting it into a different square or you can try amending a 5x5. We will try to amend a 5x5 for that number to properly illustrate the process. Let's look at the Key formula:

$$[(\text{Number} / \text{Hinge}) - \text{Door}] / 2 = \text{Key}$$
$$[(639 / 2.5) - 24] / 2 = \text{Key}$$
$$[255.6 - 24] / 2$$

At this point, we have a fraction in the formula. What we do is drop the fraction altogether. So, it looks like this: [255 – 24] / 2 = 115.50

The Key also has a fraction. We do the exact same thing. We drop the fraction from the Key and put in 115 into the 5x5 square that accepts amending.

132	124	136	128	115
126	118	130	122	139
120	137	129	116	133
119	131	123	135	127
138	125	117	134	121

However, this square isn't correct. It yields six hundred and thirty-five rather than six hundred and thirty-nine on each line. What is left is to amend the square. The first step is to figure out the remainder. We do this by subtracting the two values: 639-635 = 4. The remainder is four. To solve this problem, look at the table of the remainder. Find the cell position marked there and, from that point on to the end of the square, skip the exact number of the remainder. So, if the value in the cell is 10 and the remainder is 2, skip two numbers from 10 and put in 12, then continue with 13, 14, and so forth until you finish the square.

Amendment Guide

Magic Square	Starting Cell
3x3	7
4x4	13
5x5	21
6x6	31
7x7	43
8x8	57
9x9	73
10x10	91

This may seem a bit challenging to do, especially if you are not good with numbers. Fortunately, you can make this process easier by using software or programming a spread sheet. Here is the amended square:

225

132	124	140	128	115
126	118	130	122	143
120	141	129	116	133
119	131	123	139 (135+4)	127
142	125	117	134	121

Once you have the numbers for your square, all that is left is to insert them into the grid formed by the Elemental letters. We have given you the values for two of the Elements so far. The value to be inserted for the magic square for Water is four hundred and twenty-nine. The value to be inserted for the magic square for Earth is nine hundred and ninety-one. Now that you know the process, you can easily make those squares yourself. The finished square is then painted or drawn into the center of your talismanic scroll.

There is one remaining step before consecrating and charging the scrolls. You will need to write the charge around the square. The charge consists of the names of the spiritual forces that activate the talisman, followed by your request. The request should include what you want the talisman to do in detail and the name of the person whom it is affecting. The name is spelled out in similar fashion to what you did for deriving the HGA. This part can be in your native language. The names of the spiritual governors or angels should be in Arabic, Hebrew or a corresponding magical script. They are calculated from the numbers in the talisman. The values within the magic square are the basis from which we extract the names of angels and jinn that oversee the execution of the talisman. There are celestial angelic governors and governors from among the underworld jinn. A number of ancient teachers in our tradition considered the underworld jinn to be equivalent to satanic spirits and called upon only for destructive workings. Others considered them more neutral and used them primarily for material objectives. You will not need the underworld jinn for the Elemental scrolls and the rest of the rites in this book.

Once we have the general values for the governors, we subtract forty-one for the angels. The subtraction of forty-one represents the Arabic form of the Divine Name El or Ayl. This is done for the same

226

reason as with the calculation of your holy guardian angel. You may want to review that section, if you are uncertain, for the explanation.

MAGIC SQUARE EXTRACTION RULES

Magic Square Value	How It Is Extracted	Governor's Position
Key	First number in the square	Usurper
Lock	Last number in the square	Guide
Balance	Key + Lock	Mystery
Square	Total sum of a row	Adjuster
Area	Total value of all rows	Leader
Regulator	Area + Square	Regulator
Purpose	(Square + Area) x 2	General Governor
Origin	Lock x Purpose	High Overseer

FIRE TALISMAN EXTRACTIONS

Governor's Position	Fire	Angel
Usurper	115	74
Guide	143	102
Mystery	258	217
Adjuster	639	598
Leader	3195	3154
Regulator	3834	3793
General Governor	7668	7627
High Overseer	1096524	1096483

The next step is to convert these numbers into letters, in a process again similar to the formulation of the holy guardian angel's name. This is done by pronouncing the numbers using letters. As an example, three thousand one hundred and fifty-four is numerically 3-1000-100-50-4.

When working with larger numbers, follow the same process, where a hundred thousand is 100-1000 and a million is a 1000-1000. Then add Ayl to the equation giving the following numerical sequence: 3-1000-100-50-4-1-10-30. Next, replace these numbers with Arabic letters that share their exact same large range. Now, write those letters from right to left to form the angelic leader. You should do the same for all the angels. Once you have all of the names for the angelic governors, you then proceed to write them around the square in a magical script of your choosing, followed by the rest of the charge. The last step in the process is the actual consecration of the Elemental scrolls once they are finished. There are a variety of consecration methods available to you. It is easy to assume it all boils down to intent and some mental visualization, but traditional magical methods are a bit more complex than that. We will use the Ancient Oath Ritual or the Great Conjuration to do the consecration, which in and of itself is a very powerful ritual for general magical work.

THE ANCIENT SOLOMONIC OATH

PURPOSE: We will use this ritual to consecrate the Elemental scrolls, but the value of this ritual transcends any one given application. The medieval astrologer Abu Ma'asher says these names have great power over the Elements and the spirits of the six directions. The master Al-Boni had this to say in his book, *Sharhu Al-Barhatiah*, "Know o seeker, God aided me and you with a spirit from Him, that the names of Barhatiah are the dependable conjuration from the ancient of times. The ancients used to refer to it as the Ancient Conjuration, Powerful Binding, Guarded Mystery, Vaulted Secret and the Red Sulphur. It was spoken of by the original wise men, then by our master Solomon Ben David, peace be upon them, then by Assif Ben Barkhiah, then by the wise man Klaphitrius, and whoever apprentices with it to our current day. This is a powerful conjuration, which no angel can turn from, and which can't be refused by any Jinn, Ifreet, Mared or Shitan. Any seeker's knowledge of the arts is handicapped, who doesn't possess it or doesn't know of it."

Every ancient Arabic book on Occultism worth its mettle, dating as far back as we could get (7-8 CE), included a variation of this conjuration. The ancient magicians argue that the origin of this conjuration dates even further back than King Solomon himself and that it was transmitted orally. We are convinced that anyone in possession of the complete Barhatiah conjuration, and making a habit of its recitation sincerely at least once a day, will be able to draw upon a tremendous reservoir of energy. The conjuration is used heavily in our magical tradition and its applications are extensive. One of the most important applications is in the calling forth of jinn and other spirits.

TIMING: This ritual is usually integrated in major evocational work and in consecration of talismans. It can also be used daily as a general magical exercise. You will be using it when you are ready to consecrate the scrolls.

DIVINE NAMES: These are names that cause the spirits and jinn worlds to tremble and magic to happen. Although the names in the conjuration are written in Arabic, they are not Arabic at all. The Arabic, like the English pronunciations given in parentheses, is the phonetic spelling found in the old manuscripts. As we said, the names could be a mix of languages ranging from ancient Hebrew to Aramaic. Finding the absolutely correct spelling of the names is difficult with such an old conjuration. We have presented one of the most accurate renditions from among many sources. It is believed that these names were revealed to King Solomon and then written down by his court magician and advisor, Asef Ben Barkhiah. Some authors feel they are based on ancient Hebrew and others consider them Akkadian or a dialect of Aramaic. Considering their antiquity, it is difficult to know for sure. What is known is that these names are to magic what a switch is to a light bulb. The old masters of magic from the Middle East gave this conjuration different names ranging from the Red Sulfur to the Great Conjuration.

TOOLS: There is no known tool associated with the actual conjuration. For your currently intended use, you will need the talismans and four long threads of silk. If you have them, wear the Elemental rings. The talismans should be hung above the incense burner by the silken threads. Apart from candle light, the room should be dark . Wear your white robe of the art or do this rite sky clad.

STEP ONE: Purify and consecrate your working area.

STEP TWO: Recite the Prayer to the Queen of Heaven.

STEP THREE: Perform the Call to the Masters of Magic

STEP FOUR: Open the Magus Gate to all four Elemental planes.

STEP FIVE: Say: "Beshem El Melech Qadosh, He filled the cosmos with the radiance of the light of His face. He extended to it the power of the letters of His awe over every angel, constellation, jinn and shitan. He was feared by all of His creation, and the Kerubim heeded and obeyed from their highest places and prostrated and answered the call of His great name. They quickly answered with the special confirmations concealed in the tablets of the hearts of the administrators. I conjure you, O celestial angels and spiritual rouhaniah and servants of this ancient oath, by what was gathered from the sea of names from the lights of Malkuth to answer my call and fulfill my need, which is the charging of these Elemental scrolls with a ray from the world of the spirits of Fire [Air / Water / Earth]. Let these scrolls become a living covenant between me [full name] and the spirits of the world of Fire [Air / Water / Earth], so that by mere possession of them I shall be attuned and awakened to the awesome power and presence of the spirits of the world of Fire [Air / Water / Earth].

In the glory of Ber-hat-yah [x3], Ka-reer [x3], Tat-lee-yah [x3], Toh-ran [x3], Maz-jal [x3], Baz-jal [x3], Tahr-qab [x3], Bar-hash [x3], Ghal-mash [x3], Cho-teer [x3], Qal-in-hod [x3], Bar-shan [x3], Katz-heer [x3], Namoh Shelech [x3], Berhayola [x3], Bash-kee-lach [x3], Qaz Maz [x3], An-ghala-leet [x3], Qa-ba-rat [x3], Gha-ya-ha [x3], Kayed-ho-la [x3], Shem-cha-her [x3], Shem-cha-heer [x3], Shem-ha-heer [x3], Bak-hat-hon-yah [x3], Ba-sha-resh [x3], To-nesh [x3], Shem-cha Ba-roch) [x3]:

Respond, O hosts of spiritual spirits, O honored, pure and chaste angels, O entities of essence, and ghosts of light, by the privilege of this noble oath over you and its obedience among you. I avow and assert on you by the Knower of the all that is hidden and visible, the Great and Exalted, and by the names of your covenant on the door of great temple Ba'al Saqesh, Ba'al Saqesh, Mahraqesh, Mahraqesh, Aqshamqesh, Aqshamqesh, Shaqmonhesh, Shaqmonhesh. I swear upon these, O you spiritual rouhaniah, to the charging of these Elemental scrolls with a ray from the world of the spirits of Fire [Air / Water / Earth]. Let these scrolls become a living covenant between me [full name] and the spirits of the world of Fire [Air / Water / Earth], so that by mere possession of them I shall be attuned and awakened to the awesome power and presence of the spirits of the world of Fire [Air / Water / Earth].

By the name by which the King of Spirits Metatron spoke and felled in prostration the melachim, rouchanim, cherubim under the Throne of the Lord of the Universe and it is Yankeer [x3] Horeen [x3] Horesh [x3] Yaroch Abarach Abadach Tashteesh Yah-Nateeteeu-in Yah-Nateeteeoh Shelesh Leesh Shalesh Bakrakroak El Qadosh; fulfill your covenant with God if you pledged and don't break the faith after its confirmation; don't be aloof and come to me in peace, quickly, and obedient to the names of God, the Lord of the Universes." [x14- 49]

STEP SIX: Seal the Elemental Gates.

Once you have finished the consecration, you can wrap the scrolls in a white cloth until you need them. You can carry the talismans with you in a magical sash or by placing them near your skin under clothing. You can also use them during meditation by placing them in front of you.

Congratulations! You have completed a very challenging operation, designed and consecrated what may be your first talismanic scrolls. As you may have noticed by now, the Elemental energies are very intense and transformative. However, their effect is cumulative. While we are ready to move on now to the next chapter, it is important you come back to this chapter and work through the materials here a few times. As you will see, planetary magic is tied in strongly to Elemental concepts and philosophy. This means that Elemental magic is an important precursor to serious celestial occultism.

Works Referenced

al-Toukhi, A'adu al-Fatah. *al-bidayah wa al-Nihaya fi A'aloom al-Haref wa al-Awfaq wa al-Arsad wa al-Rouhaniah (v1-2)*. al-Maktabah al-Thaqafiah. Beirut:1991

al-Buni, Ahmed (D. 1225 C.E.). *Shamsu al-Ma'aref al-Kubrah*. Maktabat Isha'at al-Islam. Delhi, India.

al-Buni, Ahmed (D. 1225 C.E.). *Manba'a Ussol al-Hikmah*. Maktabat al-Hidayah. Surabaya, Indonesia.

al-Manzeri, Omar (D. 1747 C.E.). Kashef al-Asrar al-Mukhfiah fi A'alem al-Ajram al-Samawiah wa al-Roqoom al-Harfiah (v1-3).

8

Planecary Magic

lanetary magic is an important vehicle for the development of any magician. Planetary energies have an impact on the personality of the magician. These energies
that influence you can also influence others. Therefore,
it makes occult sense that you learn how to flow with
and eventually manipulate these tides. You can bring
out the positive aspects of your own astrological make up, overcome
the negative influences of the planets in a given day and generally live
in harmony with the cosmos as you flow with the light and spirits of
the stars. It is easy to focus, as do many magicians today, on the elements within nature as the central pillar of your magical success and
on spirit evocation. For sure, these are important areas, but planetary
magic is the backbone of success in many of these operations as well.
Let us imagine a particular scenario. Let us say you want to communicate with your boss at work on an important issue and you would
like to get his agreement. For some reason or another, you doubt this
meeting will go well. You can do general spell casting magic, as most
magicians would, to make sure your intent comes to pass. You can also
stray into a shady area of magic by sending out Air spirits to influence
your boss's mind or try to bind him. The alternative is to simply invoke into you the rouhaniat (prana) of Mercury and Venus, the planet
of communication and the planet of desire and attraction, to improve
your own charisma and communication skills for the meeting. This
will result in better success and doesn't really attempt to control another person's own decision making or will. Better still, this improved
benefit will continue with you for a long time, because it is your own
skill that has developed. This is personal growth at the highest level.

The importance of planetary magic hadn't escaped the awareness
of the ancient magicians, who made it the bedrock of their spiritual
practices. Historically, the word Chaldean has become synonymous
with astrologers as much as magicians. The Sabians of Harran built
seven planetary temples to their various divinities, since astrological

magic was central to their faith. The number seven is also part of the mysteries of the ancient Queen of Heaven and Goddess of Love. In the epic tales, Ishtar descends into seven gates of the underworld to restore the slain shepherd king. The number seven is associated with the star of the Goddess of Love, the planet Venus, and seven by seven equals the forty nine petals of the Rose of Life.

However, the seven ancient planets are not all planets, by modern astronomical definition, as they include among them the Sun and Moon. The Arabic word for a planet is Kawkab, which is almost identical to the Hebrew word Kokab or Star. The word Kawkab was also used in medieval and ancient Arabic astrological writing when referring to stars. It seems that the ancients viewed these heavenly bodies simply as stars; some were thought of as moving fast and others very slowly. The seven primary stellar bodies of the ancients are Saturn, Jupiter, Mars, Sun, Venus, Mercury and the Moon. This order is known as the Chaldean order.

The ancient magicians viewed each of these planets as alive and emanating a sentient spiritual essence or rouhaniah endowed in it by the Divine. It is the prototype of the Gaia Theory, but extends to all stellar bodies and not just those with eco-systems that support biological life. The ancients believed that this rouhaniah materializes in the form of spirits that can be contacted and lured here into our sphere on Earth. These rouhaniah orbit the planet itself. It is the rays emanating from the rouhaniah that are the cause of astrological influences, rather than the physical bodies of the celestial spheres. In the ancient world, the physical body and the rouhaniah of each planet was believed to be a chariot to one of the gods and goddesses. Some of the ancients even worshipped those planets directly as the gods and goddesses of their realm. The names of the seven planets in English correspond with ancient Roman deities such as Venus, the goddess of love and beauty, and Mercury, the Divine messenger. Similar naming practices occurred in many cultures.

Some among the ancients viewed the planets themselves as gods and goddess, but others saw them more as natural living beings acting on behalf of the Creator. They believed them to be aware enough to be entreated with prayers and addressed humbly. The spirits of their own world would respond directly to the seeker. Even when not taken to the point of worship, the ancient rites included years of devotional service, sacrifices, initiation and an entire life style change to be compatible with the nature of the planets. Even so, many argued that the planets themselves were agents of the primal creator and shouldn't be confused with the source. The father of the divinities among the Chaldeans was Anu and Anat and the Milky Way galaxy was known as Tariq Anu or the Pathway of Anu.

NAMES OF SEVEN PLANETS

Planet	Sumerian	Babylonian	Hebrew
Saturn	Uduidimsagus	Kayamanu	Shabbathai
Jupiter	Mulsagmegar	Neberu	Tzedek
Mars	Simuud	Salbatanu	Maadim
Sun	Utu	Samas	Shemesh
Venus	Ninsianna	Delebat	Nogah
Mercury	Uduidimguud	Sihtu	Kochav Chama
Moon	Suen	Sin	Yareach

Planet	Arabic	Persian	Greek
Saturn	Kevan	Zuhal	Kronos
Jupiter	Moshtari	Moshtari	Zeus
Mars	Merrikh	Bahram	Ares
Sun	Shams	Khorshid	Helios
Venus	Zuhra	Zohreh	Aphrodite
Mercury	Otaared	Tir	Hermes
Moon	Qamar	Mah	Selene

An easy way to understand the nature of the planets is to use the example of a kingdom. The Sun is like the king among the planets, with the rest acting as aids and advisors. The Moon is like the minister of state and the keeper of the covenant of the ruler. Mercury is the king's scribe. Saturn is the guardian of the vaults and treasury, as well as general over the army and police. Venus is both the queen and the maidens that serve the king. Jupiter is the court's judge and master of fortune and finance. Mars is the king's executioner and foot soldier.

The seven planets are the rulers of the twelve Zodiacal signs. Few occultists today know why the planets were attributed to the signs as they were. Most modern magicians accept the attribution as a matter of tradition. The key to understanding the attributions lies in understanding the four Elements, Fire, Air, Water and Earth, which are a combination of states. These states are a key to understanding the basic celestial cosmology of the ancients. The primordial states are cold-ness, heat, dryness and wetness.

ELEMENTS AND STATES

Element	States
Spirit	Light
Fire	Hot Dryness
Air	Hot Wetness
Water	Cold Wetness
Earth	Cold Dryness

The two celestial lights are the Sun and the Moon; they have the strongest effect on the incidents that occur in the world. The Sun is by far the stronger of the two, and thus the most important of the seven planets. Through observation, it is obvious that its elemental nature is heat and dryness, and its effect is strongest during summer. The sign of Leo is associated with the hottest month in the year. It shares with the Sun its elemental nature, masculinity and the diurnal quality. Ancient astrologers also marked that the Sun was the middle planet in their ancient order and that Leo is the middle of the Fire signs and the middle of the dry signs. The compatibility between the two and the fact that the heat impact of the Sun increases in Leo made them consider it to be its natural sign.

The moon and the sun also share compatibility in eight facets. First, the moon is also one of the brightest planets visible to the naked eye. Second, it is the one the most evident planets as far as its effect on our earthly world. Third, they are similar in their not going straight and then moving backward during their orbit. Fourth, they are both lights in this world, one by day and the other by night. Fifth, they consecutively symbolize creation and life. The symbol of the Sun is heat, and that of the moon is moisture. Heat is the strongest of the actives and moisture is the strongest of the reactives. Sixth, the ascendant of conjunction and receptivity occurs due to the Sun and the Moon. Seventh, the Moon receives its own light from the Sun. Eighth, the largest and most potent of the planets is the Sun, and the Moon is the closest one to us. The Moon thus becomes a partner of the Sun and its proxy in its influence on this world. It is because of this that the sign of the Moon was placed next to the sign of the Sun. This could have been either Cancer or Virgo. Cancer was considered more suitable, because the moon is cold and moist and feminine. Cancer has these same qualities, while Virgo is cold and dry. The moon also quickly changes from quickness to slowness, from light to darkness and from shape to shape. Cancer is considered a changing or cardinal sign and at its commencement, the season changes from one kind to the next. Astrologers therefore agreed that Cancer is the sign of the Moon.

Astrologers then divided the Zodiacal wheel in half. All the signs from Leo to the end of Capricorn were attributed to the overall dominion of the Sun. The signs from the beginning of Aquarius to the end of Cancer were then attributed to the Moon. The solar section was called the great half and the lunar section the minor or lesser half. The two lights' primary functions are the giving of power and the maintenance of composition and mixtures. The other planets share the signs with the two lights. Thus, each planet has two signs, one from the direction of the Sun and the other from the direction of the Moon.

Saturn is likened to an individual who is intent on destroying the world and thus his signs were placed opposite to those of the two lights. From the lunar half, he was given the sign Aquarius. Aquarius is hot, contrary to the coldness of Cancer, but it also shares its moisture. From the solar half, Saturn got the contrary sign to Leo, or Capricorn. Capricorn is contrary to Leo in that it is cold, but it shares dryness with it.

Jupiter follows Saturn among the planets and is beneficial. So, Jupiter received the two signs after Saturn's. The first is from the direction of the Sun and shares with Leo its elemental nature and that is Sagittarius. The other is from the direction of the Moon and shares with Cancer's elemental nature and that is Pisces. Respectively, their placement creates a one hundred and twenty degree or trine aspect with the signs of the two lights; a trine is an aspect of love and kindness.

Mars follows Jupiter and hence was given the two signs following his. Mars received from the direction of the Sun, Scorpio, and from the direction of the Moon, Aries. If he was given from the directions of the Sun a fire sign, then the combined heat would lead to combustion and destruction. He was given a water sign to help balance his nature. From the side of the moon, he was given a planet that is cold and moist and a sign that is hot and dry, so that his weakness isn't compounded. With the signs of the two lights, the two signs of Mars form a ninety degree aspect called a square, which is an aspect of conflict and challenge.

Venus follows Mars after the Sun and is given the two signs that follow his. From the side of the Sun, she receives Libra and from the side of the Moon, Taurus. With the signs of the two lights, they form an aspect of sixty degrees called a sextile, which is friendly and good. It is not as friendly as a trine, for Libra and Leo are both hot, but one is dry and the other is moist. Hence Venus is called the lesser benefic planet.

This leaves Mercury, who receives from the side of the Sun, Virgo, and from the side of the Moon, Gemini. Leo and Virgo are in harmony in the strongest reactives, which is dryness, and different in actives or heat. Mercury is considered benefic with benefics and malefic with malefics, because his signs are next to the two lights in one state and different in another. One of the Mercurial signs, Gemini, has dual bodies.

❂ PLANETARY NAMES OF POWER ❂

In a previous chapter, we introduced the Tahateel names. We will discuss them more in this chapter, as they have great benefit in awakening and bringing forth the energy and power of the planets into your life. They manifest the planetary energy in a pure and high concentration. Such an exposure will not only help you to work with planetary energies in a magical capacity, but it will also help you overcome the negative qualities brought forth by your birth chart. We have incorporated these holy names and their derivatives into basic conjurations that can fit into any busy schedule. Each one should be done daily on the appropriate planetary day, if you want your life be in harmony with the most sublime and spiritual elements of the celestial spheres. Planetary days are easy to determine: Sun (Sunday), Moon (Monday), Mars (Tuesday), Mercury (Wednesday), Jupiter (Thursday), Venus (Friday) and Saturn (Saturday). It should be noted that planetary days begin from sunrise and end at sunset. The attributions are different for night.

These seven names are each made of seven letters. The total letters composing the names are forty-nine, which is the number of the Rose of Life. The letter Ta ط occurs fourteen times. The letter Lam ل occurs eleven times. The letter Ha ه occurs nine times. The letter Ya ى occurs eight times. The following letters occur only once: Kha خ, Qaf ق, Fa ف, Nun ن, Mym م, Jym ج, Ba ب. The total number of dots appearing on all the letters of the names is twenty-three.

THE TAHATEEL NAMES

Arabic	Phonetics	Planet
للطهطيل	Lel-tah-teel	Saturn
م ه طهطيل	Mah-tah-teel	Jupiter
ق ه طيطيل	Qah-tee-teel	Mars
ف ه ط ب طيل	Fah-tob-teel	Sun
ن ه ه ططيل	Na-hah-ta-teel	Venus
ج ه ل طططيل	Jah-lah-ta-teel	Mercury
ل خ ه ططيل	Lach-ha-tot-eel	Moon

NUMBER OF LETTERS IN TAHATEEL NAMES

ب	ج	م	ن	ف	ق	خ	ي	ه	ل	ط
1	1	1	1	1	1	1	8	9	11	14

From these seven names an eighth name is derived. It is formed from the first letter of each of the seven names. It doesn't have a Ta or Ha in it and begins with Lam and ends with Lam. Names that begin with and end with the same letter are said to partake of the quality of the Great Secret Name. The first and seventh names share this, as they begin and end with Lam. The eighth name La-maq-fan-jal is especially used against artificially enchanted waters. The original seven also are very potent against disabling occult wards and traps.

DERIVED EIGHTH NAME

7th	6th	5th	4th	3rd	2nd	1st
ل	ج	ن	ف	ق	م	ل

They also have many mundane occult applications. When using them for spell casting, remember that their writing and recitation should begin in a good hour, with the degree of the mage's birth sign at the ascendant. A planetary conjuration should also be recited seven times with the proper incense. Keep in mind, as noted elsewhere in the materials, you are responsible for all the work you do before the Creator, and all things are by Divine permission. This is why we recommend that you do divination and prayers if there is ambiguity in your heart about the spiritual permission of the operation. Here are some practical ways you can use them:

✳ If you want to increase the traffic of customers to a shop, write the seventh name and the eighth using an iron implement on tin. Whoever is selling in the shop should wear this talisman around his or her neck. You should also write the seven names on seven clay pieces and place them in hidden places in the store location.

✳ If you want to terminate the effects of sorcery, write the seven names on leaves from a palm tree. Write the eighth name on a clean piece of cloth, then soak it with water and wash the affected person. The individual's body should then be dried with the leaves. Afterward, write the first name and the eighth name on seven pieces of paper or leaves. Burn them in a censor placed under the victim, one after the other, as you charge the spirits of the names to remove the bindings and sorceries.

✳ If you need to meet someone of whom you are afraid, write the eighth name on a white paper with musk, saffron and rose water and put it in your hat near to your brow and write it on your palm before you leave for the meeting.

✳ If you want to cure migraines, headaches, evil eye and general ailments, write the seventh name on a wall or a piece of wood in separate letters with a knife. Ask the affected individual to put his or her finger on the place that is aching. Place a nail on the first letter of the name and vibrate the seven names seven times. If the pain stops, then end with it, otherwise continue by repeating this with the next letters. Once the pain dies at one of the letters, hammer the nail in at that spot.

✳ If you want to help facilitate peace between two conflicting parties, write the first six names with edible ink on food or rice paper and let them eat them. The seventh name should be consumed by you or the pursuer of the reconciliation.

✳ To facilitate the return of a lost or missing person, write the seventh name in the first hour of Friday and carry it. In the hour of Mars for that day, write the name of the missing person and his or her mother, as well as the name of the seeker with his or her mother, together with the seventh name. Say, "Move, O servants of this name, by bringing the missing person N son/daughter of N to the house of N son/daughter of N, by honor of this name." Hang the papers in the air in front of the house and the missing person shall return by permission of the Divine One.

❈ If you want to banish a stubborn Jinn, write the eighth name, followed by the fourth and third on a piece of red wax. Say, "Burn, O spirits of these names," and light it.

❈ If you wish to walk where no one notices you, fast physically and spiritually for seven days and eat no animal products, as per the magical guidelines. Break your fast on steamed barley, dipped in olive oil, late at night, then write the seven names on the right side of your chest. You should be in a clean place away from people when you are doing this. Charge the servants of these names with your purpose of not being noticed. After this you will walk to your destination and no one will notice you. Speaking will break the effect.

❈ If you want to access treasures or objects guarded by enchanted waters, write the eight names on stones, pieces of cloth or other objects. Approach the enchanted water, then throw the first name in front of you, then the second, then the third. Move forward slowly until you throw the sixth name near the object or treasure. Take it quickly and if you can collect the objects with the names again, then do it; otherwise don't be bothered. Keep the last two names in your hand, as the guardians will return to their locations. If you fear betrayal from any companions with you, place the eighth name in your right hand and charge the servants of the name to hide you from the eyes of your companions.

From these seven Tahateel names, twenty-seven other mighty names are extracted for a total of twenty-eight names per planet. This brings the total names of the Tahateel to one hundred and ninety-six, divided among the seven planetary spheres. For each planet, there are seven names of Tahateel that are known as potencies, intelligence or inner power. These call forth the inner power of the spheres and their corresponding rouhaniah. These are usually used first. The second set is known as the names of charging or commanding. These names are used to compel the spirits of the sphere to respond and obey. The third are known as astrological and are used to call down the planetary rays. These are often used when attempting to consecrate or empower amulets and talismans. The fourth set is known as the burning names. These are used to fiercely charge and compel disobedient spirits or thwart adverse or evil spirits that may come at the magician.

These names are extracted from the magic square of each name. The individual name of the Tahateel is placed in a square as separate letters. Each subsequent line is permutated from the preceding one. The permutation begins with the fifth cell of the line. The fifth, sixth, and seventh letters are placed as first, second and third letters of the next lines. The remaining initial four letters subsequently become the last four letters of the next line. This process is continued for six lines. As an example, we have shown the permutation square for the first Tahateel name, with the first two lines of permutation highlighted for clarity.

TAHATEEL TABLE OF PERMUTATION

ل	ي	ط	ه	ط	ل	ل
ه	ط	ل	ل	ل	ي	ط
ل	ل	ي	ط	ه	ط	ل
ط	ه	ط	ل	ل	ل	ي
ل	ل	ل	ي	ط	ه	ط
ي	ط	ه	ط	ل	ل	ل
ط	ل	ل	ل	ي	ط	ه

The set of names for inner power is extracted from the magic square by reading its rows from right to left to form the names. The astrological names are extracted by reading its rows from left to right. The names of burning are extracted by reading its columns from top to bottom. The names of charging are extracted by reading its columns from bottom to top. We will only use the names of inner power and astrological names in this book. These will be used for the daily planetary conjurations later on in this chapter.

MOON MAGIC

The first planet to work with in your magical development is the Moon. The moon is the closest to us and has the strongest influence as one of the two lights. The key to successful planetary magic is observance of the idea of correspondence. Your success will depend on how much you surround yourself with things that are under the rulership of the Moon and try to embody its attributes. It is common for modern magicians to become too focused on the correspondences, but embodying attributes is equally as important. When you are working with the Moon, you should spend time before the ritual engaged in Lunar activities such as happy domestic evenings, spending time by the sea, and so on. The idea is that like is attracted to like. You will be more successful at attracting the rouhaniah or prana of a planet, when surrounding yourself with things that resonate with its energy and engaging with activities that they rule over. We can't go really into much detail on planetary magic in a single chapter. We will give you what you need to begin to fully awaken these energies in your life. Some of the tools we will be discussing may be too expensive or difficult to procure, or hard to make. Don't wait to have them all to begin your practice. They are the ideal tools for the work, but you need to do what you can with what you have.

TAHATEEL NAMES OF THE MOON

Inner Power Names	Inner Power Names (Arabic)	Astrological Names	Astrological Names (Arabic)
Lach-ha-tot-eel	لخهططيل	Lee-tot-ha-chal	ليططهخل
Tee-lal-cha-hot	طيللخهط	Tah-cha-la-leet	طهخليط
Chah-tot-ee-lal	خهططيلل	La-lee-tot-hach	لليطططهخ
Ya-la-lach-ha-tot	يللخهطط	Tot-hach-la-lee	ططهخللي
Ha-tot-ee-la-lach	هططيللخ	Chal-lee-ta-tah	خلليططه
Lal-chah-tot-ee	للخهططي	Ya-tot-hach-lal	يططهخلل
Totee-la-la-chh	ططيللخه	Hach-la-lee-tot	هخلليطط

LUNAR TABLET OF THE GREAT NAME

On a piece of wood paint the following magic square in white color upon a black background. You can use this tablet by placing it before you while you recite the lunar conjuration.

☆	G	ℰ	IIII	✸	⌈	𝕀𝕀𝕀
𝕀𝕀𝕀	☆	G	ℰ	IIII	✸	⌈
⌈	𝕀𝕀𝕀	☆	G	ℰ	IIII	✸
✸	⌈	𝕀𝕀𝕀	☆	G	ℰ	IIII
IIII	✸	⌈	𝕀𝕀𝕀	☆	G	ℰ
ℰ	IIII	✸	⌈	𝕀𝕀𝕀	☆	G
G	ℰ	IIII	✸	⌈	𝕀𝕀𝕀	☆

PLANETARY TIMING

The moon has Monday from sunrise to sunset and Thursday from sunset to the next sunrise and rules the 1st and 8th planetary hours of each period.

MAGIC SQUARE OF THE MOON

⊩⊲))	𝕏◻	𝕏ℰ	𝕏𝕔	♻	⊩⊲𝕔	⊩⊲ℰ	⊩⊲◻	𝕏𝖧
⊩⊲❸	𝕏◻	⇒◯	⇒	𝕏))	𝕏𝖧	𝕏♀	⇒❸	𝕏
⊩⊲◯	𝕏ℰ	𝔹ℰ	◐	𝔹))	𝔹◻	◐◯	◐𝖧	𝕏◯
⊩⊲	𝕏𝕔	𝔹𝕔	𝕋	𝕋ℰ	𝔹♀	𝕋♀	◐♀	𝕏❸
𝕩◯	⇒ℰ	◐))	))♻	𝕋◯	𝕋))	𝕏♻	⊩⊲𝖧	◯
𝕩	⇒𝕔	◐❸	𝕋𝕔	𝔹𝖧	𝕋❸	𝔹	⊩⊲♀	❸
𝕏♻	⇒))	𝔹◯	𝔹❸	𝕋	𝕋◻	𝕋𝖧	⊩⊲♻	))
𝕏♀	𝕏	𝕏◯	𝕏❸	◐♻	◐ℰ	◐𝕔	◐◻	𝕔
ℰ	◻	𝖧	♀	𝕏))	⇒♀	⇒𝖧	⇒◻	⇒♻

The Lunar magic square of 9x9 is useful for bringing reconciliation between those in disagreement. For this purpose, write the magic square on a scroll or piece of cloth when the Moon is aspected with Mars in the 29th degree of Capricorn. The Sun should be in a trine or sextile aspect to this alignment.

SCRIPT OF THE MOON

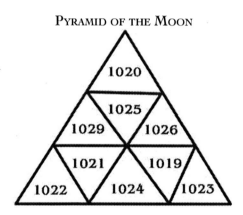

۪؍	و	ه	د	ج	ب	ا
ن	م	ل	ك	ي	ط	ح
ش	ر	ق	ص	ف	ع	س
غ	ظ	ض	ذ	خ	ث	ت

PYRAMID OF THE MOON

```
          1020
        1025
     1029    1026
       1021    1019
    1022    1024    1023
```

CONJURATION TO THE MOON

PURPOSE: The weekly conjurations are good tools to connect you with the energies of the planets and keep their flow balanced in your life. There are seven conjurations and performing each one once a week will bring the planetary forces into positive alignment into your life and surrounding. The conjurations in their expanded version utilizes the ritual of the Magus Gate. The weekly conjuration, however, can be done without the earlier steps. They are included at the end of the list of steps.

DIVINE NAMES: The sacred names used in the conjuration are the Tahateel names covered in this chapter, plus the chants for opening the various portals.

245

TIMING: The weekly planetary conjurations, at the end of the steps, should be done once a week. You can do the extended version once a month. Do each one based on the corresponding planetary day and night. Extend the process for at least three months to allow the energy to work through into your life. Planetary magic takes time to completely come to fruit, since we are working on a more cosmic scale, but the benefits are worth it. When doing the ritual you also will need to determine the placement of the planet in the sky. You can do this by casting a chart for the time you plan to do your work and looking in which house the Moon is found. You can cast a chart for the day by hand, if you know how, or you can use any astrological software. The astrological chart is divided into four quadrants with an axis representing the four directions. The ascendant or 1st house is East, the descendant or 7th house is the West, the midheaven is North or 10th house and the South is the 4th house. If you are using stationary portals and it is hard to move them, select the approximate direction. If for example, the Moon is at the end of the 11th house and transiting into the 12th, consider it to be East and face the Eastern portal. During the ritual you will be facing this portal and standing close to it.

TOOLS: You will need the planetary magic square of the Great Name somewhere before you or carried by you. You will also need the physical portal, but you can do the ritual with a visualized compliment.

SABIAN PRAYER: This specific Sabian prayer will be used throughout the conjurations, so we will reproduce it here. The prayer goes as follows: "**You are such an eternal being that all the chiefs and governorships depend on you. You are the God of all the creatures who are thought of and who exist in the region of senses. You are the chief of the worlds and the shepherd of 'realms.' You are the Lord of all the angels and their superiors. Wisdom originates from you and reaches the governor of the earth. You are the first cause. Your might envelops all those who exist. You are a boundless oneness. You are the unfathomable one. You are the supervisor of the celestial sovereigns and the sources of light whose lights are eternal. You are the sovereign of sovereigns who dictates all the good and who forewarns everything through revelations and signs. The creation and development of all creatures is caused by you. Order takes the right path with your signal. The lights emanate only from you. You are the oldest cause, existing before everything.**

I request that you purify my spirit. I wish to succeed in winning

246

your blessings, now and always, till eternity. O El, who is pure of all kinds of pollution, make my reason sound and give me health free of all kinds of ailments. Turn my worries into joy. I take refuge in you only and fear only you. I beg of you to let me succeed in expressing your immensity, which can only be expressed by manifestations. This immensity cannot be expressed by words. Everybody and everything comes from you; everything and realization of every success depends on you. You are the desire and hope of the worlds and you are the supporter of all mankind."

STEP ONE: Begin with the purifying and consecration of your working space. Close your eyes and take a very deep breath inward, then exhale forcefully. Feel the stress leaving your body. Allow your breathing to increase, sensing yourself filled with vigor and energy. Take a few minutes to perform the four fold or eight-fold breath. Take the time to meditate on the Divine that is present in all the galaxies, stars, planets, and universes.

STEP TWO: Perform the basic opening of the Magus Gate.

STEP THREE: Exhale into the pentagram the name Gabriel seven times then say, "Aid me, O archangel Gabriel [x3], peace be upon you, with your protection and by opening the gateway between me and the realm of spirits of the Moon through the portal of spirit."

STEP FIVE: Pointing toward the portal, say, "In the Holy Divine Name, Motdar Chaqlas A'amaa'a Lakma Al-lan Qossmee Rahmah [x3] move, O spirits of Light, and open the gateway between me and the world of the spirits of the Moon, Rouhaniah Kawkab al-Qamar."

STEP SIX: Recite the Sabian prayer.

STEP SEVEN: Recite the weekly conjuration of the Moon. Say, "O ye celestial chariot of Sin called Suen, Sin, Yareach, Qamar, Mah, Selene, Moon and by many other names, I call upon your rays and spirit to descend upon me. Envelop me with a cloak of your light, in the names of Lach-ha-tot-eel [x3], Tee-lal-cha-hot [x3], Chah-tot-ee-lal [x3], Ya-la-lach-ha-tot [x3], Ha-tot-ee-la-lach [x3], Lal-chah-tot-ee [x3], Totee-la-la-chh [x3]. O Kawkab al-Qamar, O Moon, fill me with the power of your sphere and aid me with the spirits of your orbit, by the mighty and sacred names Lee-tot-ha-chal [x3], Tah-cha-la-leet [x3], La-lee-tot-hach [x3], Tot-hach-la-lee [x3], Chal-lee-ta-tah [x3], Ya-tot-hach-lal [x3], Hach-la-lee-tot [x3]. O Rouhaniat Kawkab al-Qamar, by the permission of the Queen of Heaven and Earth, and authority of the archangel Gabriel, and the blessed names Lach-ha-tot-eel [x3], Tee-lal-cha-hot [x3], Chah-tot-ee-lal [x3], Ya-la-lach-ha-tot [x3], Ha-tot-ee-la-lach [x3], Lal-chah-tot-ee [x3], Totee-la-la-chh [x3], Lee-tot-ha-chal [x3], Tah-cha-la-leet [x3], La-lee-tot-hach [x3], Tot-hach-la-lee [x3], Chal-lee-ta-tah [x3], Ya-tot-hach-lal [x3], Hach-la-lee-tot [x3] come through this celestial portal before me in peace profound as a friend and infuse me with the pure magic and spirit of Luna. Fill me, through your aid, with a loving personality, vivid imagination, strong instinctual mind, balanced emotions, healthy change, love of the people, understanding of women, positive psychic qualities and personal magnetism. Let me be a vessel for noblest expression of your spirit and power, O Kawkab al-Qamar."

❊ MERCURY MAGIC ❊

TAHATEEL NAMES OF MERCURY

Inner Power Names	Inner Power Names (Arabic)	Astrological Names	Astrological Names (Arabic)
Jah-lah-ta-teel	جهلططيل	Lee-tot-la-haj	ليطططهج
Teel-jah-lot	طيلجهلط	Tal-haj-leet	طلهجليط
Hal-tot-ya-laj	هلططيلج	Ja-lee-tot-lah	جليطططله
Yal-ja-hal-tot	يلجهلطط	Tot-la-haj-lee	طططلهجلي
La-tot-yal-jah	لططيلجه	Haj-lee-tot-al	لططيطجه
La-jah-lo-tot-ee	لجهلططي	Ya-tot-lah-jal	يطططلهجل
Tot-eel-ja-hal	طططيلجهل	Lah-ja-lee-tot	لهجليطط

MERCURY TABLET OF THE GREAT NAME

On a piece of wood paint the following magic square in brown upon a light sky blue background. You can use this tablet by placing it before you while you recite the conjuration of Mercury.

ٲ	⫿	☆	؏	؟	∭	⧣
⧣	ٲ	⫿	☆	؏	؟	∭
∭	⧣	ٲ	⫿	☆	؏	؟
؟	∭	⧣	ٲ	⫿	☆	؏
؏	؟	∭	⧣	ٲ	⫿	☆
☆	؏	؟	∭	⧣	ٲ	⫿
⫿	☆	؏	؟	∭	⧣	ٲ

PLANETARY TIMING

Mercury has Wednesday from sunrise to sunset and Saturday from sunset to the next sunrise.

SCRIPT OF MERCURY

ز	و	ه	د	ج	ب	ا

ن	م	ل	ك	ي	ط	ح

ش	ر	ق	ص	ف	ع	س

غ	ظ	ض	ذ	خ	ث	ت

MAGIC SQUARE OF MERCURY

The Mercurial 8x8 magic square is beneficial for memorization, intelligence and the acquisition of knowledge. For this purpose, draw this square using saffron and honey on a washable surface when the moon is in Cancer and Mercury is in the 15ᵗʰ degree of Virgo. Wash the writing off with water and drink it. If you give it regularly to a child, it is purported to assist the child to grow up with a strong memory and reading comprehension. It is also very beneficial for illnesses that affect limbs and animals. For this purpose, construct the square when Jupiter is exalted and Mars is in positive aspect with it. The moon should also be conjunct with Mars. Write it on barley bread and give it to the ill to consume for healing. It can also be used as part of a ring for the receptivity and friendship of figures of authority. To construct this ring, take 34 grams of pure silver and form the surface for the square. Do this on a Wednesday, during a waxing moon with Mercury in good aspect. Etch or draw the square on the silver and incense it with aloes and carnation. The ancients also used this to bring about an increase in rain. They would write the square on a scroll, tie it to the shell of a tortoise, and then bury it in the middle of the village.

¥	吊¥	吊X	♈	↑	♉Ⅰ	♉♠	盃
祆X	⊁♠	⊁↑	吊Ⅰ	吊♠	⊁盃	¥	吊♠
祆盃	⊕♠	⊕Ⅰ	祆↑	祆♠	⊁X	⊁¥	祆¥
丌Ⅰ	丌↑	丌♠	⊕X	⊕¥	♠¥	♠X	⊕♠
祆	⊕♠	⊕♠	丌♠	丌♠	丌	丌盃	丌♠
♠	祆♠	祆♠	⊕	⊕盃	祆♠	祆Ⅰ	⊕↑
X	吊♠	吊↑	⊁Ⅰ	⊁♠	吊盃	吊	⊁♠
♉↑	Ⅰ	♠	♉盃	♉	♠	♠	吊♠

PYRAMID OF MERCURY

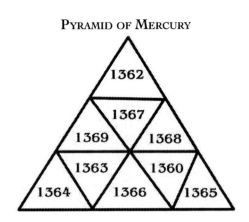

CONJURATION OF MERCURY
The purpose and requirements for this conjuration have been covered under the Lunar conjuration.

STEP ONE: Begin with the purifying and consecration of your working space. Close your eyes and take a very deep breath inward, then exhale forcefully. Feel the stress leaving your body. Allow your breathing to increase, sensing yourself filled with vigor and energy. Take a few minutes to perform the four fold or eight-fold breath. Take the time to meditate on the Divine that is present in all the galaxies, stars, planets, and universes.

STEP TWO: Perform the basic opening of the Magus Gate.

STEP THREE: Exhale into the pentagram the name Michael seven times then say, "**Aid me, O archangel Michael [x3], peace be upon you, with your protection and by opening the gateway between me and the realm of spirits of Mercury through the portal of spirit.**"

STEP FIVE: Pointing toward the portal, say, "**In the Holy Divine Name, Motdar Chaqlas A'amaa'a Lakma Al-lan Ossree Dahhmah [x3] move, O spirits of Light, and open the gateway between me and the world of the spirits of the Mercury, Rouhaniat Kawkab Otaared.**"

STEP SIX: Recite the Sabian prayer.

STEP SEVEN: Recite the weekly conjuration of Mercury. Say, "**O ye celestial chariot of Nabû called Udu-idim-gu-ud, Sihtu, Kochav Chama, Otaared, Tir, Hermes, Mercury and by many other names, I call upon your rays and spirit to descend upon me. Envelop me with a cloak of your light, in the blessed names of Jah-lah-ta-teel [x3], Teel-jah-lot [x3], Hal-tot-ya-laj [x3], Yal-ja-hal-tot [x3], La-tot-yal-jah [x3], La-jah-lo-tot-ee [x3], Tot-eel-ja-hal [x3]. O, Kochav Chama, O Mercury, fill me with the power of your sphere and aid me with the spirits of your orbit, by the mighty and sacred names Lee-tat-la-haj [x3], Tal-haj-leet [x3], Ja-lee-tot-lah [x3], Tot-la-haj-lee [x3], Haj-lee-tot-al [x3], Ya-tot-lah-jal [x3], Lah-ja-lee-tot [x3]. O Rouhaniat Kawkab Otaared, by the permission of the Queen of Heaven and Earth, and authority of the archangel Michael, and the blessed names Jah-lah-ta-teel [x3], Teel-jah-lot [x3], Hal-tot-ya-laj [x3], Yal-ja-hal-tot [x3], La-tot-yal-jah [x3], La-jah-lo-tot-ee [x3], Tot-eel-ja-hal [x3], Lee-tat-la-haj [x3], Tal-haj-leet [x3], Ja-lee-tot-lah [x3], Tot-la-haj-lee [x3], Haj-lee-tot-al [x3], Ya-tot-lah-jal [x3], Lah-ja-lee-tot [x3] come through this** celestial portal before me in peace profound as a friend and infuse me with the pure magic and spirit of Mercury. Fill me, through your aid with great reason, strong self-expression in all affairs, clear and moving speech, literary ability, graceful gestures, wisdom through knowledge, quick-wittedness, eloquence and dexterity. Let me be a vessel for noblest expression of your spirit and power, O Kawkab Otaared."

STEP EIGHT: Close the Magus Gate.

 VENUS MAGIC

TAHATEEL NAMES OF VENUS

Inner Power Names	Inner Power Names (Arabic)	Astrological Names	Astrological Names (Arabic)
Na-hah-ta-teel	نههططيل	Lee-tot-ha-han	ليططههن
Teel-na-ha-hot	طيلنههط	Tah-ha-na-leet	طههنليط
Ha-ha-tah-tee-lan	هههططيلن	Nah-lee-tot-hah	نليططهه
Ya-lan-ha-ha-tot	يلنههطط	Tot-ha-ha-na-lee	ططههنلي
Hot-teel-nah	ههططيلنه	Han-lee-tot-ah	هنليطط
Len-hah-tah-tee	لنههططي	Ya-to-tah-ha-nal	يططههنل
Ta-teel-na-hah	ططيلنهه	Hah--na-lee-tot	ههنليطط

VENUSIAN TABLET OF THE GREAT NAME

ⅠⅠⅠⅠ	✳	↑	𝗆	☆	Ϭ	℈
℈	ⅠⅠⅠⅠ	✳	↑	𝗆	☆	Ϭ
Ϭ	℈	ⅠⅠⅠⅠ	✳	↑	𝗆	☆
☆	Ϭ	℈	ⅠⅠⅠⅠ	✳	↑	𝗆
𝗆	☆	Ϭ	℈	ⅠⅠⅠⅠ	✳	↑
↑	𝗆	☆	Ϭ	℈	ⅠⅠⅠⅠ	✳
✳	↑	𝗆	☆	Ϭ	℈	ⅠⅠⅠⅠ

On a piece of wood paint the magic square of the Great Name in green upon a red background. You can use this tablet by placing it before you while you recite the conjuration of Venus. We should point out that the ancient Sabians also associated blue with this planet. This is why in our magical sources there appears to be lack of consistency concerning which color to use specifically. This problem will appear later on when we look at Jupiter. Jupiter is given also blue or green colors. The ancient Sabians elected green for Jupiter and blue for Venus. Later Arabic magical texts continued this tradition, but at times switched them. You may elect to use either blue or green since there appears to be no final consensus on this in the texts. We lean toward using green for Venus and blue for Jupiter. Venus is considered hot and dry leaning toward moist and Jupiter is cold and wet. Green is produced by mixing yellow with the blue. Yellow is associated with the Sun and adds warmth to the moist blue. Blue is the color of the ocean and water. Therefore, it would make more sense for us that green be Venus and blue be Jupiter.

PLANETARY TIMING

Venus has Friday from sunrise to sunset and Monday from sunset to the next sunrise.

SCRIPT OF VENUS

ا	ب	ج	د	ه	و	ز
ح	ط	ي	ك	ل	م	ن
س	ع	ف	ص	ق	ر	ش
ت	ث	خ	ذ	ض	ظ	غ

MAGIC SQUARE OF VENUS

ꙮ	ꙮ	ꙮ	ꙮ	ꙮ	ꙮ	ꙮ
ꙮ	ꙮ	ꙮ	ꙮ	ꙮ	ꙮ	ꙮ
ꙮ	ꙮ	ꙮ	ꙮ	ꙮ	ꙮ	ꙮ
ꙮ	ꙮ	ꙮ	ꙮ	ꙮ	ꙮ	ꙮ
ꙮ	ꙮ	ꙮ	ꙮ	ꙮ	ꙮ	ꙮ
ꙮ	ꙮ	ꙮ	ꙮ	ꙮ	ꙮ	ꙮ
ꙮ	ꙮ	ꙮ	ꙮ	ꙮ	ꙮ	ꙮ

The magic square of 7x7, being associated with Venus, is very powerful for love. As a love talisman, it should be made when Venus is in Taurus, Gemini or Libra. Make the talisman's surface on a silver coin that weighs 29.75 grams. Etch the magic square on the coin on a Friday and incense it with aloes wood. Place it in a piece of silk that you carry about you and it will have a powerful effect in the affairs of love. If you run into difficulty with a situation, just place the coin in your pocket and it will be resolved quickly. It is also beneficial for dealing with negative emotions or in areas where violence occurs. To dissipate the negative and aggressive energies of such a place, wash the silver coin in a cup and then take that water and sprinkle it at the location. It can also be sprinkled in animal barns, places of business, government, homes and so forth to repel negativity and attract all that is beneficial. If you place the coin in your bed, you will see an increase in sexual activity and a more harmonious relationship with your partner. You can also etch this square on virgin paper with musk and saffron on a Friday and then incense it with amber and aloes. Then make the paper part of an ointment and place the container under the light of Venus in the sky. Anoint your body with it to be received with awe and respect by others.

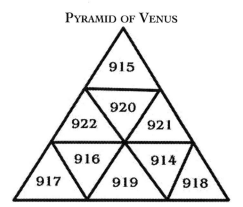

CONJURATION OF VENUS

The purpose and requirements for this conjuration have been covered under the Lunar conjuration.

STEP ONE: Begin with the purifying and consecration of your working space. Close your eyes and take a very deep breath inward, then exhale forcefully. Feel the stress leaving your body. Allow your breathing to increase, sensing yourself filled with vigor and energy. Take a few minutes to perform the four fold or eight-fold breath. Take the time to meditate on the Divine that is present in all the galaxies, stars, planets, and universes.

STEP TWO: Perform the opening of the Magus Gate.

STEP THREE: Exhale into the pentagram the name A'anael l seven times then say, "**Aid me, O archangel Aa'niel [x3], peace be upon you, with your protection and by opening the gateway between me and the realm of spirits of Venus through the portal of spirit.**"

STEP FIVE: Pointing toward the portal, say, "**In the Holy Divine Name, Motdar Chaqlas A'amaa'a Lakma Al-lan Zosshee Rahh-hah [x3] move, O spirits of Light, and open the gateway between me and the world of the spirits of the Mercury, Rouhaniah Kawkab al-Zuhra.**"

STEP SIX: Recite the Sabian prayer.

STEP SEVEN: Recite the weekly conjuration of Venus. Say, "**O ye celes-**

tial chariot of Ishtar called Nin-si-an-na, Delebat, Nogah, Zuhra, Zohreh, Aphrodite, Venus and by many other names, I call upon your rays and spirit to descend upon me. Envelop me with a cloak of your light, in the blessed names of Na-hah-ta-teel [x3], Teel-na-ha-hot [x3], Ha-ha-tah-tee-lan [x3], Ya-lan-ha-ha-ta-tot [x3], Hot-teel-nah [x3], Len-hah-tah-tee [x3], Ta-teel-na-hah [x3]. O Nogah, O Venus, fill me with the power of your sphere and aid me with the spirits of your orbit, by the mighty and sacred names Leet-tot-ha-han [x3], Ta-ha-na-leet [x3], Nah-lee-tot-hah [x3], Tot-ha-ha-na-lee [x3], Han-lee-tot-ah [x3], Ya-to-tah-ha-nal [x3], Hah-na-lee-tot [x3]. O Rouhaniat Kawkab al-Zuhra, by the permission of the Queen of Heaven and Earth, and authority of the archangel A'aniel, and the blessed names Na-hah-ta-teel [x3], Teel-na-ha-hot [x3], Ha-ha-tah-tee-lan [x3], Ya-lan-ha-ha-ta-tot [x3], Hot-teel-nah [x3], Len-hah-tah-tee [x3], Ta-teel-na-hah [x3], Leet-tot-ha-han [x3], Ta-ha-na-leet [x3], Nah-lee-tot-hah [x3], Tot-ha-ha-na-lee [x3], Han-lee-tot-ah [x3], Ya-to-tah-ha-nal [x3], Hah-na-lee-tot [x3] come through this celestial portal before me in peace profound as a friend and infuse me withthe power of attraction, cohesion of heart and mind, ability to build a coalition, personal love, social instincts, artistic talent, internal and external beauty and harmony in my life, cheerfulness and suavity. Let me be a vessel for noblest expression of your spirit and power, O Kawkab al-Zuhra."

STEP EIGHT: Close the Magus Gate.

✹ SUN MAGIC ✹

TAHATEEL NAMES OF THE SUN:

Inner Power Names	Inner Power Names (Arabic)	Astrological Names	Astrological Names (Arabic)
Fah-tob-teel	فهطبطيل	Lee-ta-bot-haf	ليطبطهف
Teel-fah-tab	طيلفهطب	Bat-haf-leet	بطهفليط
Hat-ba-tee-luf	هطبطيلف	Fa-lee-tub-tah	هبطله
Yal-fah-ta-but	يلفهطب	Ta-but-huf-lee	طبطهفلي
Tab-teel-fah	طبطيلفه	Haf-lee-ta-bat	هفليطب
Lef-hat-bot-ee	لفهطبطي	Yat-bot-ha-fal	يطبطهفل
Bah-teel-fa-hat	بطيلفهط	Tah-fa-lee-tub	طهفليطب

SOLAR TABLET OF THE GREAT NAME

𐓝	𐒆	ⅠⅠⅠⅠ	#	𐓘	𝍤	✪
✪	𐓝	𐒆	ⅠⅠⅠⅠ	#	𐓘	𝍤
𝍤	✪	𐓝	𐒆	ⅠⅠⅠⅠ	#	𐓘
𐓘	𝍤	✪	𐓝	𐒆	ⅠⅠⅠⅠ	#
#	𐓘	𝍤	✪	𐓝	𐒆	ⅠⅠⅠⅠ
ⅠⅠⅠⅠ	#	𐓘	𝍤	✪	𐓝	𐒆
𐒆	ⅠⅠⅠⅠ	#	𐓘	𝍤	✪	𐓝

PLANETARY TIMING

The Sun has Sunday from sunrise to sunset and Wednesday from sunset to the next sunrise.

SCRIPT OF THE SUN

ز	و	ه	د	ج	ب	ا
ن	م	ل	ك	ي	ط	ح
ش	ر	ق	ص	ف	ع	س
غ	ظ	ض	ذ	خ	ث	ت

MAGIC SQUARE OF THE SUN

The Solar 6x6 magic square has benefits for the pursuit of power, oratory ability and gaining respect. It is also useful for those who want the guidance of scholars and to develop their magical abilities. As well, it is good for prosperity and blessing in ownerships and for increase in money and status. When the Sun is exalted in Aries, take 1.75 grams of gold and cast it into a circular disk like a coin. Then etch the six by six magic square on it on Sunday in the hour of the Sun, making sure that at that given time the Sun is well aspected. Incense the talisman with saffron and wash it with rose water, camphor and musk. Wear it upon you to receive its power.

258

PYRAMID OF THE SUN

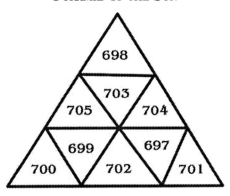

CONJURATION OF THE SUN

The purpose and requirements for this conjuration have been covered under the Lunar conjuration.

STEP ONE: Begin with the purifying and consecration of your working space. Close your eyes and take a very deep breath inward, then exhale forcefully. Feel the stress leaving your body. Allow your breathing to increase, sensing yourself filled with vigor and energy. Take a few minutes to perform the four fold or eight-fold breath. Take the time to meditate on the Divine that is present in all the galaxies, stars, planets, and universes.

STEP TWO: Perform the basic opening of the Magus Gate.

STEP THREE: Exhale into the pentagram the name Ruqiel seven times then say, "**Aid me, O archangel Ruqiel [x3], peace be upon you, with your protection and by opening the gateway between me and the realm of spirits of the Sun through the portal of spirit.**"

STEP FIVE: Pointing toward the portal, say, "**In the Holy Divine Name, Motdar Chaqlas A'amaa'a Lakma Allan Shosmee Sahhmah [x3] move, O spirits of Light, and open the gateway between me and the world of the spirits of the Sun, Rouhaniat Kawkab al-Shames.**"

STEP SIX: Recite the Sabian prayer.

STEP SEVEN: Recite the weekly conjuration of the Sun. Say, "**O ye** celestial chariot of Shamash called Utu, Samas, Shemesh, Shams, Khorshid, Helios, Sun and by many other names, I call upon your rays and spirit to descend upon me. Envelop me with a cloak of your light, in the blessed names of Fah-tob-teel [x3], Teel-fah-tab [x3], Hat-ba-tee-luf [x3], Yal-fah-ta-but [x3], Tab-teel-fah [x3], Lef-hat-bot-ee [x3], Bah-teel-fa-hat [x3]. O Shemesh, O Sun, fill me with the power of your sphere and aid me with the spirits of your orbit, by the mighty and sacred names Lee-ta-bot-haf [x3], Bat-haf-leet [x3], Fa-lee-tub-tah [x3], Ta-but-huf-lee [x3], Haf-lee-ta-bat [x3], Yat-bot-ha-fal [x3], Tah-fa-lee-tub [x3]. O Rouhaniat Kawkab al-Shames, by the permission of the Queen of Heaven and Earth, and authority of the archangel Ruqiel, and the blessed names Fah-tob-teel [x3], Teel-fah-tab [x3], Hat-ba-tee-luf [x3], Yal-fah-ta-but [x3], Tab-teel-fah [x3], Lef-hat-bot-ee [x3], Bah-teel-fa-hat [x3], Lee-ta-bot-haf [x3], Bat-haf-leet [x3], Fa-lee-tub-tah [x3], Ta-but-huf-lee [x3], Haf-lee-ta-bat [x3], Yat-bot-ha-fal [x3], Tah-fa-lee-tub [x3] come through this celestial portal before me in peace profound as a friend and infuse me with the pure magic and spirit of the Sun. Fill me, through your aid with strong individuality, truthful inner expression, vitality, will, ambition, authority, health, generosity, dignity and understanding of men. Let me be a vessel for noblest expression of your spirit and power, O Kawkab al-Shames."

STEP EIGHT: Close the Magus Gate.

 MARS MAGIC

TAHATEEL NAMES OF MARS

Inner Power Names	Inner Power Names (Arabic)	Astrological Names	Astrological Names (Arabic)
Qah-tee-teel	قهطيطيل	Lee-tee-ta-haq	ليطيطهق
Teel-qah-tee	طيلقهطي	Yot-hah-qleet	هطههقليط
Ha-tee-tee-loq	هطيطيلق	Qa-lee-tee-tah	قليطهطه
Yal-qah-teet	يلقهطيط	Teet-haq-lee	طيطهقلي
Tee-teel-qah	طيطيلقه	Haq-lee-teet	هقليطيط
Laq-hah-tee-tee	لقههطيطي	Ya-teet-ha-qul	يطيطهقل
Ya-teel-qa-hot	يطيلقهط	Tah-qa-lee-tee	طهقليطه

MARTIAN TABLET OF THE GREAT NAME

On a piece of wood paint the following magic square in deep red upon an emerald-green background. You can use this tablet by placing it before you while you recite the conjuration of Mars.

ᛃ	☆	Ꮙ	ᱛ	ᛁᛁᛁᛁ	⚹	ᚁ
ᚁ	ᛃ	☆	Ꮙ	ᱛ	ᛁᛁᛁᛁ	⚹
⚹	ᚁ	ᛃ	☆	Ꮙ	ᱛ	ᛁᛁᛁᛁ
ᛁᛁᛁᛁ	⚹	ᚁ	ᛃ	☆	Ꮙ	ᱛ
ᱛ	ᛁᛁᛁᛁ	⚹	ᚁ	ᛃ	☆	Ꮙ
Ꮙ	ᱛ	ᛁᛁᛁᛁ	⚹	ᚁ	ᛃ	☆
☆	Ꮙ	ᱛ	ᛁᛁᛁᛁ	⚹	ᚁ	ᛃ

PLANETARY TIMING

Mars has Tuesday from sunrise to sunset and Friday from sunset to the next sunrise.

SCRIPT OF MARS

𝄢	𝄢	⚓	𝄢	𝄢	𝄢	𝄢
ز	و	ه	د	ج	ب	ا
𝄢	𝄢	𝄢	𝄢	𝄢	𝄢	𝄢
ن	م	ل	ك	ي	ط	ح
𝄢	𝄢	𝄢	𝄢	𝄢	𝄢	𝄢
ش	ر	ق	ص	ف	ع	س
𝄢	𝄢	𝄢	𝄢	𝄢	𝄢	𝄢
غ	ظ	ض	ذ	خ	ث	ت

MAGIC SQUARE OF MARS

The Martian magic square of 5x5 is purported to be good for an increase in discipline and for protecting children from maladies. It is believed to help improve their character and to assist them in areas of knowledge and manners. For that effect, this magic square should be written when Venus is in the 27th degree of Pisces, with the Moon being in the same degree. The ink used in the writing is made from musk and saffron. The writing is done on a sheet of edible rice paper or placed on a scroll and then washed off. The child should then eat the paper or drink the washed out ink. It is also beneficial for an individual who is seeking to strengthen a relationship. For this purpose, when the sun is in Aries and the moon is in Cancer, write the square on an edible or washable surface; then give it to your lover to consume. Due to its Martian attributes, it has also been used to gain victory during conflicts. For this purpose, etch it on a Tuesday in the hour of Mars. Make sure that Mars is in good aspect and rising near the ascendant. Incense it with Frankincense and Blue Mukul and then place the square in a piece of red fabric and tie it around your arm. It will help you to be victorious in any conflict.

𝄢	𝄢	𝄢	𝄢	𝄢
𝄢	𝄢	𝄢	𝄢	𝄢
𝄢	𝄢	𝄢	𝄢	𝄢
𝄢	𝄢	𝄢	𝄢	𝄢
𝄢	𝄢	𝄢	𝄢	𝄢

262

PYRAMID OF MARS

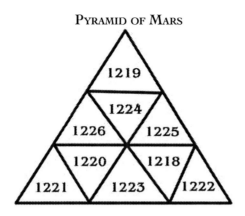

MARTIAN CONJURATION ON TUESDAY

The purpose and requirements for this conjuration have been covered under the Lunar conjuration.

STEP ONE: Begin with the purifying and consecration of your working space. Close your eyes and take a very deep breath inward, then exhale forcefully. Feel the stress leaving your body. Allow your breathing to increase, sensing yourself filled with vigor and energy. Take a few minutes to perform the four fold or eight-fold breath. Take the time to meditate on the Divine that is present in all the galaxies, stars, planets, and universes.

STEP TWO: Perform the basic opening of the Magus Gate.

STEP THREE: Exhale into the pentagram the name Semsamiel seven times then say, "**Aid me, O archangel Semsamiel [x3], peace be upon you, with your protection and by opening the gateway between me and the realm of spirits of Mars through the portal of spirit.**"

STEP FIVE: Pointing toward the portal, say, "**In the Holy Divine Name, Motdar Chaqlas A'amaa'a Lakma Al-lan Mossri Yahh-chah [x3] move, O spirits of Light, and open the gateway between me and the world of the spirits of Mars, Rouhaniat Kawkab al-Merrikh.**"

STEP SIX: Recite the Sabian prayer.

STEP SEVEN: Recite the weekly conjuration of Mars. Say, "O ye celestial chariot of Nergal called Si-mu-ud, Salbatanu, Maadim, Merrikh, Bahram, Ares, Mars and by many other names, I call upon your rays and spirit to descend upon me. Envelop me with a cloak of your light, in the blessed names of Qah-tee-teel [x3], Teel-qah-tee [x3], Ha-tee-tee-loq [x3], Yal-qah-teet [x3], Tee-teel-qah [x3], Laq-hah-tee-tee [x3], Ya-teel-qa-hot [x3]. O Maadim, O Mars, fill me with the power of your sphere and aid me with the spirits of your orbit, by the mighty and sacred names Lee-tee-ta-haq [x3], Yot-hah-qleet [x3], Qa-lee-tee-tah [x3], Teet-haq-lee [x3], Haq-lee-teet [x3], Ya-teet-ha-qul [x3], Tah-qa-lee-tee [x3]. O Rouhaniat Kawkab al-Merrikh, by the permission of the Queen of Heaven and Earth, and authority of the archangel Ruqiel, and the blessed names Qah-tee-teel [x3], Teel-qah-tee [x3], Ha-tee-tee-loq [x3], Yal-qah-teet [x3], Tee-teel-qah [x3], Laq-hah-tee-tee [x3], Ya-teel-qa-hot [x3], Lee-tee-ta-haq [x3], Yot-hah-qleet [x3], Qa-lee-tee-tah [x3], Teet-haq-lee [x3], Haq-lee-teet [x3], Ya-teet-ha-qul [x3], Tah-qa-lee-tee [x3] come through this celestial portal before me in peace profound as a friend and infuse me with the pure magic and spirit of Mars. Fill me, through your aid with dynamic energy, constructiveness, courage, enterprising spirit, enthusiasm and bravery. Let me be a vessel for noblest expression of your spirit and power, O Merrikh."

STEP EIGHT: Close the Magus Gate.

 JUPITER MAGIC

TAHATEEL NAMES OF JUPITER

Inner Power Names	Inner Power Names (Arabic)	Astrological Names	Astrological Names (Arabic)
Mah-tah-teel	مهطهطيل	Lee-tah-ta-hum	ليطهطهم
Teel-mah-tah	طيلمهطه	Hat-hum-leet	هطهمليط
Hat-ha-tee-lem	هطهطيلم	Ma-lee-tah-ta-ha	مليطهطه
Ya-lem-hot-hot	يلمهطهط	Tah-tah-ma-lee	طهطهملي
Tah-teel-mah	طهطيلمه	Ha-ma-lee-ta-hut	همليطهط
La-mah-tah-tee	لمهطهطي	Yah-tah-tah-mal	يطهطهمل
Hah-teel-mah-hot	هطيلمهط	Tah-ma-lee-tah	طهمليطه

JOVIAN TABLET OF THE GREAT NAME

⚡	٢	Ⅲ	☆	𝇍	૭	‖‖
‖‖	⚡	٢	Ⅲ	☆	𝇍	૭
૭	‖‖	⚡	٢	Ⅲ	☆	𝇍
𝇍	૭	‖‖	⚡	٢	Ⅲ	☆
☆	𝇍	૭	‖‖	⚡	٢	Ⅲ
Ⅲ	☆	𝇍	૭	‖‖	⚡	٢
٢	Ⅲ	☆	𝇍	૭	‖‖	⚡

On a piece of wood paint the following magic square in blue upon an orange background. You can use this tablet by placing it before you while you recite the conjuration of Jupiter.

PLANETARY TIMING
Jupiter has Thursday from sunrise to sunset and Sunday from sunset to the next sunrise.

SCRIPT OF JUPITER

ز	و	ه	د	ج	ب	ا
ن	م	ل	ك	ي	ط	ح
ش	ر	ق	ص	ف	ع	س
غ	ظ	ض	ذ	خ	ث	ت

MAGIC SQUARE OF JUPITER

The Jovian 4x4 magic square is beneficial against misfortune in wealth, for protecting property and for safeguarding children from evil. If you want to protect your property, write this square when the Sun is in the 29th degree of Aries. If you want a general protection for children, then write the square when the moon is in Taurus. It is also a ward against evil spirits. If you want to ward someone, write the square when Venus is in the 29th degree of Pisces and place it under the thigh of the individual. It is beneficial for entering into the presence of and seeking favours from community elders and kings, and for victory against enemies. It is also beneficial for acquiring the general love of people and for the maintenance of love. For this purpose, etch it on a ring made of red copper and draw it on a scroll when the moon is conjunct with Venus in the 15th degree of Libra or the 5th degree of Sagittarius. If you carry the scroll with you, those that see you will be attracted to you. If you run into difficulty with income, keep it in your pocket for prosperity, increase of status and protection against peoples' ill will. If you place it with some money or on a business' premises, it will increase and multiply. For general benefits, when the Sun reaches the 19th degree of Aries and the moon is in the 4th degree of Taurus, draw the square upon an amulet made from gold and jasmine or upon a paper. Generally, it is best done when the moon is waxing and well aspected.

PYRAMID OF JUPITER

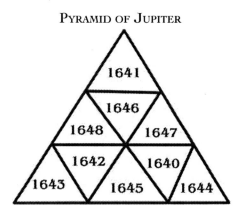

JOVIAN CONJURATION ON THURSDAY

The purpose and requirements for this conjuration have been covered under the Lunar conjuration.

STEP ONE: Begin with the purifying and consecration of your working space. Close your eyes and take a very deep breath inward, then exhale forcefully. Feel the stress leaving your body. Allow your breathing to increase, sensing yourself filled with vigor and energy. Take a few minutes to perform the four fold or eight-fold breath. Take the time to meditate on the Divine that is present in all the galaxies, stars, planets, and universes.

STEP TWO: Perform the basic opening of the Magus Gate.

STEP THREE: Exhale into the pentagram the name Sarfiel seven times then say, "**Aid me, O archangel Sarfiel [x3], peace be upon you, with your protection and by opening the gateway between me and the realm of spirits of Jupiter through the portal of spirit.**"

STEP FIVE: Pointing toward the portal, say, "**In the Holy Divine Name, Motdarach Qalsa'am A-a'alakem A-al-lan Moss-sheet Hharmee [x3] move, O spirits of Light, and open the gateway between me and the world of the spirits of Mars, Rouhaniat Kawkab al-Moshtari.**"

STEP SIX: Recite the Sabian prayer.

STEP SEVEN: Recite the weekly conjuration of Jupiter. Say, "O ye celestial chariot of Bel Marduk called Mul-sag-me-gar, Neberu, Tzedek, Moshtari, Zeus, Jupiter and by many other names, I call upon your rays and spirit to descend upon me. Envelop me with a cloak of your light, in the blessed names of Mah-tah-teel [x3], Teel-mah-tah [x3], Hat-ha-tee-lem [x3], Ya-lem-hot-hot [x3], Tah-teel-mah [x3], La-mah-tah-tee [x3], Hah-teel-mah-hot [x3]. O Tzedek, O Jupiter, fill me with the power of your sphere and aid me with the spirits of your orbit, by the mighty and sacred names Lee-tah-ta-hum [x3], Hat-hum-leet [x3], Ma-lee-tah-ta-ha [x3], Tah-tah-ma-lee [x3], Ha-ma-lee-ta-hut [x3], Yah-tah-tah-mal [x3], Tah-ma-lee-tah [x3]. O Rouhaniat Kawkab al-Moshtari, by the permission of the Queen of Heaven and Earth, and authority of the archangel Sarfiel, and the blessed names Mah-tah-teel [x3], Teel-mah-tah [x3], Hat-ha-tee-lem [x3], Ya-lem-hot-hot [x3], Tah-teel-mah [x3], La-mah-tah-tee [x3], Hah-teel-mah-hot [x3], Lee-tah-ta-hum [x3], Hat-hum-leet [x3], Ma-lee-tah-ta-ha [x3], Tah-tah-ma-lee [x3], Ha-ma-lee-ta-hut [x3], Yah-tah-tah-mal [x3], Tah-ma-lee-tah [x3] come through this celestial portal before me in peace profound as a friend and infuse me with the pure magic and spirit of Jupiter. Fill me, through your aid with benevolence, broad-mindedness, executive ability, spiritual righteousness, honor, charity, reverence, opulence, popularity and success. Let me be a vessel for noblest expression of your spirit and power, O Moshtari."

STEP EIGHT: Close the Magus Gate.

❂ SATURN MAGIC ❂

TAHATEEL NAMES OF SATURN

Inner Power Names	Inner Power Names (Arabic)	Astrological Names	Astrological Names (Arabic)
Lel-tah-teel	للطهطيل	Lee-tah-tal-el	ليطهطلل
Teel-lal-tah	طللللطيه	Ha-tel-la-leet	هطللليط
La-tah-tee-lel	لطهطيلل	La-lee-tah-tal	لليطهطل
Yal-lal--ta-hat	يللللطهط	Ta-hat-la-la-lee	طهللللي
Tah-tee-la-lal	طههطيلل	Lal-lee-ta-hat	للهيطهط
Lal-la-tah-tee	لللطهطي	Ya-tah-tal-lal	يطللطهل
Ha-tee-lala-lat	هطيلللط	Ta-lal-lee-tah	طللليطه

SATURNIAN TABLET OF THE GREAT NAME

On a piece of wood paint the following magic square in black upon a white background. You can use this tablet by placing it before you while you recite the conjuration of Saturn.

PLANETARY TIMING

Saturn has Saturday from sunrise to sunset and Tuesday from sunset to the next sunrise.

SCRIPT OF SATURN

ز	و	ه	د	ج	ب	ا
ن	م	ل	ك	ي	ط	ح
ش	ر	ق	ص	ف	ع	س
غ	ظ	ض	ذ	خ	ث	ت

Magic Square of Saturn

The 3x3 is probably one of the most important of these magic squares in the ancient magical tradition, as explained in the previous chapter. Imam Al-Ghazzali, a famous medieval Islamic philosopher, wrote a book on the qualities and mysteries of this square. His discourse on the subject was so influential, it became known as the Al-Ghazzali square. Naturally, it is much older than him and has appeared in the work of prominent occult masters, such as Al-Boni, and in Chinese and Indian texts prior. The Saturnian 3x3 square has both protective and destructive qualities. It was also believed to help women in difficult labor. One method given by the ancients was to write the square on two pieces of ceramic pottery, and place each under one of a laboring woman's feet. When placed among the belongings or worn, the square is also useful for protection against thieves. To construct it for this purpose, write it on a scroll, when the Sun is in the 12th degree of Aries or when it is in the 3rd degree of Taurus, with the Moon well aspected to it.

The magic square is also excellent for protection against the evil eye. Above the magic square, place the name of Qashemkus in magical script:

𐤎𐤟𐤟𐤟𐤟𐤟𐤟

Below the magic square, place the name of Kashrich in magical script:

𐤟𐤟𐤟𐤟𐤟

On the right of the magic square, place the name of Anukh in magical script:

𐤟𐤟𐤟𐤟

On the left of the magic square, place the name of Abba Nuch in magical script:

𐤟𐤟𐤟𐤟𐤟𐤟

Next, write the conjuration around the talisman. Once you are done, enter into a place where no one sees you. Light a candle, and burn some incense. Recite the conjuration over the evil eye amulet multiple times, until you feel confident that it has been charged. Now, wear it upon your person, or you can roll it up with a blue bead or similar jewelry and put it around your neck as a necklace. This is one example of many of the versatility of the magical application of such scripts. This is the accompanying magical conjuration to remove the evil eye: **"I conjure you by Qashemkus, Qashemkus, Qashemkus, Kashrich, Kashrich, Kashrich, Anukh, Anukh, Anukh, descend O Abba Nuch, Abba Nuch, Abba Nuch, and remove the eye and the sight from the carrier of this talisman. O every eye that contemplates N. with strange harm, swirl, you swirl, keep looking, do you see any flaw? Then look again and again; your eyes will come back stumped and conquered. There is no will and power, except by the Divine One, the Exalted and Majestic."**

PYRAMID OF SATURN

CONJURATION OF SATURN

The purpose and requirements for this conjuration have been covered under the Lunar conjuration.

STEP ONE: Begin with the purifying and consecration of your working space. Close your eyes and take a very deep breath inward, then exhale forcefully. Feel the stress leaving your body. Allow your breathing to increase, sensing yourself filled with vigor and energy. Take a few minutes to perform the four fold or eight-fold breath. Take the time to meditate on the Divine that is present in all the galaxies, stars, planets, and universes.

STEP TWO: Perform the basic opening of the Magus Gate.

STEP THREE: Exhale into the pentagram the name Kasfiel seven times then say, "**Aid me, O archangel Kasfiel [x3], peace be upon you, with your protection and by opening the gateway between me and the realm of spirits of Saturn through the portal of spirit.**"

STEP FIVE: Pointing toward the portal, say, "**In the Holy Divine Name, Motdar Chaqlas A'amaa'a Lakma Al-lan Lossmi Dahh-chah [x3] move, O spirits of Light, and open the gateway between me and the world of the spirits of Saturn, Rouhaniat Kawkab Zuhal.**"

STEP SIX: Recite the Sabian prayer.

STEP SEVEN: Recite the weekly conjuration of Saturn. Say, "**By the supervisor of the celestial sovereigns, O ye celestial chariot of Nin-**

urta called Udu-idim-sag-us, Kayamanu, Shabbathai, Kevan, Zu-hal, Kronos, Saturn and by many other names, I call upon your rays and spirit to descend upon me. Envelop me with a cloak of your light, in the blessed names of Lele-tah-teel [x3], Teel-la-lel-tah [x3], La-tah-tee-lel [x3], Yal-lal--ta-hat [x3], Tah-tee-la-lal [x3], Lal-la-tah-tee [x3], Ha-tee-lala-lat [x3]. O Shabbathai, O Saturn, fill me with the power of your sphere and aid me with the spirits of your orbit, by the mighty and sacred names Lee-tah-tal-el [x3], Ha-tel-la-leet [x3], La-lee-tah-tal [x3], Ta-hat-la-la-lee [x3], La-la-lee-ta-hat [x3], Ya-tah-tal-lal [x3], Ta-lal-lee-tah [x3]. O Rouhaniat Kawkab Zuhal, by the permission of the Queen of Heaven and Earth, and authority of the archangel Kasfiel, and the blessed names Lele-tah-teel [x3], Teel-la-lel-tah [x3], La-tah-tee-lel [x3], Yal-lal--ta-hat [x3], Tah-tee-la-lal [x3], Lal-la-tah-tee [x3], Ha-tee-lala-lat [x3], Lee-tah-tal-el [x3], Ha-tel-la-leet [x3], La-lee-tah-tal [x3], Ta-hat-la-la-lee [x3], La-la-lee-ta-hat [x3], Ya-tah-tal-lal [x3], Ta-lal-lee-tah [x3] come through this celestial portal before me in peace profound as a friend and infuse me with the pure magic and spirit of the Sun. Fill me, through your aid with faithfulness, stability, concentration, constructive qualities, tact, diplomacy, justice, prudence, deliberation, endurance and discipline. Let me be a vessel for noblest expression of your spirit and power, O Zuhal."

STEP EIGHT: Close the Magus Gate.

Continuing to apply the planetary conjurations on a daily basis for seven months will see your life and personality grow and develop in amazing ways. You will look back at this experience with astonishment. The changes will be slow and gradual, but they will be cumulative and long lasting. This journey will prepare you for future in-depth planetary magic. You can chose to specialize in this aspect of the art by following the extended initiatory procedures of the ancient Chaldeans and Sabians as detailed in some of Nabatean occult books. These planetary initiations require strong dedication and can take more than ten years to fully complete, but the results are said to be nothing short of astounding. As far as we know, they haven't been attempted in more than five hundred years. Might you be the first to do so? Whatever choice you make in this regard, if you just apply the materials in this chapter regularly, you will be walking a path of brilliance that is little trodden.

This is a focal point in your magical development program as laid out through this book. It is time to take it to the next level. This level can only reached by initiation. Magical initiation isn't easy to come by, since few groups do it any more. In the next chapter, we will provide you with a potent tool for solitary initiation that will work as an effective temporary substitute. Its success depends on purity of heart and on your efforts so far. Inexperienced occultists may find it a challenge to get any real substance from it, but you should be able to experience a profound magical change after performing it. We recommend you take this next magical gem and preform it as often as you can and let it be the fire of your magical transformation.

Works Referenced

al-Ghalani, Mohammed (D. 1740 C.E.), *al-Der al-Mantzoom wa Khilasat al-Sir al-Maktoom fi Al-Sihr wa al-Talasem wa al-Nojoom*. al-Maktaba al-Tahqafia, Beirut, Lebanon: 1992.

al-Marzooqi, Ali Abu Hai Allah, *al-Jawaher al-Lama'a fi Isthadhar Muluk al-Jinn fi al-Waqet wa al-Sa'a*. Maktabat Iqbal Haj Ibrahim. Siragh Bantan: 1962.

al-Toukhi, A'adu al-Fatah. *al-Siher al-Azeem (v1-3)*. al-Maktabah al-Thaqafiah. Beirut:1991

al-Buni, Ahmed (D. 1225). *Manba'a Ussol al-Hikmah*. Maktabat al-Hidayah. Surabaya, Indonesia.

9

Magical Initiation

agical initiations are tied in intimately with ancient celebrations and mystery rites. Very little is known about the ancient rites of magical initiations. In absence of concrete and detailed historical record, many organizations today design their own initiations. These can be simple or elaborate, but often they occur in group settings as theatrical psycho-drama full of esoteric symbolism. The ceremony is often divided into different stages that represent being invited *in* to the group after having undergone a journey of some kind. Many of the ceremonies recreate the process of death and rebirth or some other historical mystery or event, in a symbolic way. Many modern magical ceremonies owe much to the structure and initiations of Freemasonry.

Is there a reason that we should all aspire to such an experience? The answer will depend on you, but we can say that as magicians we want more than the process of playing out a symbolic passage from one stage to the next and the ceremonial act of being invited to the group or raised within its structure. When we think of magical rites of passage, we think of something truly magical or at least deeply spiritual. There is a drastic difference in our minds between someone walking us around an elaborate stage saying extended speeches and then tapping us on the shoulder as initiates, and going on a deep vision quest such as the First Nations do. Those kind of spiritual journeys in challenging circumstances are not only common to Shamans. There is a story of a magical initiation ceremony that occurs somewhere in either the Middle East or Africa. There is a cave that is known as cave of prophet Daniel, who was a chief of the Magi in Chaldea, or more often as cave of Harut and Marut, the two angels that taught magic in Babylon. This cave is sealed except for once a year. The candidates seeking initiation must first learn of its location. Some say it is in one of the mountains of Iraq and others give its place in North Africa. On this one given day, the cave door opens, and those seeking initiations approach at sunrise. They carry with them enough dried food for nine months. The nine months within the cave is equivalent to twelve normal months outside the cave. Time is known to flow differently inside the cave. They also bring with them magical talismans prepared beforehand. They enter the cave and the entrance is sealed behind them. Inside the cave is a spring for the candidates to drink from and there is a source of air. Near the entrance are pedestals upon which the candidates place the talismans. The candidates then begin performing the initiation ceremony and reciting the conjurations. Assuming the candidates can withstand the beings that appear and the manifestation that follow, they continue reciting for the next nine months. If a candidate fails, often insanity or death is known to follow. Upon the completion of the nine months, the nineteen levels of magical initiations have been completed. The candidates then readies the talismans and, drawing on everything learned and experienced, challenges the guardian of the entrance. If the candidates overcomes the guardian, the entrance is opened and the candidate leaves, allowing the next set of candidates in. If a candidate fails, then the candidate is trapped till death. Whether this is a real account or a mythical lore passed in magical circles of the Middle East, we can't say for sure. What is obvious is the underlying theme that magical initiations were challenging, life and death trials.

Why would someone want to do something like this? The short answer is because it is worth it to them. Those who were initiated lifted many veils that would take many years of their life to do, otherwise, and gained tremendous amounts of spiritual and magical insight and power. It is accelerated growth for those who felt ready for such a challenge. The idea that someone would risk their lives for magic seems odd to Western minds. But back then and in many cultures, even to this day in many Islamic countries, magic is considered a capital punishment crime. Being a magician entailed a threat to one's life. Even in Europe, witches were burnt during the inquisition, many falsely accused, but that didn't stop the real witches and magicians from continuing and even finding recruits. There is no room for fear in our art, it leads to failure and it is an enemy of love.

Naturally, we don't expect you to find this cave or to go through something similar, even though there are still stories to this day of those who have found it and undergone this initiation, or died trying. The important lesson to draw from this is that initiations are: a) a magical experience, b) require personal action from the seeker, c) challenging, d) can take more than a few hours of one's life to accomplish, and e) have a mechanism of failure to weed out those who are not ready. Each of the ancient cultures had its own version, but rarely any in which the candidate passively passed through the whole process experiencing nothing but drama, with guaranteed passage. The reason for this lay in the actual purpose of the magical initiation. Part of the initiation focused solely on testing the candidate's worthiness and on opening the aspirant to the magical currents and lifting the veil between the candidate and the spiritual world. In a modern version, the function of initiation remains the same. The process doesn't have to be drastic, but if it doesn't do those things at some level, the initiation lacks something or another.

Those who experience magical initiations should come out of them empowered, infused with the Sacred Light, and having had the veil between them and the inhabitants of the spiritual realms lifted. Upon successfully completing the process they should feel connected with the magical stream that has flowed from the beginning of time. We have ourselves seen many people walk out of magical initiations almost speechless and feeling as if they have been reborn as a child of Light. Many of them soon grow and expand in amazing ways, often spiritually, but sometimes also on a mundane earthly level. There are also those who fail the initiation trials and realize that this path isn't for them. That is also wonderful, as it frees them to go back on their search, instead of dabbling for years before coming to that conclusion.

From experience, we can say that magical initiations of any kind are amazing and intense and very spiritually important and transformative. Sadly, not everyone has the opportunity to undergo such remarkable initiations, primarily because very few groups offer true magical initiations. First, as we mentioned, many modern occult initiations are hybrids between esoteric plays and group ordinations, with the emphasis on the drama. Second, most candidates who want magical initiations still end up having to travel thousands of miles to undergo those rites and few can afford the expense. Third, gaining entry into them is a difficult process, as the candidate must prove him or herself ready for such a step through spiritual growth, development of skills in the magical lifestyle and extensive preparation. There is no easy solution to this dilemma; when the seeker is ready, she must be willing to make the jump, because it may be twenty years before such an opportunity is made available again.

As an alternate method, a number of groups began offering astral or distant initiations. If the purpose of initiation is the bringing a candidate into membership of a magical order or group or to initiate the candidate onto the tradition of that path, then it is really easy. As long as the group itself and you agree that a given process accomplishes this fact, you are initiated. This could be an elaborate play, a tap of the wand, or an astral play done while you are cooking dinner thousands of miles away. What is key is that you both agree to its effectiveness and accept its result. For any serious magician, such initiations are considered exoteric and not esoteric. They are social and not magical, even if the act itself is considered as such. Therefore, you need a process that produces magical change in you and in your connection with the spiritual world. This means that most of the onus of the initiation's success depends on you directly. You have to be involved through the whole process and in more than just intent. Intent is good, but you need to walk the talk or, in this case, the thought. Distant or astral initiations alone are not sufficient, as magical initiation requires the physical participation of the candidate to an extensive degree.

An alternate solution for someone who is solitary or unable to attend a given physical magical initiation would be a solitary initiation. Those initiations work by petitioning the Divine for the initiation to manifest. Magical initiations can be conducted in a solitary facet, with a higher degree of success if they are coupled with distant initiations. A distant initiation should be coordinated so that it is conducted at the same time as the candidate is conducting the solitary initiation rite. There needs to be a physical magical link between the candidate and the earthly initiators. Distant initiations coupled with solitary initiations are referred to as Spirit Initiations, due to their reliance on the Divine, angels, spirits and the cosmic magical currents that transcend physical limitations. They are not a replacement for direct group initiation, but an augmentation of that process. After the first Spirit Initiation, a solitary initiation can be done at any point, even after attending physical initiation, to reinforce the magical connection. It is best done once a month, for years to come, to keep the connection fully open.

In this chapter, we present the solitary initiation for those who wish something deep and empowering, but who may be beginners on the path. The ceremony focuses on empowerment of the Elements and entry into the magical current. Before beginning this initiation, the candidate should select a magical name that represents their highest spiritual aspiration, dedication, and power as a magician. This name should be kept confined to your magical environment, as it represents your spiritual identity in the magical realm. It is used in the solitary magical initiation as the name by which you are known before the spirits, instead of the name by which you are known among the people.

The initiation ritual has been divided into segments. Each segment is based on previous materials covered in the book and can be performed independently as the need arises. These segments have been combined to provide a comprehensive and cohesive formula. We recommend that you take each segment separately and practice it until you achieve a high stage of proficiency. Only then do we recommend that you combine all the separate elements into one setting and perform the rite of magical initiation. The complete rite may take between three to four hours to perform adequately. For many Westerners this may feel like lots of work, but keep in mind that some advanced magical initiations in group settings can take up to a week to complete. If you have done all the rites outlined previously, this initiation shouldn't be too daunting. Take your time with each step and don't feel rushed or pushed. You will find it manageable and doable once a month on a weekend or on one of your days off. For maximum effect, we recommend you repeat this process monthly for at least six months.

Each segment will be marked with a sub-header. Many parts of the rituals have been covered in earlier chapters in the book. We will make references to them without actually reproducing them. When you type the ritual up on your computer, make sure to replace the references with the actual procedures. Let's take a quick look at each segment, what it does and why it is there. The first segment is the opening prayer of dedication. This is a devotional ritual that primarily functions as a praise and adoration of the Holy One. It is also a ritual of thanks, reaffirmation and a greeting to the spirits of Light. The rite contains a Quranic chapter, the Opener. This chapter is a beautiful prayer with many esoteric layers that relate to the seven planets and the seven fold secret name. It is also used in Arabic occultism as a means of opening doors and lifting veils. The entire segment helps open you to spirit and allows you to shift your consciousness into a more mystical state. In essence, this rite opens you and your working area to the influx of Light.

The second segment is the purification and consecration of your space. This is done using symbols of the Elements and it helps raise the vibration of your surroundings. It also declares your working area as a sacred place for the rest of the operation. This purification assumes that you have already done the traditional self-preparation by undertaking the illumination wash, wearing clean clothing or ritual garb and so forth. The third segment is vital to the success of all magical rites. It involves the release of resident jinn that inhabit the place. The fourth segment is the Bane Breaker to remove any prior occult restraints that could hinder you from fully connecting to the currents. The fifth segment is the Shield of the Magi to protect you from any surprising intrusions. This completes the opening and basic preparation.

The sixth segment follows this basic preparation and opening of the rite. It begins with the invocation of the Supreme Being, in the facet of the Queen of Heaven and Earth. The Divine One is the source of initiations. So, we turn to the Creator of the Garden of Eden and the Source of Magic as our first step within the initiation. Unless this connection is built strong, it is doubtful that the rest of the rite will carry much weight.

The seventh segment involves opening the Elemental gateways. You will need all four portals for this ritual. This is important, since the principle of this initiation is to open you up to the currents of magic as it interplays through the five Elements, Spirit, Fire, Air, Water and Earth. Therefore, we open the portals to the Elemental worlds through the portal of Spirit, under the auspices of the Queen of Heaven and Earth. You will feel the connection with the spirits of each quarter as you move along. Doing this segment of the initiation alone, repeatedly, for many months will attune you strongly to the Elements.

The eighth segment is the calling up of your guardian angel. The ninth segment is the Solomonic invocation of Red Sulphur, also known as the Ancient Oath, which was covered earlier in the book. This is one of the most important and powerful of magical conjurations and by this stage should be very familiar to you. The recitation of it will awaken to you the presence of many beings at all different levels. It will gain their attention and it is up to you to earn their friendship and cooperation. Doing this ritual by itself, forty-nine times for forty-nine days, is an empowerment all on its own. It is also believed to be part of the cave initiation ceremony. During this initiation ritual, you should do it as many times as necessary to make you feel that you are simply not alone in your working area. You will sense, feel and even see many things around you that are not human or of this world. Get used to it, as you are a magician now.

The tenth segment is the empowerment part of the initiation procedure. It uses the Divine Name of the Elements, which we have introduced earlier as well. This is also the name that is said to have been used to bring the Throne of Sheba to Solomon. The chanting of the name will empower you on many levels and will transform your aura. You will not be the same person if you make a habit of putting this segment only to daily practice. Do not be surprised by your experiences or be afraid of the changes. You will develop and grow from them at an accelerated rate.

The eleventh segment is the conjuration of the sun. This conjuration is based on a more elaborate Arabic version, where you enlist the aid of all manner of spiritual beings to help you in all forms of magical workings. If the previous steps of this ritual have taken root, this is equivalent to receiving your charge. Become accustomed to working with and calling upon many of the beings mentioned in this conjuration, for they will assist you in all manner of workings mentioned in it. You may choose to make a point of reciting this conjuration daily for maximum benefit. Anyway, this is the point of receiving magical influxes, so take your time with it and enjoy it.

The twelfth segment follows the closing of the portals. This is a time to reaffirm your spiritual connection and your aspiration to the virtues. Now that we have discussed the segments, let's go through the actual rite.

PREPARATION AND TOOLS: You will need a magical robe or you can go sky clad. You will also need candles and incense. It is recommended that you have the four portals built and ready. If you can't have physical portals, then just use your imagination to create etheric pentagrams. Finally, you should be fasting from all animal products and by-products the day of the ceremony. Consider the time it will take you to complete this initiation and ensure that you have an empty room (remove all furniture) or a dedicated sacred space where you can do this ceremony. To ensure that there will be no interruptions, turn off the ringer or unplug your phone and put a 'do not disturb' sign on your door.

STEP ONE: Perform the illumination wash.

STEP TWO: Dress in your magical robe or go sky-clad and enter into your working space. Light the incense and candles. Face the direction of Sunrise or the Pole Star or any other sacred direction.

Opening Prayer of Dedication

Step Three: Raise your hands beside your ears, where the thumbs are near to or touching the ears. The palms are facing out. Vibrate out loud three times: "El Gedul."

Step Four: Hold your hands facing up before your chest like a cup. Repeat the following three times in English or Hebrew:

"In the name of God, most gracious, most merciful. (1)
Praise be to God, Lord of the Universe; (2)
most beneficent, most Merciful; (3)
Owner of the Day of Faith, (4)
Thee we worship; Thee we ask for help. (5)
Guide us on the straight path, (6)
The path of those whom Thou hast favoured; not of those who
earn Thine anger nor of those who go astray. (7) (Amen)"

"Beshem Ha-El Ha-Rachman Wa Ha-Rachum (1)
Ha-Shebach La-El Reebun Ha-Oulemym (2)
Ha-Rachman Wa Ha-Rachmun (3)
Rebun Yum Hae'muna (4)
Autcha Naavud U'Becha Ne'azer (5)
Hanchenu Shveel Meysharim (6)
Aurach Elah Shechnuth Authem Asher La Ha-Cherun Oleehem
Wa-La Men Ha-Shuetim. (7) (Amen)"

Step Five: Say: "Beshem Elat."

Step Six: Bend down so that your hands are touching your thighs. People with bad backs should only stretch as far as is possible for them. Say at this point: "**Halelu El Elyon.**" [x3]

Step Seven: Say: "**Beshem Elat,**" while standing back up to an upright position.

Step Eight: Say "**Beshem Elat,**" while prostrating yourself with your head on the ground. We recommend that you put most of the weight on your arms with your head slightly touching the floor. As with other steps, do what you can if you suffer from any health disabilities. Then say in multiples of three: "**Halelu-El Qadosh Adonoi Malachim Wa-Ruachim.**"

STEP NINE: Say: "**Beshem Elat**," while you sit up with your hands on the floor before you or on your knees. Say three times: "O Divine One, forgive my sins and aid me with magic from you."

STEP TEN: Say: "**Beshem Elat**," then prostrate yourself again with your head on the floor. Then say three times: "Halelu-El Qadosh Adonoi Malachim Wa-Ruachim."

STEP ELEVEN: Say: "**Beshem Elat**" and stand up again to full position. This counts as one full prostration cycle.

STEP TWELVE: Repeat Step 4 to Step 10 again.

STEP THIRTEEN: Say "**Beshem Elat**", while you sit up with your hands on the floor before you or on your knees. Say: "**O Light of Lights, Mystery of Mysteries, I thank You for all the blessings in my life. I thank You for opening my heart to Your love, and my mind to your occult mysteries. I thank you for placing my feet on this straight path to You via spiritual occultism and holy magic. O Holy of Holies! O El Chai! Strengthen me in my path and in my aspirations. I thank you for aiding me with celestial angels, spiritual spirits, and faithful jinn.**" (Add also if in a group gathering, "**and this company of the children of light**")

Turn your head to the right and say: "**Peace profound be upon you O celestial angels, spiritual spirits, and faithful jinn.**" (Add also if in a group gathering. "**and this company of the children of light.**")

Turn your head to the left and say: "**Peace profound be upon you, O celestial angels, spiritual spirits, and faithful jinn.**" (Add also if in a group gathering, "**and this company of the children of light**"). This step ends the second prostration cycle.

SACRED SPACE OPENING
STEP FOURTEEN: Purify and consecrate your working area with the four Elements.

STEP FIFTEEN: Perform the Bane Breaker ritual.

STEP SIXTEEN: Perform the Shield of the Magi.

STEP SEVENTEEN: Recite the prayer of the Queen of Heaven.

RITUAL OF ANCIENT OATH

STEP EIGHTEEN: Say: "In the name of the Divine One, the Ancient One, the Eternal One, the Encompasser who encompasses all the creatures with His knowledge; the Ancient One and Eternal One that has no beginning to His ancientness and has no end. He dawned all the universes with the radiance of the light of His face and emanated in them with the power of His awe upon every angel, constellation, jinn, shitan and ruler. He was feared by all of His creation, and the angels of closeness heeded and obeyed from their highest places and prostrated and answered the call of His great name to whom called by it. They quickly answered with the confirmation fastened and written in the tablets of the hearts of the users of the mystery of Baduh Ajhazat. I conjure you, O rouhaniah spirits from the above and below and ask the servants of this ancient oath to enable me to see and hear the jinn and to aid me with jinn rouhani khadem Baduh wa al-Malek al-Sadeq. Answer my conjuration and fulfil my need in the glory of Ber-hat-yah [x3], Ka-reer [x3], Tat-lee-yah [x3], Toh-ran [x3], Maz-jal [x3], Baz-jal [x3], Tahr-qab [x3], Bar-hash [x3], Ghal-mash [x3], Cho-teer [x3], Qal-in-hod [x3], Bar-shan [x3], Katz-heer [x3], Namoh Shelech [x3], Berhayola [x3], Bash-kee-lach [x3], Qaz Maz [x3], An-ghala-leet [x3], Qa-ba-rat [x3], Gha-ya-ha [x3], Kayed-ho-la [x3], Shem-cha-her [x3], Shem-cha-heer [x3], Shem-ha-heer [x3], Bak-hat-hon-yah [x3], Ba-sha-resh [x3], To-nesh [x3], Shem-cha Ba-roch [x3]. O Rouhaniah al-Nuraniah, come and aid me in this rite of magical passage by infusing me with that holy emanation from the Divine Presence." [x3]

EMPOWERMENT OF THE SACRED NAMES

STEP NINETEEN: Recite the following chant of empowerment one thousand, one hundred, and eleven times: "Ashiaaloh Alyahoshin Wa-anwashaal Tattayloosh Nahtooshaal."

STEP TWENTY: Recite the following prayer three times: "Elat, I ask you, by the sanctity of Your being and the generosity of Your attributes, by the majesty of Your name, by the light of Your face, by the expanse of Your bounteousness, by the enforceability of Your decrees and by the fulfilment of Your promise, to make available to me the Rouhaniah of this noble name. I ask you to initiate my spirit and soul into the mysteries of the magic of Light. May the Rouhaniah aid me in the fulfilment of this initiation into

Your mysteries, O Lady of the Universe."

STEP TWENTY-ONE: Chant the Divine name over the Elements and the Key of the Mysteries: "**Aham Saqak Hhala'a Yass Toren.**" [x1111]

After every hundred, say the following: "O Holy of Holies, I ask of you a spiritual emanation that strengthens the total and partial powers of my soul. Lift the veil that separates me from the Cosmic Pole, the Divine Throne, the Emerald Chair, the Cosmic Tablet, the Pen of Creation, the Pad, the Divinity, the Power and the Light. I ask you to open for me the doors of magic by the mystery of Your greatest of names, that you love and to which you answer, Aham Saqak Hhala'a Yass Toren.

Initiate me into the mysteries of the magic of Light. Let me be reborn as a magician in Your name. I ask You by that with which You have endowed Melechi Tzedeq and the Master Metatron from Your power and Light. Adorn me from the same mysteries with whatever my spirit can contain. I swear before You, and let be my witness all the beings of lights and the spirits of all the magi of old, that I will follow the path of the magic of Light to the day that I shall return unto Thee.

While I walk this earth, let my eyes behold through Your eyes. Let my tongue speak Your truth. Let my heart feel Your love for Your creation. Let my hands labor in the works of Your transformation. Let my feet walk the path of holiness. I surrender unto You what You have given unto me from the senses so that I may be reborn by You as a magician of the white, a servant of the Queen of Heaven and Earth. Send unto me Your servants to aid me in all my works of magic and teach me the Divine arts, so that by them I can do the work of Light." [x3]

ELEMENTAL PORTALS AND INITIATION:
STEP TWENTY-TWO: Perform the opening of the Magus Gate.

STEP TWENTY-THREE: Move toward the East Portal and open the Fire Gateway. Proclaim before all the spirits that reside on the other side: "Blessed be Your name O limitless Light, Ilah al-Nar wa Ilahat al-Nar, who are the King and Queen of the Universe, and from whose paradise flows the river of Fire throughout Your creation. Grant unto me who is known among the people as ___N___ and before your spirits as ___N___, yet in truth I am naught but Your

Light made manifest, the power and help of the Great Archangel Ghassdaiel that he may command unto my assistance the Rouhaniat al-Nar, that working through them, I may cause to appear visibly and physically into my spiritual and physical form the Rouhaniat al-Nar.

By the power and brilliance of Elat, I call you O mighty and powerful Mala'ikat al-Nar, under the command of Ghassdaiel, who prepares the way for you, to send a ray of the spiritual essence and magical force of the Element of Fire into my spiritual body. In the name of Gerra and Ishum, command O angels the Rouhaniat of al-Nar to speedily come through this gateway and initiate me into the currents of Ash. O Armin Yazad, manifest the current, light, force and power of the Element of Fire in me in a physical form and teach me the great magic of Light and that of the Element of Fire.

I stand here before the Gateway of Anu to the realm of Fire, in the presence of Elohim Ha-Ruach, and declare that I submit myself for initiation unto the currents of Fire and that I hold your gift unto me in greatest of trust to be used under the guidance and auspices of the Queen of Heaven and in service of the Divine Light. I invoke and charge you, that even as within these currents is concealed the knowledge of the magic of Light, so shall you pass from concealment unto manifestation visibly in my spiritual body and fill it with the currents of Fire. Aham Saqak Hala'a Yass, thou secret of secrets in the vast kingdom of Fire, grant unto me the presence and power of the Rouhaniat al-Nar. O Rouhaniat al-Nar bestow upon me the spiritual power whereof ye are masters in the element of Fire, that I may evoke unto visible appearance in my life the power and force of Fire. Let the light and wisdom of the Divine One descend upon my head and through this initiation manifest unto me the perfect purity and the unsullied vision of the mysteries of the magic of Fire, so that by its assistance I may ever pursue the sacred mysteries in the pathway of Light and thus be better able to aid your beloved children.

O ye Ancient Masters of the Magic of Light, who reside in the Holy Kingdom, which is the throne of the Queen of Heaven, ye Spirits of Life who preside over the souls in the cosmic hall of rebirth before Anu, give me your aid and empower me with your tremendous magical power. Breathe into my spirit the power and might irresistible to compel the Rouhaniat of al-Nar to manifest through me and unto me, that I may be a living channel for the magic of sacred Fire. Initiate me into the current of sacred Fire, for thou art the ancient initiators of magic."

STEP TWENTY-FOUR: Move toward the South Portal and open the Air gateway. Proclaim before all the spirits that reside on the other side: "Blessed be Your name O limitless Light, Ilah al-Hawa' wa Ilahat al-Hawa', who are the King and Queen of the Universe, and from whose paradise flows the river of Air throughout Your creation. Grant unto me who is known among the people as ___N___ and before your spirits as ___N___, yet in truth I am naught but Your Light made manifest, the power and help of the Great Archangel Gathssaiel that he may command unto my assistance the Rouhaniat al-Hawa', that working through them, I may cause to appear visibly and physically into my spiritual and physical form the Rouhaniat al-Hawa'.

By the power and brilliance of Elat, I call you O mighty and powerful Mala'ikat al-Hawa', under the command of Gathssaiel, who prepares the way for you, to send a ray of the spiritual essence and magical force of the Element of Air into my spiritual body. In the name of Enlil, command O angels the Rouhaniat al-Hawa' to speedily come through this gateway and initiate me into the currents of Air. O Armin Yazad, manifest the current, light, force and power of the Element of Air in me in a physical form and teach me the great magic of Light and that of the Element of Air.

I stand here before the Gateway of Anu to the realm of Air, in the presence of Elohim Ha-Ruach, and declare that I submit myself for initiation unto the currents of Air and that I hold your gift unto me in greatest of trust to be used under the guidance and auspices of the Queen of Heaven and in service of the Divine Light. I invoke and charge you, that even as within these currents is concealed the knowledge of the magic of Light, so shall you pass from concealment unto manifestation visibly in my spiritual body and fill it with the currents of Air. Aham Saqak Hala'a Yass, thou secret of secrets in the vast kingdom of Air, grant unto me the presence and power of the Rouhaniat al-Hawa'. O Rouhaniat al-Hawa', bestow upon me the spiritual power whereof ye are masters in the element of Air, that I may evoke unto visible appearance in my life the power and force of Air. Let the light and wisdom of the Divine One descend upon my head and through this initiation manifest unto me the perfect purity and the unsullied vision of the mysteries of the magic of Air, so that by its assistance I may ever pursue the sacred mysteries in the pathway of Light and thus be better able to aid your beloved children.

O ye Ancient Masters of the Magic of Light, who reside in the Holy Kingdom, which is the throne of the Queen of Heaven, ye Spirits of Life who preside over the souls in the cosmic hall of rebirth before Anu, give me your aid and empower me with your tremendous magical power. Breathe into my spirit the power and might irresistible to compel the Rouhaniat al-Hawa' to manifest through me and unto me, that I may be a living channel for the magic of Air. Initiate me into the current of Air, for thou art the ancient initiators of magic."

STEP TWENTY-FIVE: Move toward the West Portal and open the Water gateway. Proclaim before all the spirits that reside on the other side: "Blessed be Your name O limitless Light, Ilah al-Ma' wa Ilahat al-Ma', who are the King and Queen of the Universe, and from whose paradise flows the river of al-Ma' throughout Your creation. Grant unto me who is known among the people as ____N____ and before your spirits as ____N___, yet in truth I am naught but Your Light made manifest, the power and help of the Great Archangel Ghadha'aaiel that he may command unto my assistance the Rouhaniat al-Ma', that working through them, I may cause to appear visibly and physically into my spiritual and physical form the Rouhaniat al-Ma'.

By the power and brilliance of Elat, I call you O mighty and powerful Mala'ikat al-Ma', under the command of Ghadha'aaiel, who prepares the way for you, to send a ray of the spiritual essence and magical force of the Element of Water into my spiritual body. In the names of Nammu and Ea, command O angels the Rouhaniat al-Ma' to speedily come through this gateway and initiate me into the currents of Water. O Armin Yazad, manifest the current, light, force and power of the Element of Water in me in a physical form and teach me the great magic of Light and that of the Element of Water.

I stand here before the Gateway of Anu to the realm of Water, in the presence of Bari al-Rouh, and declare that I submit myself for initiation unto the currents of Water and that I hold your gift unto me in greatest of trust to be used under the guidance and auspices of the Queen of Heaven and in service of the Divine Light. I invoke and charge you, that even as within these currents is concealed the knowledge of the magic of Light, so shall you pass from concealment unto manifestation visibly in my spiritual body and fill it with the currents of Water. Aham Saqak Hala'a Yass, thou secret of secrets in the vast kingdom of Water, grant unto me the presence and power of the Rouhaniat al-Ma'. O Rouhaniat al-Ma' bestow upon me the spiritual power whereof ye are masters in the element of Water, that I may evoke unto visible appearance in my life the power and force of Water. Let the light and wisdom of the Divine One descend upon my head and through this initiation manifest unto me the perfect purity and the unsullied vision of the mysteries of the magic of Mayim, so that by its assistance I may ever pursue the sacred mysteries in the pathway of Light and thus be better able to aid your beloved children.

O ye Ancient Masters of the Magic of Light, who reside in the Holy Kingdom, which is the throne of the Queen of Heaven, ye Spirits of Life who preside over the souls in the cosmic hall of rebirth before Anu, give me your aid and empower me with your tremendous magical power. Breathe into my spirit the power and might irresistible to compel the Rouhaniat al-Ma' to manifest through me and unto me, that I maybe a living channel for the magic of Water. Initiate me into the current of Water, for thou art the ancient initiators of magic."

STEP TWENTY-SIX: Move toward the North Portal and open the Earth gateway. Proclaim before all the spirits that reside on the other side: "Blessed be Your name O limitless Light, Ilah al-Turab wa Ilahat al-Turab, who are the King and Queen of the Universe, and from whose paradise flows the river of Earth throughout Your creation. Grant unto me who is known among the people as ___N___ and before your spirits as ___N___, yet in truth I am naught but Your Light made manifest, the power and help of the Great Archangel Ghasheezaiel that he may command unto my assistance the Rouhaniat al-Turab, that working through them, I may cause to appear visibly and physically into my spiritual and physical form the Rouhaniat al-Turab.

By the power and brilliance of Elat, I call you O mighty and powerful Mala'ikat al-Turab, under the command of Ghasheezaiel, who prepares the way for you, to send a ray of the spiritual essence and magical force of the Element of Earth into my spiritual body. In the name of Enkido, command O angels the Rouhaniat al-Turab to speedily come through this gateway and initiate me into the currents of Earth. O Armin Yazad, manifest the current, light, force and power of the Element of Earth in me in a physical form and teach me the great magic of Light and that of the Element of Earth.

I stand here before the Gateway of Anu to the realm of Earth, in the presence of Elohim Ha-Ruach, and declare that I submit myself for initiation unto the currents of Earth and that I hold your gift unto me in greatest of trust to be used under the guidance and auspices of the Queen of Heaven and in service of the Divine Light. I invoke and charge you, that even as within these currents is concealed the knowledge of the magic of Light, so shall you pass from concealment unto manifestation visibly in my spiritual body and fill it with the currents of Earth. Aham Saqak Hala'a Yass, thou secret of secrets in the vast kingdom of Earth, grant unto me the presence and power of the Rouhaniat al-Turab. O Rouhaniat al-Turab bestow upon me the spiritual power whereof ye are masters in the element of Earth, that I may evoke unto visible appearance in my life the power and force of Earth. Let the light and wisdom of the Divine One descend upon my head and through this initiation manifest unto me the perfect purity and the unsullied vision of the mysteries of the magic of Earth, so that by its assistance I may ever pursue the sacred mysteries in the pathway of Light and thus be better able to aid your beloved children.

O ye Ancient Masters of the Magic of Light, who reside in the Holy Kingdom, which is the throne of the Queen of Heaven, ye Spirits of Life who preside over the souls in the cosmic hall of rebirth before Anu, give me your aid and empower me with your tremendous magical power. Breathe into my spirit the power and might irresistible to compel the Rouhaniat al-Turab to manifest through me and unto me, that I maybe a living channel for the magic of Earth. Initiate me into the current of Earth, for thou art the ancient initiators of magic."

 INVOCATION OF THE GOLDEN SUN

STEP TWENTY-SEVEN: Face East again and say: "O Rouhaniat Kawkab Zuhal, by the permission of the Queen of Heaven and Earth, and authority of the archangel Kasfiel, and the blessed names Lele-tah-teel [x3], Teel-la-lel-tah [x3], La-tah-tee-lel [x3], Yal-lal--ta-hat [x3], Tah-tee-la-lal [x3], Lal-la-tah-tee [x3], Ha-tee-lala-lat [x3], Lee-tah-tal-el [x3], Ha-tel-la-leet [x3], La-lee-tah-tal [x3], Ta-hat-la-la-lee [x3], La-la-lee-ta-hat [x3], Ya-tah-tal-lal [x3], Ta-lal-lee-tah [x3], send to me the radiant ghosts and illuminated presences from your sphere to help in my operation to call forth the spirits who move under the sway of the rays of Kawkab Zuhal. Be a friend to me and aid me this day/night in my spiritual aspiration in the name of the Queen of Heaven and Earth in whose womb we all swim.

O Rouhaniat Kawkab al-Moshtari, by the permission of the Queen of Heaven and Earth, and authority of the archangel Sarfiel, and the blessed names Mah-tah-teel [x3], Teel-mah-tah [x3], Hat-ha-tee-lem [x3], Ya-lem-hot-hot [x3], Tah-teel-mah [x3], La-mah-tah-tee [x3], Hah-teel-mah-hot [x3], Lee-tah-ta-hum [x3], Hat-hum-leet [x3], Ma-lee-tah-ta-ha [x3], Tah-tah-ma-lee [x3], Ha-ma-lee-ta-hut [x3], Yah-tah-tah-mal [x3], Tah-ma-lee-tah [x3], send to me the radiant ghosts and illuminated presences from your sphere to help in my operation to call forth the spirits who move under the sway of the rays of Kawkab al-Moshtari. Be a friend to me and aid me this day/night in my spiritual aspiration in the name of the Queen of Heaven and Earth in whose womb we all swim.

O Rouhaniat Kawkab al-Merrikh, by the permission of the Queen of Heaven and Earth, and authority of the archangel Semsamiel, and the blessed names Qah-tee-teel [x3], Teel-qah-tee [x3], Ha-tee-tee-loq [x3], Yal-qah-teet [x3], Tee-teel-qah [x3], Laq-hah-tee-tee [x3], Ya-teel-qa-hot [x3], Lee-tee-ta-haq [x3], Yot-hah-qleet [x3], Qa-lee-tee-tah [x3], Teet-haq-lee [x3], Haq-lee-teet [x3], Ya-teet-ha-qul [x3], Tah-qa-lee-tee [x3], send to me the radiant ghosts and illuminated presences from your sphere to help in my operation to call forth the spirits who move under the sway of the rays of Kawkab al-Merrikh. Be a friend to me and aid me this day/night in my spiritual aspiration in the name of the Queen of Heaven and Earth in whose womb we all swim.

O Rouhaniat Kawkab al-Shames, by the permission of the Queen of Heaven and Earth, and authority of the archangel Ruqiel, and the blessed names Fah-tob-teel [x3], Teel-fah-tab [x3], Hat-ba-tee-luf [x3], Yal-fah-ta-but [x3], Tab-teel-fah [x3], Lef-hat-bot-ee [x3], Bah-teel-fa-hat [x3], Lee-ta-bot-haf [x3], Bat-haf-leet [x3], Fa-lee-tub-tah [x3], Ta-but-huf-lee [x3], Haf-lee-ta-bat [x3], Yat-bot-ha-fal [x3], Tah-fa-lee-tub [x3], send to me the radiant ghosts and illuminated presences from your sphere to help in my operation to call forth the spirits who move under the sway of the rays of Kawkab al-Shames. Be a friend to me and aid me this day/night in my spiritual aspiration in the name of the Queen of Heaven and Earth in whose womb we all swim.

O Rouhaniat Kawkab al-Zuhra, by the permission of the Queen of Heaven and Earth, and authority of the archangel A'aniel, and the blessed names Na-hah-ta-teel [x3], Teel-na-ha-hot [x3], Ha-ha-tah-tee-lan [x3], Ya-lan-ha-ha-ta-tot [x3], Hot-teel-nah [x3], Len-hah-tah-tee [x3], Ta-teel-na-hah [x3], Leet-tot-ha-han [x3], Ta-ha-na-leet [x3], Nah-lee-tot-hah [x3], Tot-ha-ha-na-lee [x3], Han-lee-tot-ah [x3], Ya-to-tah-ha-nal [x3], Hah-na-lee-tot [x3], send to me the radiant ghosts and illuminated presences from your sphere to help in my operation to call forth the spirits who move under the sway of the rays of Kawkab al-Zuhra. Be a friend to me and aid me this day/night in my spiritual aspiration in the name of the Queen of Heaven and Earth in whose womb we all swim.

O Rouhaniat Kawkab Otaared, by the permission of the Queen of Heaven and Earth, and authority of the archangel Michael, and the blessed names Jah-lah-ta-teel [x3], Teel-jah-lot [x3], Hal-tot-ya-laj [x3], Yal-ja-hal-tot [x3], La-tot-yal-jah [x3], La-jah-lo-tot-ee [x3], Tot-eel-ja-hal [x3], Lee-tat-la-haj [x3], Tal-haj-leet [x3], Ja-lee-tot-lah [x3], Tot-la-haj-lee [x3], Haj-lee-tot-al [x3], Ya-tot-lah-jal [x3], Lah-ja-lee-tot [x3], send to me the radiant ghosts and illuminated presences from your sphere to help in my operation to call forth the spirits who move under the sway of the rays of Kawkab Otaared. Be a friend to me and aid me this day/night in my spiritual aspiration in the name of the Queen of Heaven and Earth in whose womb we all swim.

O Rouhaniat Kawkab al-Qamar, by the permission of the Queen of Heaven and Earth, and authority of the archangel Gabriel, and the blessed names Lach-ha-tot-eel [x3], Tee-lal-cha-hot [x3], Chah-tot-ee-lal [x3], Ya-la-lach-ha-tot [x3], Ha-tot-ee-la-lach [x3], Lal-chah-tot-ee [x3], Totee-la-la-chh [x3], Lee-tot-ha-chal [x3], Tah-cha-la-leet [x3], La-lee-tot-hach [x3], Tot-hach-la-lee [x3], Chal-lee-ta-tah [x3], Ya-tot-hach-lal [x3], Hach-la-lee-tot [x3], send to me the radiant ghosts and illuminated presences from your sphere to help in my operation to call forth the spirits who move under the sway of the rays of Kawkab al-Qamar. Be a friend to me and aid me this day/night in my spiritual aspiration in the name of the Queen of Heaven and Earth in whose womb we all swim.

O Rouhaniat Kawkab al-Qamar, Kawkab Otaared, Kawkab al-Zuhra, al-Shames, Kawkab al-Merrikh, Kawkab al-Moshtari, and Kawkab Zuhal, who swim in the path of Anu, come to me and lift from me the seven veils so that I become an incarnation of the word of Enki and the beating heart of the Ishtar. Let my nature that is against me be for me, and let my nature that is for me, be for others, so that I may become an instrument of wisdom and love in the temporal world. O guardians of the cross-roads and Lords of Time, hear my cry as I utter it, for I am naught but a drop of dew from the fountain of spirit that engulfs us all. Yet, in me is contained a mirror of all that came before me and from me will spark the life of all that will come after me. For I am more than my body, and my body is more than the clay that formed it. Lift from me the seven veils of darkness and let me pass from the womb of the below to the chambers of the above. Let me glimpse the four rivers of paradise that flow from the heavens above and fill the world with life. Let those hidden masters who oversee those rivers judge me now and if I am worthy, let them aid me with a charge of magic. Empower me and infuse me with magical potency for I am a seeker of the Children of Light."

STEP TWENTY-EIGHT: Speaking with strength and authority say: "Beshem Qadush Elat va-El Elyon Ha Malachim, I ask You by Your divinity, compassion and inclusive mercy, which encompasses all things. O Elah of those that came first, and those that will come last, I ask You with links of glory from Your Throne, the extremity of Your spirit and mercy, O whom to the Universe is a Divinity.

By the Sun and its heat, I ask You, O Lord, O Lady, with the Waw of Your singularity, to pour out upon me from the suns of the knowledge of Your caring light what dawns in my heart and in my world of senses like the dawning of the Sun in the day. O Knower of the Mysteries, a veil had cloaked what is between the knowledge of Your Holiness and me, with the darkness of forgetfulness, but when the revelations of Your caring dawned upon it, the twilight of ignorance was removed by the Lights of the Light.

By the moon that follows it, O Creator of the illuminating crescent, Who has bestowed upon it Your radiating Lights and through this vanished the darkness, remove from my mind the veil of ignorance and the subtlety of human nature, so that the lantern of my heart may shine with the crescent of Your guidance.

By the day and its brightness, O Thou Who created the day and arranged the labors and destined fates upon Your creation and bestowed upon the select of Your servants the Mysteries, via the Being of Your care; O Thou, Who made the spiritual souls, and earthly kings pure and answerable to those who recite this conjuration with subtle knowledge from the oceans of evocations and oaths of Your book; I swear by this exalted evocation, upon the Master Metatron who is entrusted with the pattern of the meaning of the numerals on the Throne, who is engulfed by the seas of bestowal of the wondrous of the Lights. Be charged, O Master Metatron, and command the spiritual archangel who leads the mightiest choir, who has the highest status in the greatest mystery. O Master, come with your spirits, your aid and all that enter obediently under your command.

Come forth, O spiritual hosts, and descend upon the earthly jinn kings. Come, O ye benevolent kings of the jinn, with your tents, flames, birds, thunder, lightning; come between my hands and do whatever I command of you. Come so that I can see you with my own eyes and talk to you with my tongue. Obey me in all that I ask of you in the work of magic from manifestation and materialization, attraction and repelling, transformation, restoration, the bringing of the missing, invisibility, teleportation and all that I ask you about, of what occurs in the year and what the Divine has ordained to happen in the Universe. For you have knowledge and awareness of what is concealed. You are informed of this by the spiritual beings. The spiritual beings are informed by your leaders. Your princes are informed by the Master Metatron, who beholds all that occurs on the right side of the Throne of Divine Orders from the archangel Michael.

By the honor of the status of the Master Metatron among the heavenly spirits, you will but answer this conjuration. Serve me in all things that are miraculous and magical, so that I may finish my work and succeed in the magic of Light. I conjure you, O masters of the jinn, and spiritual orders, by the angel Barjyl who reveals the Ring of the Mysteries to do with all that I asked. Let it be that the master of spirits and crown of glory, the Master Metatron, calls unto them: Listen and obey if _(your full name)_ calls you and don't disobey the names of the Queen of Heaven and the conjuration that called you. If you refuse, you will be hit by a penetrating comet from the highest heaven.

By the elevated sky upon the mountains, by the occult and the gathered Light, aid me by the reproduction of the spiritual mysteries. O ye Jinn Kings who follow the Master Metatron, whether you be earthly, aerial, watery or fiery, in the sky or under the oceans, come to me and aid me by the honor of these great names: Lele-tah-teel [x3], Teel-la-lel-tah [x3], La-tah-tee-lel [x3], Yal-lal--ta-hat [x3], Tah-tee-la-lal [x3], Lal-la-tah-tee [x3], Ha-tee-lala-lat [x3], Lee-tah-tal-el [x3], Ha-tel-la-leet [x3], La-lee-tah-tal [x3], Ta-hat-la-la-lee [x3], La-la-lee-ta-hat [x3], Ya-tah-tal-lal [x3], Ta-lal-lee-tah [x3], Mah-tah-teel [x3], Teel-mah-tah [x3], Hat-ha-tee-lem [x3], Ya-lem-hot-hot [x3], Tah-teel-mah [x3], La-mah-tah-tee [x3], Hah-teel-mah-hot [x3], Lee-tah-ta-hum [x3], Hat-hum-leet [x3], Ma-lee-tah-ta-ha [x3], Tah-tah-ma-lee [x3], Ha-ma-lee-ta-hut [x3], Yah-tah-tah-mal [x3], Tah-ma-lee-tah [x3], Qah-tee-teel [x3], Teel-qah-tee [x3], Ha-tee-tee-loq [x3], Yal-qah-teet [x3], Tee-teel-qah [x3], Laq-hah-tee-tee [x3], Ya-teel-qa-hot [x3], Lee-tee-ta-haq [x3], Yot-hah-qleet [x3], Qa-lee-tee-tah [x3], Teet-haq-lee [x3], Haq-lee-teet [x3], Ya-teet-ha-qul [x3], Tah-qa-lee-tee [x3], Fah-tob-teel [x3], Teel-fah-tab [x3], Hat-ba-tee-luf [x3], Yal-fah-ta-but [x3], Tab-teel-fah [x3], Lef-hat-bot-ee [x3], Bah-teel-fa-hat [x3], Lee-ta-bot-haf [x3], Bat-haf-leet [x3], Fa-lee-tub-tah [x3], Ta-but-huf-lee [x3], Haf-lee-ta-bat [x3], Yat-bot-ha-fal [x3], Tah-fa-lee-tub [x3], Na-hah-ta-teel [x3], Teel-na-ha-hot [x3], Ha-ha-tah-tee-lan [x3], Ya-lan-ha-ha-ta-tot [x3], Hot-teel-nah [x3], Len-hah-tah-tee [x3], Ta-teel-na-hah [x3], Leet-tot-ha-han [x3], Ta-ha-na-leet [x3], Nah-lee-tot-hah [x3], Tot-ha-ha-na-lee [x3], Han-lee-tot-ah [x3], Ya-to-tah-ha-nal [x3], Hah-na-lee-tot [x3], Jah-lah-ta-teel [x3], Teel-jah-lot [x3], Hal-tot-ya-laj [x3], Yal-ja-hal-tot [x3], La-tot-yal-jah [x3], La-jah-lo-tot-ee [x3], Tot-eel-ja-hal [x3], Lee-tat-la-haj [x3], Tal-haj-leet [x3], Ja-lee-tot-lah [x3], Tot-la-haj-lee [x3], Haj-lee-tot-al [x3], Ya-tot-lah-jal [x3], Lah-ja-lee-tot [x3], Lach-ha-tot-eel [x3], Tee-lal-cha-hot [x3], Chah-tot-ee-lal [x3], Ya-la-lach-ha-tot [x3], Ha-tot-ee-la-lach [x3], Lal-chah-tot-ee [x3], Totee-la-la-chh [x3], Lee-tot-ha-chal [x3], Tah-cha-la-leet [x3], La-lee-tot-hach [x3], Tot-hach-la-lee [x3], Chal-lee-ta-tah [x3], Ya-tot-hach-lal [x3], Hach-la-lee-tot [x3], and the great archangels Ruqiel, Gabriel, Semsamiel, Michael, Sarfiel, A 'aniel, and Kasfiel. Come to me now, O spiritual jinn, and send to me those who will aid me in my magical and spiritual work and support me in service of the Queen of Heaven and Earth, the Queen of angels, humans, and jinn kind.

Elat, inspire me to righteousness in actions and words. Inspire me with Your knowledge, through all that increases my heart with revelation and power, so that I may witness from You the inspiration. So that from my vision is not hidden what will occur of events in the days. Make me one of the winners, who are the people of virtue, accomplishment and success. Cleanse my self with your forgiveness, mercy and acceptance. Drop upon me the curtains of Your Lights. Amen."

Closing Prayer

Step Twenty-Nine: Say: "Elat, place upon my head a crown of lights like the crown you have placed upon the head of the prophets of the Children of Light and endow me with the virtue of spirituality." Feel the Light of the Divine upon you and meditate on the virtue of Spirituality.

Step Thirty: Say: "Elat, shine from my face a Light like the light you have emanated from the face of the prophets of the Children of Light and endow me with the virtues of humility and honesty." Feel yourself loved by all that is in heaven and earth and meditate on the virtues of humility and honesty.

Step Thirty-One: Say: "Elat, consecrate my tongue with your sanctity as you consecrated the tongue of the prophets of the Children of Light and endow me with the virtue of justice." Meditate for about a minute on the fact that everything you utter is of the Light and on the virtue of justice.

Step Thirty-Two: Say: "Elat, consecrate and empower my hands like you have empowered the hands of the prophets of the Children of Light and endow me with the virtue of honor." Focus on the fact that all that behold you are awed by your presence and meditate on the virtue of honor.

Step Thirty-Three: Say: "Elat, strengthen my heart as you fortified the heart of the prophets of the Children of Light and endow me with the virtue of valor." Meditate for about a minute on your courage and willingness to face death in your pursuit of Light and on the virtue of valor.

Step Thirty-Four: Say: "Elat, consecrate and anoint my spirit with your chrism as you consecrated and anointed the spirit of the prophets of the Children of Light and endow me with the virtue of love and sacrifice." Meditate on the universal love and purity in your heart and the virtue of sacrifice.

STEP THIRTY-FIVE: Say: "Elat, engulf me with your peace like you covered the prophets of the Children of Light with its garment and endow me with the virtue of compassion." Focus on the peace profound filling every ounce of your body and meditate on the virtue of compassion.

STEP THIRTY-SIX: Say: "Elat, Elat, Elat you are my shield from calamity and your Light is the Magic that runs in my veins. Holy is your name to the end of time." Feel the Divine Spirit all around, without and within you.

STEP THIRTY-SEVEN: Close the Elemental Gates

In the next chapter, we will discuss the art of jinn magic. Jinn magic is the most powerful magic known to humankind. It can also be very dangerous and thus requires a strong heart and resolute will and faith in the Divine. We will be drawing from the materials in this chapter for use in th next. Jinn magic is strongly connected to planetary magic. This shouldn't come as a surprise. The jinn's magic and many aspects of their culture are tied in with one of the oldest civilizations in the world. In Babylon, it is said the angels taught man magic and from there the first images and names of the jinn began to emerge. The Chaldean faith and their lore of the planets was the dominant one in Babylon and hence from early on became entwined with the art of the jinn.

Works Referenced

al-Ghalani, Mohammed (D. 1740 C.E.), *al-Der al-Mantzoom wa Khilasat al-Sir al-Maktoom fi Al-Sihr wa al-Talasem wa al-Nojoom*. al-Maktaba al-Tahqafia, Beirut, Lebanon: 1992.

al-Marzooqi, Ali Abu Hai Allah, *al-Jawaher al-Lama'a fi Isthadhar Muluk al-Jinn fi al-Waqet wa al-Sa'a*. Maktabat Iqbal Haj Ibrahim. Siragh Bantan: 1962.

al-Toukhi, A'adu al-Fatah. *al-Siher al-Azeem (v1-3)*. al-Maktabah al-Thaqafiah. Beirut:1991

10
Magic of the Jinn

Jinn magic is an amazing art that can make magical tales come true. It is also an art that can lure many unsuspecting beginners who get addicted to the rush of summoning a spirit, into spending years of their lives pursuing power and inviting dangerous forces into their lives. Jinn magic is an important part of the magical art, but it isn't the defining element of the craft. Most ancient magicians didn't spend their entire lives summoning jinni after jinni. The focus was on summoning one or two who would become brothers or sister companions on the path. These new found family members would help the magician in all affairs, magical and mundane. Capable magicians would expand the number to a dozen, but beyond that it was considered playing with fire. The ancient tales of a covenant between the magician and the spirit are based on the required deal between the magician and the jinni. This deal is essential, but it doesn't involve the magicians selling their souls or any thing like that. It is a direct equal exchange of friendship and an acceptance that both parties would honor the terms of the relationship. If you summoned a spirit without a pact, you opened yourself to a free-for-all relationship. You would have succeeded in proving to yourself that these beings exist, assuming you did it right and physical manifestations occurred, but they would not be bound to aid you or honor their promise. Needing a pact made it impractical to summon a different jinni every day. The actual rituals also required months upon months of preparation and performance for a single summoning. It took so much energy that it wasn't practical to do too many. The idea that you could summon a spirit in an hour or two for trivial mundane purposes would have been anathema to the ancients. This was only possible once you had a working pact with a jinni. This is a vast art and although many grimoires are available, many of its mysteries remain a secret.

In this chapter, we will introduce you safely to the art of jinn magic. We can't cover this complex art in a single chapter. However, we can give you the basics. Let us begin with an often unheeded piece of advice: don't expect to see jinn physically. You will have tangible physical evidence that they are there and you may even get glimpses of them, but don't expect to see them as you see any other physical object. This doesn't mean it will never happen, it may very well do, but don't make that an axiom of your magical pursuit. It may seem counter intuitive to us physical beings, but the jinn by definition are invisible to us. They are invisible to us because they choose to be and because it is their natural instinct. They can be felt and their actions can be seen. When they are felt by you, they are felt by all those around you. When their actions are seen, it is pure physical action. For example, one of our students performed an earthly jinn chant. The chant was meant to be performed over many weeks and for hundreds of repetitions, a couple of times a day. After his first attempt, he fell asleep alone in his apartment and when he woke up the lights that he had turned off were now on, also the fan that he had turned off was on, and he had a cockroach in his hand. This may not be much of a manifestation, but you can imagine what could happen on the sixth or seventh day. Other students reported a jinn occurrence in their bedroom, where the being removed a mirror from their wall and a tray from their dresser, placing them both on a high, hard to reach, shelf, and even scattered their shoes on the ground. They heard and saw the evidence of its handiwork, but didn't see the jinni physically.

The second piece of advice we would like to share with you is to approach them as you would approach any intelligent race of beings. Avoid wielding weapons in their presence unless you fear them, or it will be seen as sign of aggression. Weapons will protect you only if they are effective deterrents. Most earthly weapons are not. Don't communicate with them in a hostile fashion unless they are hostile or threatening. Make sure your tone and words during the conjurations, while stern, are not demeaning or unnecessarily aggressive. Don't try to bind them since you can't; instead call them to help you and aid you. Finally, don't assume because you have asked them to leave that they will not return. It is necessary to ensure that they are on friendly terms with you and that they will not come back to harm you or any of your family. Finally, use common sense in all of your dealings with them, as if you are dealing with any other human beings.

The third piece of advice is to know the signs of the jinn. Many people are not familiar with the jinn and they confuse them with other kinds of spiritual experiences. The last thing you want to do is think you have contacted a jinni when you are actually indulging in mental fantasy. Different jinn have different signs; a common one is a sense of electrical sensation around your body, a sense of something tugging at the back of your head, a sudden penetrating migraine that makes it hard to think, and increased room and body temperature. The more benevolent a jinni is, the less uncomfortable these signs will be. Ifreets are literally painful to have around and may cause people around you to be angrier and edgier. Shadow creatures will fill you with a total sense of fear and dread. Upper jinn will be electrical and magnetic, but you will not get the migraine or headache and you will also sense a real feeling of being uplifted emotionally and spiritually. In all cases, you and those around you will feel like there are invisible people there. You will sense them fully even if you are engaged at the time in purely mundane activities.

Knowing a jinni is around is by no means a sign that your request will be fulfilled or that the jinni will obey you. The signs of agreement and obedience are varied. Most specific jinn operations include definite things to look for. If a sign doesn't appear, you need to wait till it does before you call your operation finished. If it still doesn't happen, you need to look back and see what you may have done wrong. If there is no error, then repeat the operation again and again, for that means the jinni is simply hoping that you will quit before it has to respond to you. You can either force obedience or select a different jinni. If the operation has no specified sign of responsiveness, then it can be one of a number of signs recorded by the ancients. These are as follows:

✳ Strong winds inside your working area although there are no winds outside.

✳ The place expands until you imagine yourself in a wide desert.

✳ The place feels as if its shrinking until you imagine it collapsing it around you.

✳ You will hear loud noises, musical instruments, or the sound of things breaking or crashing.

✳ You will see fires or storming waters.

✳ Your index finger will move spontaneously without your intending to move it.

✳ Your body will itch unusually.

✳ You will speak in tongues or speak strangely during the recitation of the conjuration.

✳ Your voice will rise unintentionally.

✳ Your heart will suddenly beat erratically.

✳ You see between your hands scorpions, serpents, insects, birds, cats, or other small animals and insects.

When one of those signs appear, you know your intent has been accomplished and you can finish up your work. If none of those signs appear, chant the name Shemechaheer from the Berhatiah one hundred times, then say: **"If you have come, O ye spirits, then show me from the rays of your lights."** If they are present, you will see whiteness or light. When the angels and kings are present, greet them with: **"The Divine aid you with the Greatest Light and from the pure noble presence increase you in that for which He prepared you."** When the aids of the kings and servants appear, say unto them: **"The Divine blessings be in you and upon you."** When you have finished a scripted conjuration, state to the beings present: **"The Divine aid you with piety and aid you against every calamity."** If they are from among the residents of the place, say to them: **"The Divine thanks your endeavour."**

✸ THE SUMMONER'S WAY ✸

Eighty percent of the summoner's time is spent on protection and twenty percent on the actual process of summoning and communicating with the jinn. Before beginning any Jinn evocation, a shield of protection needs to be erected around you. There are two kinds of shields. The first is physical and the other is spiritual. Physical shields involve the magic circle. The magic circle protects you from jinn that may come from below the ground. It also helps against those that come at you from the sides. You normally would supplement that with magical wards buried or placed in the four corners of the room. The circles are used when you fear for your safety from an evil jinni. This isn't as necessary when you are dealing with upper jinn, which is why it will not really be required for the rituals in this book. You should be fine with the Shield of the Magi ritual. However, we will discuss the basics of the magic circle since it is an integral part of the art.

The magic circle was originally developed due to the need for locational protection in times of danger. It was used to protect travelling magicians from thieves and wild animals. It is said that when the magic circle was approached by hostile people, it appeared to them as if they were facing a mountain, a valley, or some other major obstruction. The magic circle was initially drawn on the sand or ground. Magicians added a mixture of salt and the ashes of a burnt talisman or amulet. This became the basis for the salt circle of future generations.

There are various circle designs that have been handed down through time. The most famous in the West are the ones found in the Lesser Key of Solomon and various other medieval grimoires. These are generally made from a single or double circle with magical inscriptions and prayers. One of the oldest designs of the magic circle, known as al-Hhutah, is recorded in ancient Arabic texts. This design appears to be of Chaldean origin, using various inscriptions ranging from Nabatean conjurations to Quranic chapters, or surahs. However, the design remained standard among the masters of the craft until it was exported to Europe.

This particular design for the magic circle consists of seven concentric circles, with an outside square with four gates containing them. There are a number of things to take into consideration when drawing or establishing your circle. First, the drawing of all the lines that forms the circles and square is to be made by steel. The best tool is a long spear with a steel tip. The line is usually drawn after you have sprinkled a mixture of dirt, ashes and salt over the place. The ashes are commonly the result of burning certain amulets or magical incantations. Second, the spaces between the circles should be equal. Third, each circle should have a piece of steel impaled on it, at the point where the circle completes itself. The outer square doesn't have any metallic pieces. Fourth, the directions of these metallic pieces should each be different. They shouldn't all be facing one direction. Each piece is impaled at the point where a circle starts and then is completed; therefore the direction of the starting point of each circle should be different. For example, to draw the first circle, you might face the starting point to the east, then turn to draw the circle; the second circle's starting point could then be facing to the east southeast, and so on. Fifth, all circles should be drawn clockwise. Sixth, the inner circle, which is the smallest, should be wide enough to encircle the length of your body. This way, if you fall unconscious for any reason, your body remains within the circle. Seventh, you begin with the outer square and then you move back from circle to circle until you reach the interior. Eighth, each circle has to have inscriptions. Most inscriptions are taken from the scriptures. There is no consensus on what those inscriptions are, as each is drawn from what the magician considers sacred and holy. Ninth, three of the gates on the outside square are usually sealed, leaving one open. The open door is the direction from which the jinn will enter and walk around your circle and sit to talk to you. The sealing of the doors is also done by certain magical inscriptions.

The second form of protection needed is a spiritual one and should be done regardless of what kind of jinn you plan to work with. The aura of protection is acquired by reciting special protective prayers and by wearing a warding amulet. The amulet is composed of magical prayers and written addresses and commands to the jinn that you should be left unharmed. They contain a command from the Divine to angels to watch over the carrier or to the evil spirits to leave the magician alone. The letter is placed into a cloth bag and worn around the neck all the time, except when you are entering unclean places. A few of those amulets have been translated into or written in Arabic. Many of them also include scriptural quotations and Divine Names from numerous languages.

We will be delving into an introductory jinn evocation later on in this chapter. You should take the time now to learn how to establish these specific wards and protection rituals. You want to get as comfortable as possible with them, so that you are fluent when the time comes. We will provide a working example of every level of protection that you need before you actually begin the conjuration.

To make the warding amulet, write on thin sheets of paper the letter Qaf in Arabic one hundred times and the letter Nun upside down fifty times, the great name of the Elements one hundred and eleven times, the Tahateel names seven times each, the names of the Berhatiah three times each, the seven angels and the four archangels seventy times each, and the four Elders twelve times each, in Arabic as separate letters or in a magical script. Follow it with the writing of the following charge in your own language. It should be modified for the person who is to wear this amulet:

"O familiars, O stalkers, O you rebellious Jinn, O you host of the evil eye, O all you who come with malign intent, O children of Iblis, all of you, Gabriel has come to you with wrath from al-Nur.

Michael has come to you with ferocity from al-Nur, and Israfel has come to you with a blow of shock, and Azrael with a mighty grip. If you disobey the name of al-Nur, each angel will come to you with a spear to remove you by the names of al-Nur, the Exalted. Light upon Light, al-Nur guides to His Light who He wishes. He also torments by His fires all who He wishes. The torment of your Lord shall be occurring and it has no obstructor.

Depart, depart, O familiars, O stalkers, O you rebellious Jinn, O you host of the evil eye, O all you who come with malign intent, O children of Iblis, from the face of N (son/daughter) of N, as by the name of Who sprouted the heath and made it contain swamps, al-Nur will take care of them and He is All Knowing and All Hearing. A thousand, thousand, angels of al-Nur fall upon the shoulders of N (son/daughter) of N, so that any harmful calamities and ill fate will be removed from (him/her). O angels of al-Nur, push away from N (son/daughter) of N the evil of every male and female Jinn, male and female Mared, male and female familiar, male and female stalker, male and female sender of the evil eye, male and female interceptor, the evil of every harmful wind and the evil of every beast. My sufficiency is al-Nur, upon Him do I depend and He is the Lord of the Magnificent Throne, and prayers of al-Nur be upon the angels, higher jinn and their pure hosts."

Once you are done with the writing, burn some incense and recite all the names and the charge. The chanting of the names and letter should be equivalent to how many times they were written on the paper. Basically, you are reading all that is written in a magical setting as a charge. You should do the charge three or seven times, before you wear it. It is wise to recite it again at least once a month. You can wear this amulet all the time or only during magical workings involving the Jinn.

This is the first stage of protection. The next step is a protective ward spoken out loud within the ceremony itself. Before you begin your magical conjuration recite the following protective prayer seven times: "O Divine One, by the hidden gentleness of the Divine, by the gentle action of the Divine, by the beautiful veil of the Divine, I have entered into the side of the Divine and sought intercession of the messengers of the Divine and there is no will nor power except by the Exalted Divine, Ehieh Asher Ehieh. I protect myself by the protection of the Divine and His fortification and with the wise invocation. By the honor of He who brings the bones to life after they have decomposed, Gabriel is on my right, Israfel is behind me, Michael is on my left, and my guardian angel is before me. The staff of Moses is in my hand, so whomever sees me is awed by me. The seal of Solomon is upon my tongue, so whomever I talk to will complete my request. The light of Joseph is on my face so that whomever sees me will love me. The majestic and exalted Divine One surrounds me and upon Him is my reliance against enemies. There is no god but the Great and Exalted Divine One, and there is no will or power except by the majestic and exalted Divine One and may the prayers of the Divine be upon the children of Light with peace profound."

The next step is the release of the residents so they don't interfere with your magical working. Burn pure frankincense resin and say the release of the residents seven times. Keep in mind that the release of the residents only works on jinn that inhabit your working area. It won't release jinn kings or other beings that you may have invited. This release works specifically for those jinn under the domain of the King Taresh. The conjuration of release is as follows: "**I charge you, O jinn and residents in this location that you evacuate and leave from this place: you, your elders, your young, and your women. Let there be no failure in my work or in my writing or in my recitation or in my circles by the honor of the King Taresh that rules over you, Tinah [x3] Mazaq [x3] Maqer [x3], so that kings and their aids may come and be of assistance to me in completing my task without harm nor failure. By the honor of Taresh [x3], Maresh [x3], Mareesh [x3], Mareeosh [x3], Baresh [x3], Radash [x3], Latmash [x3] Batash [x3] and by the honor of the most compassionate and merciful, the glorious owner of the Great Name. Be charged O Ruqiel, O Gabriel, Semsamiel, O Michael, O Sarfiel, O A'aniel, and O Kasfiel with their evacuation until I complete my task, by the honor of Ehieh Asher Ehieh Adonai Tzabaoth El Shaddi. Now [x3] Quickly [x3] This Hour [x3].**"

If you need to kick out a stubborn jinni immediately, you will need to resort to more than the release. Kicking out stubborn jinn isn't an easy task, considering their own advanced magical ability. There is a basic method that has been found to be successful and was used by many ancient masters, including Al-Buni. On clean pieces of paper write the following words: هليشا مليشا ملاهه (Haleesha Maleesha Malahah). Hang the papers on the four walls of the room, while saying the words written on them aloud. Then say a few times, in an authoritative voice: "**Yastates Mates Alehates Yastates Mates Sahates Yates Satates Ye-**

mates Ma'aates Seltates Semates Ma'ates; get out, O uninvited jinn, from this place ~ Warkeekum Bakom Kakom Bakom Rass." Point at the jinn as you say the last set of words and it will be unable to harm you. Continue to repeat the chant and command, forcing it to flee.

THE CONJURATION OF THE JINN

PURPOSE: This conjuration will slowly lift the veil between you and the jinn world. It will empower you and prepare you for further jinn workings. It is also a safe introduction to the art of evocation. Through this operation you will invite a benevolent jinn that is a servant of Baduh and Melchizedek.

TIMING: This ritual will require a two week commitment on your part and a place where you can retreat and do your working undisturbed and away from people. This could be your dedicated sealed temple space or a place in nature. You only need to do this ritual once a year.

TOOLS: You will need your magical robe. You will also need enough incense for regular burning over three days. The incense mixture is dried cilantro and aloes wood. You should have the warding amulet written and consecrated for use during the operation.

DIVINE NAMES: The primary names in the conjuration are the same as those of the Ancient Oath. You should be familiar with them by now. The conjuration used in this chapter is expanded from previous ones. There are a number of variations and this is one of the longer ones.

FIRST FOUR DAYS: Recite the three names Berhatiah, Kareer, and Tatleeyah three hundred times once in the morning and once in the evening for four days before the three day retreat begins. This phase is to bring the jinn into your sphere and to help you see them.

NEXT THREE DAYS: Fast and stay within your retreat for as long as you can during this period. Keep your conversation with people that may live with you to as little as possible and only in cases of emergency. The first two days, recite the Ancient Oath seventy times. On the third day, recite it one hundred times.

LAST SEVEN DAYS: Recite the name Toran ten thousand times for seven nights following the three day retreat. This is useful to ensure long term obedience.

JINN CONJURATION: Say: "In the name of the Divine One, the Ancient One, the Eternal One, the Encompasser who encompasses all the creatures with His knowledge; the Ancient One and Eternal One that has no beginning to His ancientness and has no end. He dawned all the universes with the radiance of the light of His face and emanated in them with the power of His awe upon every angel, constellation, jinn, shitan and ruler. He was feared by all of His creation, and the angels of closeness heeded and obeyed from their highest places and prostrated and answered the call of His great name to whomever called by it. They quickly answered with the confirmation fastened and written in the tablets of the hearts of the users of the mystery of Baduh Ajhazat. I conjure you, o rouhaniah spirits from the above and below and ask the servants of this ancient oath to enable me to see and hear the jinn and to aid me with jinn rouhani khadem Baduh wa al-Malek al-Sadeq. Answer my conjuration and fulfill my need in the glory of Ber-hat-yah [x3], Ka-reer [x3], Tat-lee-yah [x3], Toh-ran [x3], Maz-jal [x3], Baz-jal [x3], Tahr-qab [x3], Bar-hash [x3], Ghal-mash [x3], Cho-taeer [x3], Qal-in-hod [x3], Bar-shan [x3], Katz-heer [x3], Namoh Shelech [x3], Berhayola [x3], Bash-kee-lach [x3], Qaz Maz [x3], An-ghala-leet [x3], Qa-ba-rat [x3], Gha-ya-ha [x3], Kayed-ho-la [x3], Shem-cha-her [x3], Shem-cha-heer [x3], Shem-ha-heer [x3], Bak-hat-hon-yah [x3], Ba-sha-resh [x3], To-nesh [x3], Shem-cha Ba-roch [x3].

O Divine One by the honor of Kah-ka-heej, Yach-tash, Yal-tash-ghesh-weel, Am-weel, Jal-dam, Mah-jama, Haj-leej, Mah-fee-aj; nothing is like unto Him and He is All Hearing and All Seeing. Come to me, listen and obey and be my aides in everything I have commanded you to do in the honor of the name that is majestic and magnificent, that begins with El and ends with El and it is El Shala'a, Ya'ao, Yubiah, Yahuah, Ah, Betekmah, Betekefal, Busa'aee, Ka'aee, Memial, we obey You O El, how grand is Your name Jal Raziel. No spirit heard Your name and disobeyed but was stricken down and burnt with Your Light, O Greatest Light. I avow and assert on you by the Knower of the all that is hidden and visible, the Great and Exalted, and by the names of your covenant on the door of great temple of Babel: Ba'al Shaqesh [x3], Mahraqesh [x3],

Aqesha Maqesh [x3], Shaqmonhesh [x3], Raksha [x3], Kashalach [x3], A'akesh [x3], Tahesh [x3] and whomever disobeys his Lord to him is ascending torment. I swear upon these, O you spiritual rouhaniah, asking you to enable me to see and hear the jinn and to aid me with jinn rouhani khadem Baduh wa al-Malek al-Sadeq, by the honor of Ehieh Asher Ehieh Adonai Tzabaoth El Shaddi and by the honor of AbjadHawaz Hhuti and by honor of Batad Zahej Wah and by honor of Baduh Ajhazat and it is an oath if you but know great. Now [x3] Quickly [x3] This Hour [x3]."

❂ THE SEVEN JINN KINGS ❂

PURPOSE: The seven jinn kings are the most popular jinn of ancient occult lore. They are regularly summoned for almost all major magical operations involving jinn. Most often they are summoned once to give seven jinn aides and then called upon to command the aides. It is rare that they are summoned directly on a regular basis for magical work, although they are mentioned in ancient rites and spells. The ancients made that clear. The seven jinn kings are powerful beings and belong to the earthly plane and, some say, to the underworld. This is hinted at, as they are called the children of the domain of the underworld Tartaros, also known as the Pit. They are connected with the Titans and this makes them at least dangerous to most beginners. Our experience with them has been that, while not necessarily evil, they are exceedingly powerful and ambivalent toward us as humans and can be easily angered. We don't recommend them except for the most experienced and determined of jinn summoners. This doesn't mean that you can't work with the jinn of the planets. They are not the only ones, only the most known and famous. In this ritual, you will get an opportunity to enlist the aid of seven more positive and spiritual jinn associated with the planets. You will have to discover their names and seals on your own, but this ritual will set you upon the path to this discovery.

TIMING: This conjuration is to be done seven times in the morning and seven times in the evening for forty-nine weeks. The basics of fasting and avoidance of animal by-products should be observed. Once you have acquired the names and covenants of these jinn, you can call on them with this conjuration by reciting it any multiple of seven times.

TOOLS: You will need the planetary tablet of the arts, drawn on a piece of cloth or etched into or painted on wood. You should make every triangle on its appropriate planetary day. We introduced these pyramids in an earlier chapter, so you should be familiar with them. This tablet is placed before you in your magical space. Place the corresponding magical square of the planet on the outside of the pyramids. In the center of the planetary tablet, place the magical square of the name that corresponds to that name and have it also written and worn around your neck.

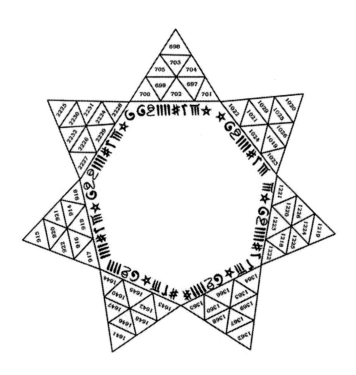

DIVINE NAMES: There are no new Divine names introduced in this conjuration. Make sure you are familiar with all the major names used so far in the book, especially the planetary names.

STEP ONE: Purify and consecrate your working space.

STEP TWO: Perform the prayer of protection, shield of the magi, and the release of residents.

STEP THREE: Say: "In the name of the Divine, by the Divine, from the Divine, to the Divine. There is no victor that can overcome the Divine. There is no will or power except by the majestic and exalted Divine. I conjure you O ye spiritual rouhaniah that are pure and clean, O ye individuals that have scintillating inner being. O brilliant, rising, beautiful lights that are charged with the constellations, the lunar mansions, and planetary hours by He who revealed Himself to the mountain and it trembled and Moses fell in shock.

I conjure you O ye clean rouhaniah of malkut by the fast name that is veiled, and it is the Divine Name with seven letters. Is he who was dead and then we brought him to life and made for him a light to walk by among the people similar to the one who is in darkness and never leaving it? I charge you, O Ruqiel, Gabriel, Semsamiel, Michael, Sarfiel, A'aniel, and Kasfiel, to command a servant from the jinn to appear before me and tend to my rights and the Divine has upon me its oath and binding that I will never send him into sin. Answer my conjuration and fulfill my request in the glory of Ber-hat-yah [x3], Ka-reer [x3], Tat-lee-yah [x3], Toh-ran [x3], Maz-jal [x3], Baz-jal [x3], Tahr-qab [x3], Bar-hash [x3], Ghal-mash [x3], Cho-taeer [x3], Qal-in-hod [x3], Bar-shan [x3], Katz-heer [x3], Namoh Shelech [x3], Berhayola [x3], Bash-kee-lach [x3], Qaz Maz [x3], An-ghala-leet [x3], Qa-ba-rat [x3], Gha-ya-ha [x3], Kayed-ho-la [x3], Shem-cha-her [x3], Shem-cha-heer [x3], Shem-ha-heer [x3], Bak-hat-hon-yah [x3], Ba-sha-resh [x3], To-nesh [x3], Shem-cha Ba-roch [x3].

I conjure you O rouhani king and queen of the jinn from the orbit of Keyamanu, Kewan, Zuhal and Shabbathai and by whatever other names it may be called, in the blessed names of Lele-tah-teel [x3], Teel-la-lel-tah [x3], La-tah-tee-lel [x3], Yal-lal--ta-hat [x3], Tah-tee-la-lal [x3], Lal-la-tah-tee [x3], Ha-tee-lala-lat [x3] to command a servant from the jinn to appear before me and tend to my rights and the Divine has upon me its oath and bind that I will never send him into sin.

I conjure you O rouhani king and queen of the jinn from the orbit of Neberu, Moshtari and Tzedek and by whatever other names it may be called, in the blessed names of Mah-tah-teel [x3], Teel-mah-tah [x3], Hat-ha-tee-lem [x3], Ya-lem-hot-hot [x3],

Tah-teel-mah [x3], La-mah-tah-tee [x3], Hah-teel-mah-hot [x3] to command a servant from the jinn to appear before me and tend to my rights and the Divine has upon me its oath and binding that I will never send him into sin.

I conjure you O rouhani king and queen of the jinn from the orbit of Salbatanu, Merrikh, Bahram, and Maadim and by whatever other names it may be called, in the blessed names of Qah-tee-teel [x3], Teel-qah-tee [x3], Ha-tee-tee-loq [x3], Yal-qah-teet [x3], Tee-teel-qah [x3], Laq-hah-tee-tee [x3], Ya-teel-qa-hot [x3] to command a servant from the jinn to appear before me and tend to my rights and the Divine has upon me its oath and binding that I will never send him into sin.

I conjure you O rouhani king and queen of the jinn from the orbit of Samas, Shams, Khorshid and Shemesh and by whatever other names it may be called, in the blessed names of Fah-tob-teel [x3], Teel-fah-tab [x3], Hat-ba-tee-luf [x3], Yal-fah-ta-but [x3], Tab-teel-fah [x3], Lef-hat-bot-ee [x3], Bah-teel-fa-hat [x3] to command a servant from the jinn to appear before me and tend to my rights and the Divine has upon me its oath and binding that I will never send him into sin.

I conjure you O rouhani king and queen of the jinn from the orbit of Delebat, Zuhra, Zohreh, and Noghah and by whatever other names it may be called, in the blessed names of Na-hah-ta-teel [x3], Teel-na-ha-hot [x3], Ha-ha-tah-tee-lan [x3], Ya-lan-ha-ha-ta-tot [x3], Hot-teel-nah [x3], Len-hah-tah-tee [x3], Ta-teel-na-hah [x3] to command a servant from the jinn to appear before me and tend to my rights and the Divine has upon me its oath and binding that I will never send him into sin.

I conjure you O rouhani king and queen of the jinn from the orbit of Sihtu, Otaared, Tir and Kochav Chama and by whatever other names it may be called, in the blessed names of Jah-lah-ta-teel [x3], Teel-jah-lot [x3], Hal-tot-ya-laj [x3], Yal-ja-hal-tot [x3], La-tot-yal-jah [x3], La-jah-lo-tot-ee [x3], Tot-eel-ja-hal [x3] to command a servant from the jinn to appear before me and tend to my rights and the Divine has upon me its oath and binding that I will never send him into sin.

I conjure you O rouhani king and queen of the jinn from the orbit of Sin, Qamar, Mah, and Yareach and by whatever other names it may be called, in the names of Lach-ha-tot-eel [x3], Tee-lal-cha-hot [x3], Chah-tot-ee-lal [x3], Ya-la-lach-ha-tot [x3], Ha-tot-ee-la-lach [x3], Lal-chah-tot-ee [x3], Totee-la-la-chh [x3] to command a servant from the jinn to appear before me and tend to my rights and the Divine has upon me its oath and binding that I will never send him into sin.

O Divine One by the honor of Kah-ka-heej, Yach-tash, Yal-tash-ghesh-weel, Am-weel, Jal-dam, Mah-jama, Haj-leej, Mah-fee-aj; nothing is like unto Him and He is All Hearing and All Seeing. Come to me, listen and obey and be my aides in everything I have commanded you to do in the honor of the name that is majestic and magnificent, that begins with El and ends with El and it is El Shala'a, Ya'ao, Yubiah, Yahuah, Ah, Betekmah, Betekefal, Busa'aee, Ka'aee, Memial, we obey You O El, how grand is Your name Jal Raziel. No spirit heard Your name and disobeyed but was stricken down and burnt with Your Light, O Greatest Light. I avow and assert on you by the Knower of the all that is hidden and visible, the Great and Exalted, and by the names of your covenant on the door of great temple of Babel: Ba'al Shaqesh [x3], Mahraqesh [x3], Aqesha Maqesh [x3], Shaqmonhesh [x3], Raksha [x3], Kashalach [x3], A'akesh [x3], Tahesh [x3] and whomever disobeys his Lord to him is ascending torment. I conjure these, O you spiritual rouhaniah, to command a servant from the jinn to appear before me and tend to my rights and the Divine has upon me its oath and binding that I will never send him into sin, by the honor of Ehieh Asher Ehieh Adonai Tzabaoth El Shaddi and by the honor of AbjadHawaz Hhuti and by honor of Batad Zahej Wah and by honor of Baduh Ajhazat and it is an oath if you but know great. Now [x3] Quickly [x3] This Hour [x3]."

THE JINNI OF THE MAGIC LAMP

Purpose: In previous rituals, we provided basic ways to summon a jinni to aid you and befriend you. In this ritual, you will be enlisting the aid of the jinn for whatever earthly need you may have, without having to enlist the jinni itself. Enlisting the aid of the jinn is like enlisting the aid of humans. You have no real say or control over how your request is executed. Also a jinni will not do something against its own ethical or moral compass, whatever that is, no matter how many times you ask. You will be responsible for the outcome, even though you are just making a request or giving orders. You should resort to jinn assistance only if you are confident it is something you can't accomplish on your own with ease. If the jinni feels that your request mocks it, it will retaliate against you. Keep these points in mind when you do make a request and you will have a powerful new magical tool in your arsenal.

TIMING: When you do this ritual, avoid the common Western tendency to do something once and expect an immediate response. You may have to repeat this ritual daily for many weeks. Continue to do so until a sign of acceptance has occurred or the purpose has been achieved, whichever comes first. The ancients recorded various signs of success in such rituals. We have listed them earlier in the chapter, so refresh your memory before doing this.

TOOLS: Before you do this ritual, you will need to make the magic tablet of the jinn elders. You will also need four candles, one colored red, one white, one blue and one green or black. You will also need an oil lamp and thin fabric material, such as cotton muslin, for the wick. On the lamp, paint the following magic square:

750	753	758	743
757	744	749	754
745	760	751	748
752	747	746	759

Take the muslin and paint on it the magical figures on the following page; then roll it very tight into a wick for the oil lamp.

MAGICAL FIGURES

ﭏﺲﭏ ﺱﻵﻝﭏ ﺱﭖ ﺝﻵﺱ ﺱﭏﻵ ﻝﭏﺍ

ﭖﻩﻵﺍﺝ ﺱﭏ ﻝﭏﺍ ﺝﺝ ﻙﻵﺝﺝﭖ

ﻵﺝﻝﻵ ﺝﺱﭏﻩ ﻙﺝﭏﺍﺱﺱ ﺱﭖ

ﺱﻵﭖﭏ ﻩﻩﺍﺝﻝ

Note: The first letter at the top-right and the fifth letter to its left may look similar, but are actually two different letters. Notice the curve in the bottom finial of the first letter.

314

You will also need the magical tablets of the four elders of the jinn. These elders also have a major tablet that is placed on the central altar or working area during any attempt to contact them. The tablet can be painted on cloth, wood or any clean surface. The ancient text gives no color instructions. The tablet consists of a front and a back. The numbers on the front of the tablet are place holders for the four Jinn Elders. They are: 1) طيكل, 2) قسورة, 3) كمطم and 4) مازر. The number one in the back corners of the table is the place holder for your intent or charge, such as: 'Do this and that.'

ELDER TABLET (FRONT)

G	Ə	IIII	#	٢	III	★	III	٢	#	IIII	Ə	G
Ə	4	ح	١	و	ج	ه	ز	د	ط	ب	١	Ə
IIII	ب	ب	ط	د	ز	ه	ج	و	١	ح	ح	IIII
#	ط	ط	ت	م	خ	م	ج	ق	ف	١	١	#
٢	د	د	م	ر	١	ت	ش	١	ق	و	و	٢
III	ز	ز	خ	١	ح	١	و	ش	ج	ج	ج	III
★	ه	ه	م	ت	ز	ه	ج	ت	م	ه	ه	★
III	ج	ج	ج	ش	ب	ط	د	١	خ	ز	ز	III
٢	و	و	ق	١	ش	ت	١	ر	م	د	د	٢
#	١	١	ف	ق	ج	م	خ	م	ت	ط	ط	#
IIII	ح	ح	١	و	ج	ه	ز	د	ط	ب	ب	IIII
Ə	3	ب	ط	د	ز	ه	ج	و	١	ح	2	Ə
G	Ə	IIII	#	٢	III	★	III	٢	#	IIII	Ə	G

ELDER TABLET (BACK)

1	اجب يا مازر	اجب يا كمطم	اجب ياقسورة	اجب ياطيكل	1
وانت يا مازر	وانت ياطيكل	وانت ياقسورة	وانت يا كمطم	وانت يا مازر	وانت ياطيكل
وانت يا كمطم	وانت ياقسورة	ح	ب	وانت يا كمطم	وانت ياقسورة
وانت ياقسورة	وانت يا كمطم	و	د	وانت ياقسورة	وانت يا كمطم
وانت ياطيكل	وانت يا مازر	وانت يا كمطم	وانت ياقسورة	وانت ياطيكل	وانت يا مازر
1	اجب ياطيكل	اجب ياقسورة	اجب يا كمطم	اجب يا مازر	1

Make sure you are in a secluded room with only candlelight for light. Place the magic tablet in the center of your working area. On the red candle, carve the names of Michael and Mazer. On the blue candle, carve the names of Gabriel and Kamtam. On the white candle, carve the names of Israfiel and Qaswarah. On the green or black candle, inscribe the names of Azriel and Taykal. (You can refer back to the chapter on Angels and Jinn for the Hebrew and Arabic writing of these names.) Place the four candles on their respective four corners on the tablet. Place the lamp in front of the tablet or on its center. Light the four candles and the lamp, putting out any other candles, and burn some sweet incense that contains cilantro.

STEP ONE: Recite the prayer of the Queen of Heaven.

STEP TWO: Recite the release of the residents at least three times.

STEP THREE: Do the ritual of the Shield of the Magi.

STEP FOUR: Recite the Ancient Oath at least seven times with the intent of enlisting the aid of the four Elder Kings.

STEP FIVE: Recite the following three thousand and four times with a strong and commanding voice: **"An Ifreet from the Jinn said, 'I will bring it to you before you get up from your chair and I am upon this task powerful and to be trusted.'"** Every hundred recitations from the three thousand and four times, intone the following conjuration:

"Answer me O Mazer, O Kamtam, O Qaswarah and O Taykal by honor of the Creator of the prophet Shelomah ben David, who was a king of men and jinn. Be friendly to me and send to me from among your rank a spiritual ifreet to help me with my affair, which is (insert it), quickly and peacefully. Answer me by the honor of Ehieh Asher Ehieh Adonoi Tzabaoth El Shaddi and the names written on the door of the Great Temple: Ba'al Saqesh Mahraqesh Aqshamaqesh Shaqmonhesh. Answer me and let your aid manifest to me (insert goal) quickly, even before I stand up from my seat, for I have conjured you with the Great Names. Bring (insert goal) about for me, quickly, and set upon this task a powerful and trusted ifreet who fears the Creator. By the honor of the grandiose king and the spiritual angels Chabaeel, Chaktahaeel, Ghatsabaeel, Baghthahsajaeel, and the Jinn Jafeshatysh, Amtahtysh, afeq'ghetish, Hafechaghabtish, hurry, O Mazer, O Kamtam, O Qaswarah and O Taykal and send to me one who will manifest to

me (insert goal) quickly and peacefully. May the blessings of El Elyon be upon you and within you."

Note: If you need to take a break during the recitation, then say: "Excuse me, O spirits and jinn, for I shall return to finish this work shortly." Leave things undisturbed and return to your work. Keep track of the count. You may also divide the number of repetitions between seven or fourteen days. It isn't a requirement that it all be done at once or in a single setting. Just remember not to quit the operation or slack off on it. If you start it, then finish it and work on it daily. The jinn will not take you seriously if you can't keep your word or maintain the vigilance needed to achieve your goal. If you are planning on stretching this operation, don't do any release in the meantime.

This brings us to the end of the magic of the jinn in this book. For many people, jinn magic is a point at which their faith in magic becomes solidified. We hope that it has had this kind of effect on you.

Works Referenced

al-Ghalani, Mohammed (D. 1740 C.E.), *al-Der al-Mantzoom wa Khilasat al-Sir al-Maktoom fi Al-Sihr wa al-Talasem wa al-Nojoom*. al-Maktaba al-Tahqafia, Beirut, Lebanon: 1992.

al-Marzooqi, Ali Abu Hai Allah, *al-Jawaher al-Lama'a fi Isthadhar Muluk al-Jinn fi al-Waqet wa al-Sa'a*. Maktabat Iqbal Haj Ibrahim. Siragh Bantan: 1962.

al-Buni, Ahmed (D. 1225). *Shamsu al-Ma'aref al-Kubrah*. Maktabat Isha'at al-Islam. Delhi, India.

al-Buni, Ahmed (D. 1225). *Manba'a Ussol al-Hikmah*. Maktabat al-Hidayah. Surabaya, Indonesia.

al-Toukhi, A'adu al-Fatah. *al-Siher al-Azeem (v1-3)*. al-Maktabah al-Thaqafiah. Beirut, Lebanon:1991

Barchiah, Assef. *al-Ajnas*. Mu'asasat al-Nur Lil-matbua'at. Beirut, Lebanon: 2005

11
Next Step

Congratulations on having got this far in your magical journey. As you probably know, there is much more to magic than what we covered in this book. There are hundreds of books on the subject from various traditions, many of which were written in the last hundred years. This brings up the question of where to go next in your magical growth. The answer depends on what tradition you feel an affinity toward. Not every reader will be pulled to this tradition, but even if all you got from it is one technique that helped your life, then it did what it was intended to do. If you do feel an affinity for this tradition and want to know more and do more, then you will be excited to know that this book just scratches the surface of this ancient and venerable magical tradition. It is a living tradition and not only a set of ancient and rare books. People still practice it today across the world, and have been doing so for hundreds, if not thousands, of years. You will have to wait for more books to be translated and find yourself a teacher to learn the oral aspects of the craft. If you try to wait for all the secrets to be in the bookstore, you will be waiting for a long time. Unlike modern trends in the West, the general rule is that only fragments of this tradition are put into print for public consumption.

Keep in mind also that the ultimate objective of this form of magic is to give you the tools to really know divinity and achieve your true spiritual potential. It is a system whose goal is the illumination of humanity and giving a taste of paradise in each person's life. It is also a balanced system, in that it provides us with the tools to deal with our material lives without getting chained to them. As you progress and apply yourself to the system, you will work toward achieving the station of a magical adept.

319

The word adept itself can refer to two categories of magical accomplishment. The first describes an individual who has reached a high state of proficiency in the methods of a given magical system. This is a functional title. Various occult orders give their initiates such titles to reflect their mastery of their own specific rituals, techniques and theories, or to reflect their position within a political hierarchy. There is no direct relation between the titles and any advanced spiritual or magical level of development.

The second describes an individual who has reached a very high level of spiritual development and has become what others may refer to as a magical or spiritual master. Magical adepts of this kind are special humans who should be treasured, because they spiritually labor when others play, they love when others hate and they show compassion when others judge. Magical adepts see life for what it is, a transitory period. They try to take care of their world, so it will be in better shape for the gardeners who come after them. They seek to plant fruits of goodness with their hands, and tender words flow from their mouths.

Disappointment can occur when someone encounters an individual who claims to be an adept, yet reflects a very unspiritual and unhealthy lifestyle. This dichotomy exists because the person was awarded the title of an adept based on the first category, while one's expectations were of the second. The importance of adepthood lies not with its status, but as an ideal and measure of aspiration.

What does being a magical adept mean to you? What are the characteristics of such people? Why don't you write up your own list of ten attributes you think each magical adept should have and ten attributes you think should be absent from a magical adept? With your list in your hand, ask yourself if you can acquire these attributes on your list and, if so, how you get there. Figure out also how many of those traits unbefitting an adept you possess, and how you can outgrow them. When thinking about this, keep in mind that all living magical adepts, no matter their state of achievements, remain human with imperfections. Perfection is only attributable to the Divine, because when beholding the Divine, the existence of error itself is eliminated.

Looking at such a list, it becomes obvious that almost no one begins as a magical adept. You must develop the nature of one. This is accomplished by mundane and magical deeds, and is also shaped by the Spirit of Light as it fills you. This is the reason for the importance of both mystical and magical rituals and meditative practices. You are not considered an adept until you have a footstool, placement, state, station, and mystery. The footstool is the path or system that you follow to reach the knowledge of the Divine. The placement is the effort you put toward transformation through the Light. It is built by years of spiritual labor, rituals of illumination and virtuous acts of righteousness. The state is with what the Divine blesses you, bestowing upon you from all that is good. The personal spiritual nature is known as the individual power of the magician. The station is the revelation to you of your achievement and of what is hidden. The Divine will reveal your placement within the Divine Order after many years of magical work. The Divine will reveal the mysteries to you as well. The occult keys consist of the hidden mysteries of Light, which will be given to you by the Holy One and spiritual messengers.

As you continue on this path of magic, you will get to study many ancient and modern works of magic. The most important of those mysteries were handed down by adepts that came before us, by intellectual means, as well as by angelic revelations. This helps to provide a path that you can follow and you too can then contribute to this body of knowledge that will be handed down to future generation. More important than techniques, methods, and information is that you pass down a good legacy. Often, we hear of great magicians that came before us, just to discover their lives were, to put it bluntly, a spiritual mess. We owe it to future magicians to establish good spiritual role models for them to follow. This is partly the job of the adepts and those aspiring to be that state. When you do encounter someone who claims to be a magical adept, don't be taken in by their external knowledge of occultism, charisma or social stutus. You can validate their claim by observing the 3-fold sign: 1) a magical adept's impetus is from the Divine; 2) a magical adept relies on the Divine for all spiritual and magical acts; 3) a magical adept aspires toward the Divine reality above all things.

🏵 MAGICAL GROUPS 🏵

Although we wrote this book while keeping in mind that you will be solitary, we continue to encourage you to find a teacher and a good group to work with. It is easier said than done. Where would you look for an authentic magical group that provides adequate training, a safe environment, and a valid initiatic stream? With the recent occult revival many groups emerged, mostly modelled on the Freemasons. Many of those orders are centered on the people that found them, and they tend to be very hierarchical in nature. The only way to really get to the top is to start your own. Many established groups have become too focused on personality, titles, and lineage. It isn't unusual to see more and more people advocate a solitary path to students, because some group leaders appear to be worse off spiritually and magically than their lower grade members.

This problem is because the revival has not been the product of awakening and tradition, but of the mass popularity of what very little of the ancient wisdom survived in the West. It is also due partially to a loss of focus on spirituality to secular humanism or power. It is no wonder that such organizations spend more time in setting up 'by-laws' than they do in seeking knowledge and union with the Divine Light. Some modern organizations are very successful and survive for many years, while others collapse in short order. Unfortunately, there are also many cases of abuse that emerge from within their framework, regardless of fame and success. This is not the fault of the path, for unscrupulous people use all venues in their endeavours. The modern group killers are egotism, despotism, paranoia, manipulation, politics and fighting, both within and between groups. You are better off going solitary than being part of any such group. You may indeed reach the top of the social ladder in such a group, but at what price?

Even amidst all these problems, magical groups remain vital and essential conduits of transmission. Groups serve another very important purpose in the path, other than social bonding and company. History is replete with examples of self-deceived individuals who, by their own anti-social tendencies, developed a twisted idea of their own importance, and of the path itself. The reality is that the path has been a solitary one for thousands of years. It was solitary because withdrawal from external and internal distractions is a key to achieving success. However, it was also common practice for these solitary occultists to gather and reflect upon each other. This is one of the many safeguards against self-deception. It is also pleasing to the beings of Light to see spiritual human choirs, as they themselves are arranged in hosts. The love that grew from individual union with the Divine was usually nourished by reaching out and sharing with people on the path and interacting with them and society.

In essence, groups were collections of solitary magicians who met on a regular basis to do work. They were also a venue for qualified teachers to instruct new aspirants, to test new aspirants for initiations, and to celebrate the mysteries of the magic of Light. The need for good groups has increased, not decreased. They are more important now than they were a thousand years ago.

Still, how is one to contend with the extremes and excesses of modern groups? The answer lies in reorganization of the structure and dynamic. The current model is very stable and effective, but in our modern society, it remains open to much abuse. Some argue that it isn't the model at fault, but the existence of group-think. This also is inaccurate, as families are groups and suffer from an extreme case of group-think, yet most families are not abusive. Many of us, regardless, long to have a partner and raise children.

As we look at a new model, we need to address some common myths. The first myth is that lineage or charters have any practical value. Lineal descent and charters are no guarantee of a group's worth, efficacy or authenticity. When a group puts emphasis on legal forms of verification, such as charters and lineage, including trademarks, then keep your eyes open as to whether they are using this as the only justification for their existence or legitimacy.

The second myth is the sacredness of a group or organization. Groups serve a purpose and they are not the end themselves. When people tell you that any given group or organization is indispensable or sacred or holy, then be careful that this isn't being used to manipulate you to support the group's policies or to pull you into a cultish mentality built on the idea of the chosen versus the profane. Once you accept such a concept, it becomes easy for the group leaders to pull you away or separate you from your loved ones or friends, especially if they are not sufficiently supportive of the group. Watch the group's literature to see how many times the group itself is exalted on a pedestal. Remember that exaltation of the group's sacredness is no different from exaltation of the self. They are both signs of spiritual pride and egotism.

The third myth is that any given group is the sole representative or solely contacted by secret masters. At best, it is sign of delusion and lack of experience, and at its worst, it is a sign that it is a cult in the making. We know those beings exist, but it is against their nature to support only one group of light seekers exclusively.

The fourth myth is that of personality worship. If you notice a group putting too much emphasis on a founder, alive or dead, you may want to check out an alternative. In a spiritual organization that focuses on raising your consciousness to the Divine state, such personality worship is inappropriate. Successful magicians, working a living tradition, don't immortalize and follow the dead leaders of their tradition in the form of personality cults.

The fifth myth is that a magical group has multiple vows of secrecy and demands loyalty to hierarchy. Privacy is understandable and private documents should be honored as such. However, excessive focus on secrecy is a sign of a cultish mentality.

When searching for a good magical group, watch out for unscrupulous people. However, don't be paranoid to the point of avoiding groups altogether. There are sincere groups, led by devoted individuals who really strive for noble causes and who are more than willing to help you along your path. The key to telling them apart is the amount of love and freedom you experience within the dynamic. Cult leaders generally are paranoid of internal betrayal or seek to have control of the group members.

A good magical group is founded on service, dedication, volunteerism and cooperation. You will feel loved and supported, even if you go against the group norm. Another good sign is that qualified individuals within the group can freely become guides and teachers without strong interference or control from the group's leaders. Good magical groups also provide services to other aspirants without needing to prove themselves or even talk about lineage and charters. This is the approach that we take in the group that we are part of, the Magic Society of the White Flame. We believe that magical groups should be places that nurture love and not politics. They are at their best as a tight family of magicians, pursuing similar goals and spiritual aspirations. They nurture in their members a spirit of joy within the sacred work of the craft.

This leads us to the final piece of advice in this book. Don't do any ritual repeatedly till it becomes a chore. Understand the benefits and purposes of each and do them when you feel an impetus. Learn to strike a balance and avoid the extremes of being a non-practising magical theorist and a magician who is stuck in routine and ritual habits. You can't be a magician by just reading about it, but you will not do yourself a service by being stuck in routine ritual work. Our general advice to beginners is to do magic daily. Make sure that magic is wilful and joyous. Study and learn as many of the magical systems that are out there as you can. You don't need to put them all into practice or adhere to all their approaches, just be aware of the variety of things and ways of approaching them. Don't be fooled into thinking that any one approach defines the totality of magic, and avoid the tendency of associating group systems with magic in general. This way magic remains fresh, alive and vibrant in your life. May you lead a magical life filled with enchanting companions.

Appendix One
Cursive Arabic

The Arabic letters can be grouped by shapes, which will help the reader familiarize herself with them. We will present the non-cursive form at this point, and discuss the cursive later on. If you are trying to learn the alphabet, work with only one category until you have full mastery. The first category is letters that have a unique shape. They are as follows:

Arabic Letter	English Name	English Written Form
ا	Alef	A
ه	Ha	H
و	Waw	U, W, O
ي	Yah	I, Y, Ee
ك	Kaf	K
ل	Lam	L
م	Mym	M

The next group is of letters that have a crescent body and one, two or three dots either on top or below. They are as follows:

Arabic Letter	English Name	English Written Form
ب	Ba	B
ن	Nun	N
ت	Ta	T
ث	Tha	Th

The third group of letters is composed of a dash connected to a right-facing vertical crescent below it. The variations are based on the

325

existence or lack of dotting and their placement. They are as follows:

Arabic Letter	English Name	English Written Form
ح	Ha (guttural H)	H, Hh
ج	Jym	J, G
خ	Kha	Kh, Ch (As in German loch)

The fourth group of letters is composed of a leftward slanting half-crescent. The differences again are based on dotting. They are as follows:

Arabic Letter	English Name	English Written Form
ر	Ra	R
ز	Zyin	Z

The fifth group is composed of a leftward angle forming intersecting lines. The top line can be straight or a bit slanted, but the bottom line is always straight. This group can easily be confused with the fourth by most beginners. The differentiation is also based on dotting. They are as follows:

Arabic Letter	English Name	English Written Form
د	Dal	D
ذ	Zah (bite your tongue when pronouncing the Z)	Zh

The sixth group is composed of two rightward facing vertical crescents. The top one is half the size of the one below it. The differences are again in dotting. This group is the hardest to pronounce for English speakers. They are as follows:

326

Arabic Letter	English Name	English Written Form
ع	Ayin (Guttral growled A)	‘a or A‘a
غ	Ghyin (Baby talk Gh..gh..gh)	Gh

The seventh group is composed of an upward facing crescent with a small circle on top of its right tip. The difference is again based on dotting. The letters are as follows:

Arabic Letter	English Name	English Written Form
ف	Fa	Ph, F
ق	Qaf	Q

The eighth group is composed of a loop with a vertical line protruding near its extended termination. The difference is again based on dotting. The letters are as follows:

Arabic Letter	English Name	English Written Form
ط	Tah (Guttral T)	T, Tt
ظ	Tzah (Bite your tongue at Z)	Tza

The ninth group is composed of the loop attached to the upper right tip of an upward crescent. The difference is again based on dotting. The letters are as follows:

Arabic Letter	English Name	English Written Form
ص	Sad (Deep Guttral S)	Sah, Tz
ض	Dhad (Deep Guttral Dh)	Dh

The tenth group is composed of a small round-bottomed w attached to the upper right tip of an upward crescent. The difference again is based on dotting. The letters are as follows:

327

Arabic Letter	English Name	English Written Form
س	Syin	S
ش	Shyin	Sh

If you have memorized the appearances of the non-cursive Arabic letters, then you will not run into any difficulty with many of the exercises in this book. This should be sufficient for most Western occultists. An occasion could arise where you need to write or read cursively. You don't need to memorize all the cursive forms, but you should be able to look them up and use them as required. Unlike most other languages, the cursive shape of each Arabic letter changes, based on its position within a word. To complicate matters, some letters don't change shape, causing you to apply a beginning of word shape for a letter in the middle of an actual word. We will detail the shapes based on their groups. We will also write examples, forming non-meaningful words with these letters. You are not expected to memorize these shapes, unless you have intentions of reading complex Arabic texts. You can just look them up here if you need them. Let's look at the cursive permutations for the first group:

Arabic Letter	**Beginning of a Word**	**Middle of a Word**	**End of a Word**
ا	ا ئـ	ـا ـئـ	ى
ه	هـ	ـهـ	ـه
و	و	ـو	*ـو
ي	يـ	ـيـ	ـي
ك	كـ	ـكـ	ـك
ل	لـ	ـلـ	ـل
م	مـ	ـمـ	ـم

You will note that the letter Alef has two beginning and two middle forms. The second form with small crescent shape is pronounced differently. It doubles the a sound as in accessory, very, cat or alarm, versus late. You will also notice that the letter Waw's middle and end have the same exact shape. This is an important clue that the letter following it will be treated as if beginning a new word, even when not. In any case, we will place a * beside a letter to indicate that what follows is always written in the form of the start of the word, no matter its actual location.

Let us form the word Allah in Arabic. We will show them disconnected and connected. The cursive letters disconnected would look like this:

ا ل ل ه

They would look like this connected:

الله

Let's take the Divine Name Ehieh in Arabic as another example. We will show them disconnected first like this:

ا ه ﻴ ه

This is how they would look connected:

اهيه

Let's show one more example, this time of the letter Waw. We will form the word Hua (He) in Arabic. This is how the letters would look, disconnected:

ه و ا

Notice how the waw was followed by the beginning of the word form of alef. It would look like this connected:

هوا

Let us now look at the cursive permutations of the other groups.

2nd Group Cursive Letters

Arabic Letter	Beginning of a Word	Middle of a Word	End of a Word
ب	بـ	ـبـ	ـب
ن	نـ	ـنـ	ـن
ت	تـ	ـتـ	ـت
ث	ثـ	ـثـ	ـث

3rd Group Cursive Letters

Arabic Letter	Beginning of a Word	Middle of a Word	End of a Word
ح	حـ	ـحـ	ـح
ج	جـ	ـجـ	ـج
خ	خـ	ـخـ	ـخ

4th Group Cursive Letters

Arabic Letter	Beginning of a Word	Middle of a Word	End of a Word
ر	ر	ـر	ـر
ز	ز	ـز	ـز

5th Group Cursive Letters

Arabic Letter	Beginning of a Word	Middle of a Word	End of a Word
د	د	ـد	ـد
ذ	ذ	ـذ	ـذ

6th Group Cursive Letters

Arabic Letter	Beginning of a Word	Middle of a Word	End of a Word
ع	عـ	ـعـ	ـع
غ	غـ	ـغـ	ـغ

7th Group Cursive Letters

Arabic Letter	Beginning of a Word	Middle of a Word	End of a Word
ف	ف	ـفـ	ـف
ق	ق	ـقـ	ـق

8th Group Cursive Letters

Arabic Letter	Beginning of a Word	Middle of a Word	End of a Word
ط	ط	ـطـ	ـط
ظ	ظ	ـظـ	ـظ

9th Group Cursive Letters

Arabic Letter	Beginning of a Word	Middle of a Word	End of a Word
ص	صـ	ـصـ	ـص
ض	ضـ	ـضـ	ـض

10th Group Cursive Letters

Arabic Letter	Beginning of a Word	Middle of a Word	End of a Word
س	سـ	ـسـ	ـس
ش	شـ	ـشـ	ـش

Let's try another exercise for fun. Why don't you try writing your name in Arabic script? First, we will guide you using a historical name: Arthur Pendragon. The first step would be to convert the letters to Hebrew. Dropping the extra vowels that don't exist in Hebrew, we get the following English vocal equivalents:

ARThR PhNDRAGWN

In Hebrew it is written, from right to left (note we are not using Hebrew finals):

ארתר פנדראגון

Looking at the table of Arabic to Hebrew, we find the equivalent Arabic for the Hebrew:

ارث ر فن د راغون

We chose the second Arabic correspondence for letter ת, which is ث, because the sound is Th versus T and the same for the letter غ for ג, due to it being hard. Now, we need to write the name cursively. Here is the cursive form of the preceding:

ا+ر+ث + ر فـ + ـنـ + ـدـ + ر + ا+ غـ + و + ن

The complete spelling of the name of King Arthur in Arabic is as follows:

ارثر فندراغون

Now, try doing that with your name. This will be good practice for Arabic cursive writing. For most people, Arabic is more difficult to learn than Hebrew, so don't feel discouraged. If you know your Hebrew letters well, the Arabic isn't that much harder. The only real obstacle is in writing and reading cursive Arabic. Getting a grip on this fluently will take some time, but isn't necessary beyond having to write out a limited number of Angelic and Divine Names. We also acknowledge that, without audio, it is difficult to really capture the pronunciation correctly; therefore, free audio samples are available at our site at: www.sacredmagic.org. While we don't expect you to learn the languages presented in this book, you still need to be sufficiently familiar with the Arabic and Hebrew alphabets to work with this system. You don't need to memorize the letters all at once, though it is highly recommended that you do memorize them as you progress.

INDEX

INNER AND OUTER ORDER INITIATIONS
OF THE HOLY ORDER OF THE GOLDEN DAWN

"At last, you can have the most amazing ceremonies ever to emerge from the Golden Dawn"

The Golden Dawn is one of most prolific and legendary of all Western secret and esoteric societies. Hundreds of people from the rich and famous to the common man have walked through its halls of the neophyte. Empowering, beautiful, transformative and unique, are ways to describe the original initiation rites. Even more can be said of another set of ceremonies penned by one of the Golden Dawn's early members, a writer, a scholar, and a deep mystic. He is the renowned occult personality, Arthur Edward Waite, the creator of the Rider Waite Tarot Deck. For the first time in more than 80 years, these secret ceremonies are revealed and made available to you. This is an excellent opportunity for you to:

• Learn the secrets of a magical magus
•Experience spiritually uplifting ceremonies
• Gain better understanding of the ancient mysteries.
• Enrich your life by ascending the Tree of Life
• Be part of a historical moment in the tradition of the Golden Dawn

If you are an aspirant of the Golden Dawn and looking for wondrous initiations that combine Golden Dawn genius with a mystical heart, you should buy this book.

0-9735931-7-2, 332 pages, Hardback $65

Printed in the United Kingdom
by Lightning Source UK Ltd.
133056UK00001B/184/A